Nature and Tourism

Nature and Tourism

R.K. Malhotra

2006

Cyber Tech Publications
4230/1 Ansari Road, Daryaganj, New Delhi-110002

Nature and Tourism

© Reserved

First Edition 2006

Published by G.S. Rawat
For **Cyber Tech Publications**
4230/1 Ansari Road, Daryaganj, New Delhi-110002
E-mail : cybertechpublishers@yahoo.com
Phone : 011-23244078
Fax   : 011-23280028

Type setting by
Shah Computer Graphics
9868853786

Printed at
Tanwar Offset, Moujpur, # 9810878184

PREFACE

It is undoubtedly true that man is the creation of nature and the increasing urbanisation in the world is making the lives of human beings very artificial and full of tensions. The man therefore, rightly hankers for natural spots like rivers, ocean, mountains, forests, and lakes. There are some natural spots in the world which are very rare. The tourists of the world want to come to India to see the Taj Mahal and to climb the Everest of Nepal. They also come to enjoy the scenic beauty of the ocean around Goa. Besides this other spots in the Himalayan Region, the Jammu & Kashmir and Kerala, also provide the spots for enjoyment of the nature. There is a close relationship between nature and tourism and the policies of the states especially of the Govt. of India is to attract tourists from all over the world which gives sufficient funds for the country also. This book considers all these aspects in detail and it is expected that the book will prove of immense value to the various Ministries of Tourism and the tourists of the world.

The Editor is grateful to the Ministry of Tourism and Civil Aviation for their kind assistance in the preparation of this book.

EDITOR.

Contents

Contents

1

The Nature and Tourism

The ice has frozen on Kotzehue Sound, and only a few "salt water" families are still at the coast, where we bunt seal at breathing holes and fish for tomcod through the ice. The sod-covered igloos are warm but we miss our friends. The "fresh water" Inuit left before freeze-up, going upriver to winter homes to hunt caribou and to set trap lines. But someone will come later by dog team and invite us to their camp, may be up the Noatak (River) for a visit. . . we can be the guests, and our sledges will carry muktuk and fish as gifts. With our good dog teams, we can arrive in two sleeps. We love to travel in winter, in the clear, cold nights when the stars sparkle and sheets of colour swish across the sky. We bear the sound, and know it is the Spirits playing football.

If it is a good year, with enough food, may be we will stay 5 or 6 sleeps. . . and dance and sing. We look forward to these visits with our ilyaga (relatives) and our friends. They have stories to tell, and new babies to see, and so do we. . . .

Anthropologists describe the events of birth, marriage, and death—with their respective rites of passage—as the age markers of an individual life. Often one has little control over these rituals—in much of the world even marriage was arranged or spousal choice limited by population size, as was true for Inuit. The events of travel were the social time markers of Inuit lives, just as tourism defines our lives today. As Graburn noted, our journeys are often our best remembered events. Aboriginal tourism, with its activities of the journey, the visiting, the social-izing, and the learning, provided the same break in the monotony of their lives as does the weekend "get-away" or vacation for modern society.

The term to *tour* derives from a Latin origin: to make a circle trip and return to one's home. To vacation comes from a verb, *vacare,* meaning to vacate the house. To *travel,* from *travail,* means to labour or to work and, by contrast, a *holiday* is a day exempt from work. Although these subtle meanings are now blurred, some individuals readily admit that travel is "hard work," involving hours of waiting for transportation, sleepless night, poor food, and uncomfortable conditions. The range of experience between luxury and discomfort is often great, at least in activity if not in price. Some adventure travellers—especially those making long treks in high mountains, rock climbing, and river rafting—seek hardship as a form of physical or mental self-testing. Other tourists anticipate vacation as a time *for fun,* to be carefree, and to socialize, and disdain rigorous activity to relax on a beatch or to sightsee. The travel industry has developed an enormous range of options, to meet all tastes, but many maintain the essence of the social time markers. An American travel agent (Tansey, 1999) adopted for her agency the slogan, "Memorable Vacations to Recreate Yourself," because a vacation is "a time of re-creation ... a journey of the mind and spirit."

Tourist Motivations

The recreational travel that now spans all seven continents provides multiple levels of comfort and exertion. It involves transportation ranging from supersonic jets to camel safaris and walking tours. This vast contemporary diversity is the byproduct of consumer interest, and forms the *demand* side of tourism. The vast array of products, including modes of transportation, types of accommodation, large- and small-boat cruises, and literally thousands of tours, stems from the *supply* side of the industry. These offerings are constantly adjusted as tourist motivations change, under the aegis of fashion, crisis, new technology, and world view. The motivations for travel rest on the basic philosophical foundation (Dann, 1981) that tourists are

simultaneously "pushed" from their homes by the desire to escape what Graburn terms the "profane" and are "pulled" by the
destination and its attractions, to fulfill some vague illusory
expectations. Tourist motivations are thus a mix of push-pull and
multiple other factors, including the role and the influence of
the culture broker. Motivations are also influenced by time
(calendrical, historical, and generational), by age and gender, by
the ethnicity of the guest and also that of the host. Other
motivational influences include the nature of the attractions, the
destination, and the strength and nature of the media, including
motion pictures, advertising, infomercials, and the available
descriptive literature including travel magazines and guidebooks
(Dann, 1996). The media and the Internet are progressively more
important elements in the decision-making process. The
combined magnitude of these factors contributes to the difficulty of defining and describing travel motivations.

Research Interests

The "why" of travel and the choice of destination are
important topics for the planning and management of tourism. The
scholarly community has broad interests in human behaviour,
and it seeks data about the psychological and social processes
involved in travel motivation and destination decision-making.
Three examples of motivational research—descriptive,
psychological, and quantitative— are presented below.

By contrast, the travel industry strives to meet visitor demand
and satisfy expectations with product diversity suitable for a
range of ages and interests. The preferred industry data are
usually obtained from market surveys, which are largely
conducted in-house or by consulting agencies. Unfortunately,
most surveys are not published or are copyrighted because they
are product specific in a highly competitive market environment.
However, Travel Industry of America (TIA)' holds an annual
Travel Outlook conference at which industry speakers

summarize the year's business and forecast the year to come. A published summary appears annually as *(Year) Outlook for Travel and Tourism* (the 2000 volume is US$195).TIA also undertakes industry-level research on requested topics. Their publication, *The Minority Traveller* (TIA, 200), is an update of a focused study (non-TIA members US$195) that surveys education and occupation in relation to travel habits of three ethnic minorities: African-Americans, Hispanic-Americans, and Asian-Americans, compared with all Americans (dominantly white). Combined, these three minorities represent 26% of the US population. The sample included 50,000 US households. Summary data identified the Asian-Americans as the minority group that traveled the most, spent more money per trip, stayed longer in a single hotel, traveled less frequently with their children, and spent the least amount of time shopping. However, distinctions in travel behavior among the three named minorities and the general population were all almost negligible. Linking historic origins the primary domestic destinations for African-Americans were southern states such as Texas and Georgia; Hispanic Americans went to California, Texas, and Florida, while Asian-Americans who were more likely to gamble than all others listed their top destinations as California and Nevada. This information assists industry carriers to develop special fares of interest to ethnic travelers.

A 2001 TIA publication, *The Profile of Travellers who participate in Gambling* (nonmembers US$195), noted that gambling accounts for 7% of all US travel, or 72.8 million person trips in 2000 (see Chapter 5). Research of this type identifies market niches and helps direct advertising funds to appropriate peer and special interest publications.

Other research interests include the preferred travel modes of older versus younger travellers. Why are some people nontravelers, and how could they be encouraged to travel? What factors support the popularity of cruises? Is here a significant market for space tourism? Answers to these questions are marketing guidelines and are specifically useful in the allocation of advertising funds.The identified market niches—whether youth travel, singles travel, senior travel, or business travel—focus advertising copy into peer group publications.

The travel agent researches individual clients. In a single meeting, the agent must try to satisfactorily match the stated interests (or vague ideas) of a previously unknown client with a specific product. Here, observation and intuition depend on a rapid assessment of the would-be traveller in terms of the "threeAs": Age (a potential guide to gender and peer group interests); Ability (to pay, which suggests a recommended category of services); and Agility (mental and physical appearance, indicative of mobility, stamina, and health). The agent thus becomes the *initial* mediator between the client, his/her motivations for travel and expectations, and the selection of an appropriate product. Sometimes termed "dealers in dreams," the agent as culture broker is often the first to be blamed for a poor choice or a bad experience. The three interest levels—academia, travel industry, and travel agent—support the need for research as a planning tool but with due regard for the enormous diversity of people. All tourist-travellers are individuals whose ideas have been shaped by heritage and education, and whose personal and professional lives are structured by training and occupation.Their motivations are often time and place specific. Riley, Baker, and Van Doren (1998) document that movie-induced tourism frequently draws increased visitation to the site of a motion picture scene, with the percentage of visitors increasing annually after its release. Conversely, a terrorist act or war can have an immediate and chilling negative impact upon travel. Mega-events such as the World Cup or Olympic Games often spur habitual nontourists to travel as sports spectators, although they might deny they were "tourists." Whatever the motivation for travel, efforts to understand travel behaviour have both theoretical and practical value.

Academic Motivational Research

The Descriptive Approach

Early in post-World War II travel, the psychologist authors of *Individual in Society* (Krech,Crutchfield,& Ballachey, 1962) undertook an analysis of tourist behavior and drafted a 12-point approach based on the travel appeals to the visitor and the resulting experiential rewards (Table 1.1).The concept is historically signifi-

Table 1.1. Twelve Types of Travel Appeals

Types of Potentially Rewarding Experience	Potential Type of Reward			
	Rationale	Sensory	Social	Ego-Satisfying
Direct-result experience	Northwest: fastest way to the Orient	Arrive relaxed and refreshed	Pleasant people await you in Mexico	Virginia is for lovers
In-use experience	You'll never wait in line at Hyatt	Escape the winter's cold in warm sunny Florida	Fly the friendly skies of United	Equatoriana's attractive, mutilingual stewardesses are chosen and trained to pamper and please you
Incidental-to-use experience	Coming or going nobody gets you out of the airport faster than Hertz	Just to dig a toe into the soft sand of Bermuda is to feel young	You'll want to be seen in Barbados	A tour for the discriminating traveller

Note: The peak of an earlier main class of wants must be passed before the next "higher" want can being to assume a dominant role. Generally, as psychological development takes place, the number and variety of wants increase.

Source: Reproduced from D. Krech, R. Brutchfield, and E. Ballachey, 1962, *Individual in Society*, p. 77, with permissiom from McGraw-Hill Book Company.

cant, as the era predates mass tourism, and the content phrases are essentially-advertising slogans of destinations or carriers.

Soon after, J.Thomas (1964), writing in the journal of the American Society of Travel Agents (ASTA), offered to the travel industry a list titled "Eighteen important travel motivations" (Table 1.2).The time frame again predates mass tourism, and the topics were useful classificatory devices for an industry at the threshold of new growth.

In 1973, Stanley C. Plog published his first diagram, Distribution of Population by PsychographicTypes (Figure 1.1), shown here in its 1991 format.The descriptive bell-shaped curve, rooted in demographic data, has become a much-cited indicator of tourist types and associated destinations.

In brief, allocentrics are the travel doers, ready to try new products, and they exercise more intellectual curiosity about the tourism experience. The psychocentrics prefer hospitality that is more like home and activities that are physically less challenging.The case study on the Finnish tourists is a near-classic example of psychocentric tourism.

Plog (1998), as Chief Executive Officer (CEO) of Plog Research Inc., updated his nomenclature of tourist types, substituting Venturers for Allocentrics, and Dependables for Psychocentrics. Further, and somewhat parallel to the Resort Cycle, Plog suggests that the rise and fall of destinations is related

Table 1.2. Eighteen Important Travel Motivations

Education and Culture
To see how people in other countries live, work, and play
To see particular sights
To gain a better understanding of what goes on in the news
To attend special events

Relaxation and Pleasure
To get away from everyday routine
To have a good time
To achieve some sort of sexual or romantic experience

<u>Ethnic Heritage</u>
To visit places one's family came from
To visit places one's family or friends have gone to
<u>Other</u>
Weather
Health
Sports
Economy
Adventure
One-upmanship
Conformity
Participation in history
Sociology, a desire to get to know the world

Source: Reproduced from J. Thomas, 1964, "What Makes People Travel," in *ASTA Travel News,* p.65, with permission.

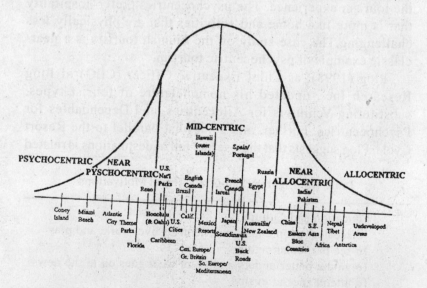

Figure 1.1. Psychographic positions of destinations. (Reprinted from Stanley C. Plog, 1991, *Leisure Travel,* with permission of John Wiley & Sons, Inc.)

to the interests and activities of these two tourist types. Venturers are usually frequent travellers who also spend more income on travel and, having visited an area once, they move on to new adventures. The Near-Venturers follow, and they are described as the "destination planner's dream "because they have plenty of money to spend, like what they find, and are welcome guests. However, when they leave due to excessive commercialization, they are followed by the Centrics and Near-Dependables, who prefer to visit the touristy well-known spots "because the very-image of popularity suggests to them that it must be a good place or it wouldn't attract so many people" (Plog, 1998). The Dependables follow, stay fewer days, and spend less per diem, so the type of guest has changed.

In summary, as the quality of the experience changes, the number of visitors initially increases but the per person visitor yield (or income) declines (Plog, 1998). As numbers increase, it literally "wears out" the physical and social environment. This sequential development is singularly important because it is the usual progression of *ecotourism* that initially attracts the upscale adventure market but, following the adage that success breeds success, as more facilities are constructed to service more visitors, the pristine area devolves into mass tourism. The profitability associated with consumerism often destroys the original product.

In the US, residential address lists are compiled (and available for purchase by advertisers) based on census data, and can detail household income, ethnicity, household size, number of children, and/or other statistics as needed. To tie his Venturer/Dependable categories with actual tourist markets, Plog (1994, p. 254) links the annual Venturer household income level with specific travel industry suppliers, as airlines target annual household incomes above US$60,000; first-class and luxury hotel chains target US$80,000; distant travel operators target US$100,000; and luxury cruise lines target US$125,000. Tourism to Antarctica exemplifies the Plog model, as it was a Venturer destination beginning with the first annual cruise season in 1966 (Headland, 1994) with small ice-reinforced vessels carrying about 70 passengers. In 1981, the cruise ship *World Discoverer* pioneered the route from Chile to New Zealand via Antarctica. Minimum tariff for this 30-day voyage was US$ 11,000, identified in a front-page *Wall Street Journal* article (January 11, 1981) as "the world's most expensive cruise." Seventy venturesome Allocentrics were aboard (V. Smith, 1994). By 1999 there were 12 ships regularly cruising Antarctica each austral summer, some with 500 passengers and occasionally one with 1200 passengers. The cost is now sharply reduced to US$4000-5000 but the Dependable Psychocentrics seem not to mind that the vessels pass like ferry boats and passengers wave to each other.

The Psychologic Approach

The American psychologist Abraham Maslow (1970) developed the theory of self-actualization as a succession of incremental steps through which an individual could achieve his/her full potential (although few actually did so). P.Pearce (1993) suggests that "like a career at work, people have a career in their tourist behaviour". Using a Maslow-type diagramme, the Tourist Career Ladder (Figure 1.2) is a series of steps that show an individual's concerns for biological needs, safety and security needs, relationship development and extension needs, special interest and self-development needs, and, finally, fulfillment or self-actualization. Tourists can enter the hierarchy at different stages, assuming that "while tourists initially enjoy physiological type experiences, more experienced travellers may use travel for the development of relationships, self-esteem purposes and even self-actualization motives" (P Pearce 1988, p. 28).

Pearce further examined the relation between tourist motivations and their attitudes and behaviour in relation to the chosen activity or destination. It is relatively apparent, for example, that even allocentrics, looking at a destination as distant and forbidding as Antarctica, would have different motivations

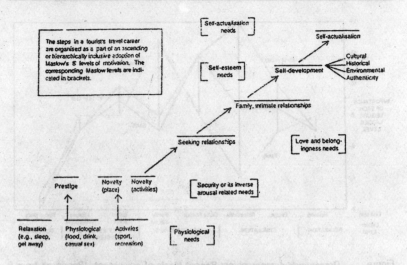

Figure   Suggested steps in tourists' travel careers. (Reprinted from P. Pearce, 1988, *The Ulysses Factor: Evaluating Visitors in Tourist Settings,"* p. 29, with permission from Springer-Verlag.)

and select their itinerary accordingly. Young, hardy adventurers might opt to ski across the continent, as some have done; the young but not so hardy might be content to fly into the South Pole, another realistic option. Able-bodied but older visitors might choose to explore aboard an ice-breaker whereas the mature sightseer would select a comfortable cruise ship that offered a casino and nightly entertainment. All four options are currently available. Age and gender are obvious variants in travel motivation but so are education, affluence, prior travel experience, and the all-important, word-of-mouth information provided by friends and travel companions.

Theme parks are an important domestic travel destination, with particular appeal to youths (an age group whose tourist motivations are seldom considered). In a theme park adaptation of the five stages of the travel career ladder, Pearce (1993, p. 127) collaborated with the management at Dreamworld, a Townsville, Australia theme park. Using a 4000-person survey,

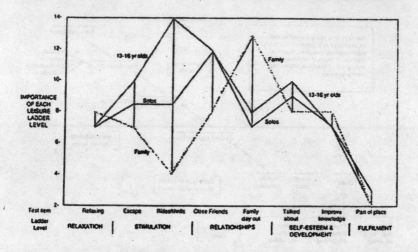

Figure   *Dreamworld* demographics: Recent levels of enjoyment. (Reprinted from P. Pearce, 1993, "Fundamentals of Tourist Motivation," in *Tourism Research: Critiques and Challenges*, p. 126, with permission from International Academy of Tourism.)

the data were divided into three demographic segments: youths (age 13-16), single adults, and family groups (Figure 1.3). Youths were excited and stimulated by the rides and thrills, whereas the family most valued the dav of togetherness, but few attendees came away "really feeling a part of the place," inasmuch as "place" was a virtual reality. This psychological research illustrates the dynamic aspect of tourist motivations. Further, using this example as model, the authors were able to explain and predict attendance at three competitive theme parks, and successfully evaluate new development proposals.

The Quantitative Approach

Visitor surveys, conducted in person, by phone or by mail, have considerable attraction because they represent human input, not just an assemblage of numbers or vague theorizing. However, C. Ryan and Glendon (1998) openly acknowledge that the results of their survey are less than perfect because of human diversity.These authors reviewed numerous quantitative studies by other investigators on travel motivation, using the much-tested Beard and Ragheb (1983) Leisure Motivation Scale.The survey instruments consisted of 113 questions relevant to recent holidays, which were mailed to 6000 residents in the East Midlands of UK, using a well-tested geodemographic database. The usable replies numbered 1127 (or 18.8%) of the sample. From this, the authors identified 11 cluster groups (Table 1.3), and their stated preferences for Holiday Destination Attributes (Table 1.4).

Ryan and Glendon note that their sample proved to be somewhat overweighted in terms of one cluster (young families with children) but that this group is known to be an important purchaser of British holiday packages. Therefore, the study distinctly has marketing validity for British tour operators. Replication of this study in other British locales could identify other clusters with significantly different holiday preference.

Table 4.3. Social Characteristics of Cluster Groups

Cluster	Characteristic
Friendly discoverers	Male, young
Relaxed discoverers	Married, middle aged
Competent intellectuals	Youngish, tendency not to be married
Relaxing moderates (i.e., not particularly	Tend to follow the characteristics of sample population young or old, high or low income)
Social relaxers	Middle age, lower income, slight tendency to be single
Positive holidaytakers	Akin to relaxing moderates
Active relaxers	Tend to be male, with higher income
Unimaginative holidaytaxers	Tend to be married
Intellectual active isolates	Skewed to higher income groups
Noisy socializers	Male, young, low income
Mental relaxers	Married, male, with children

Source: Reproduced from C. Ryan and I. Glendon, 1998, "Application of Leisure Motivation Scale to Tourism,", p. 180, in *Annals of Tourism Research*, with permission from Elsevier Science.

Table 1.4 Mean scores of Holiday Destination Attributes

	Nightlife	Bars	History	Scenery	Accomm-odation	Comfort	Locals	Culture	Get Away	Child Facil.	Mix With Others	Need Courier Input	Climate
Friendly discoverers	2.9	1.8	6.0	6.7	6.3	6.1	5.7	6.1	5.6	1.7	4.4	4.5	6.6
Relaxed discoverers	2.2	1.8	5.7	6.6	6.3	6.4	6.1	5.8	6.4	2.6	3.2	4.2	5.9
Competent intellectuals	4.3	3.1	4.9	5.8	5.1	5.3	5.7	5.3	5.0	2.3	4.4	3.1	4.9
Relaxing moderates	3.1	2.0	4.2	5.9	6.2	6.3	5.8	4.7	6.3	3.6	3.8	3.9	6.0
Social relaxers	2.4	2.3	4.1	6.0	6.4	6.1	6.0	4.0	5.9	1.9	5.2	3.1	6.8
Positive holidayakers	3.3	2.6	5.5	6.5	6.3	6.3	6.2	5.8	6.3	3.2	4.8	4.7	6.1
Active relaxers	1.8	1.5	4.3	6.2	5.3	5.5	5.4	4.6	6.2	1.9	1.7	3.0	5.6
Unimaginative relaxers	1.9	1.6	5.1	6.1	5.9	5.9	5.6	5.3	5.8	2.9	2.7	3.7	5.8
Intellectual active isolates	2.0	1.7	5.4	6.2	5.4	5.4	5.3	5.5	4.9	2.3	2.2	2.9	5.3
Noisy socializes	4.1	3.9	2.6	4.2	5.3	5.4	4.8	3.0	3.8	2.3	4.3	3.0	5.4
Mental relaxers	1.8	1.4	3.5	5.3	5.7	6.1	4.9	3.2	5.6	3.2	1.6	2.7	5.2
Total smaple score	2.5	2.0	4.9	6.1	5.9	6.0	5.7	5.1	5.8	2.9	3.2	3.7	5.7

Source: Reproduced from C. Ryan and I. Glendon, 1998, "Application of Leisure Motivation Scale to Tourism,", p. 181, in *Annals of Tourism Research,* with permission from Elsevier Science.

The three investigative styles—descriptive, psychologic, and quantitative—illustrate the interest and need for knowledge of tourist motivations and behaviour. Taken together these data have immediate value in marketing and long-term value in planning. However, P. Pearce (1988) correctly observes that "all such studies are socially and culturally bound in a time frame; tourists of the 1970s are different from the tourists of the 1990s— due to changes in perceptions, transportation, better health, greater longevity and multiple other factors". One cannot build a tourism industry without the knowledge of the special, unique defining characteristics of the tourist, which are the core of each traveller's interests, activities, and desired experiences. The rise and demise of tourist centers, described by the Butler Resort Cycle model, is built upon this premise and is well illustrated in the case study of Atlantic City in 1886.

Tourist Classifications

Classification systems are linguistic shortcuts. A tourist classification describes a population group, or cluster, whose members share some preferences or characteristics that differentiate that group from other clusters. Many classificatory terms are now in use, and are commercially used to segment the travel market. For example, business travellers, from World War II to the late 1980s, were predominantly male. As women have broken the glass ceiling into middle and upper management positions, the percentage of women business travellers has soared. Metropolitan hotels now solicit this market niche, and advertise special rooms, or even special floors, for businesswomen. The latter want rooms with more security, more in room amenities such as hair dryers, coffeepots, and irons, and sometimes semi-public lounges for committee meetings or entertaining.

Traditional Classifications

E. Cohen (1972) published one of the first post-World War II tourist classifications, based on research in Thailand. He identified four categories. First were the noninstitutional travellers, as "drifters," who searched for exotic and strange environments, and "explorers," who arranged their own travel, to visit places "off the beaten track." Second were the institutional travellers, which included the "individual mass tourists," who made arrangements through a travel agency to visit popular destinations, and the "organized mass tourists," who traveled in the security of the environmental "bubble" of an organized tour.

Cohen's definition was excellent in its day, for it expressed the interaction between visitor and destination at a time when the options for tourism were much less extensive than is true today. Subsequently, V Smith (1977), in the original *Hosts and Guests,* elaborated a similar theme, using the broad spectrum of international travel to reflect the greater differentiation in modes of travel, and the significant increase in tourist numbers, including mass and charter tourism. In both the Cohen and Smith classifications, the orientation was patently Western. In the early 1970s, the proportion of non-Western travellers was very small.

The 1977 V. Smith classification is compared with its updated 2000 counterparts (Table 1.5) The terminology is now essentially international, for all travelers, regardless of country of origin, participate in most designated categories, although

Table 1.5. Comparison of Tourist Type Classifications: 1977- 2000

1977 Tourist Types	2000 Market Terms	Numbers of Tourists	Desired Tourism Characteristics	2000 Cost*
Explorer	Adventure travel	Very few	Unusual: space tourism, submersibles, skiing in Antarctica	$ 1000 +
Elite	Soft adventure: upscale, "high end"	Increasingly "high end"	Deluxe resorts/cruises: exotic destinations	$1000
Off-beat	Off-beat	Uncommon	Unusual destinations: backpacking in Tibet, camel safaris (ecotourism?)	$500-1000
Unusual/ Incipient mass	Special interest tours: FIT/DIT	Diverse, numerous, and seasonal	Usual destinations in unusual style: small group walking, wine, music tours	$300-500
Mass	Mass, bulk tours	Continuous influx	Popular destinations; package tours	$200-300
Charter	Charter	Massive arrivals	Place marketing: Cancun, Canary Islands	Under $200

Costs per day (excluding airfare) in US dollars.

their costs are sometimes less than the US dollar amounts listed. In general, Asian tourists are reported to spend less money on hotels and meals than Westerners but proportionately more on shopping (Mok & Lam, 1997). Some original 1977 terms have been redefined, such as *explorer* and *elite,* by the industry creation of new terms: *Adventure travel* and *high end* or *npscale. There* are few areas on this planet left to "explore," and "elite" seemed pejorative. Other terms, particularly *mass tourism* and *charter tourism,* are now common place and are routinely used in both scholarly literature and industry publications. Other categories have changed, commensurate with changes in the global economy. For non-Western readers, the daily cost seems excessive—often 1 day of travel is equivalent to a month's salary in some LDC destinations. However, the costs must be correlated with American earnings. For perspective, using US data, in 1998 1.3 million Americans earned more than US $ 200,000, of whom 86,000 earned more than US $ 1 million. According to a *Wall Street Journal* survey, 1999 MBA graduates from leading US universities (Harvard, Pennsylvania, and Stanford, among others) may expect a starting salary of US $ 130,000 per year in the high-tech industries and as entry-level stockbrokers These young employees are current examples of a 10-year-long trend associated with the burgeoning US economy and bullish Wall Street. Combined, it has created a substantial market for what is now termed upscale or high end. Until the 1997-1998 Asian financial crisis reduced Asian travel, the Japanese had been a major source for upscale travel, and the Taiwanese and Koreans were entering that market in growing numbers.

Adventure travel now replaces most explorer travel, leaving to the latter principally the emerging space travel and use of submersible vehicles as the only areas left to be, expensively, "explored". Several American tour operators market (and fill) a 2-week jet charter flight around the world, with selected stops, for US$50,000 (1999 prices)—as a trip that meets the travel interests for high-salaried management with limited vacation time. Luxury travel also includes numerous five-star resort properties and several cruise companies, using small vessels with all-suite cabins, and a high ratio of guest/service personnel, at a minimum cost of US$1000 per person per day. *Travel Weekly* (April 29, 1999, p. 56) reports an industry survey of data from 3500 affluent clients (defined as those who spent an average of $6000 per trip) that 35% prefer adventure travel, 21% favour family travel, and bus and group tours are on the decline. For the younger affluent travellers (ages 34 to 52), cruises on luxury and expedition ships are highest in priority (31 %) followed by adventure travel (22%), with a further emphasis on more frequent shorter trips, and biking and walking trips abroad. Similarly, what was originally described as "off-beat" travel has now become a variant of more traditional routes. Grand Circle Travel, the travel division of the American Association for Retired Persons (AARP), operates extended stay vacations and middle-income tours for senior citizens.They expanded in 1998 with OAT (Overseas Adventure Tours) with a maximum group size of 15 persons and include itineraries such as Tibet and desert camping (in Outer Mongolia and Morocco). This company has popularized many former "off-beat" and "unusual" destinations for the travellers who have "been everywhere else," and thereby reduced costs to US $ 200 per day. Incipient Mass Tourism is now best described in terms of Foreign In dependent Travel (FIT) or Domestic Independent travel (DJT) that includes Fly-Drive packages and Hotel Vouchers available at a fixed price per night. Mass tourism continues with package tours and cruise vessels with 1000-2000 passengers. The 1979 deregulation ot American airlines and subsequent airline mergers brought about more competitive pricing. Further, the global population is progressively more knowledgeable about travel, thanks to multiple daily television programmes that showcase documentary travel footage.

Business and Convention Travel

Business travel, buiit on the principle that a one-on-one relationship best cemented commercial relationships, has gradually shrunk during the 1990s, due to tightened fiscal budgets and more effective video-conferencing. However, demand for centrally located hotels and fine restaurants were the mainstays for many metropolitan facilities. Hotels added conference centers and trained staff so that small group meetings are now characteristic of many industries, to showcase products, provide consumer support, and inform potential customers Site selection is important to convention success because attendees are drawn toward attractive venues, such as to cities noted for: their hospitality qualities such as Atlanta or Amsterdam; their dramatic setting as in San Francisco or Sydney; their cultural composite as in New Orleans or Singapore; or for the outdoor amenities as at Whistler in British Columbia or Orlando. The opportunity for attendees, and quite possibly their spouses and family members, to extend their visit beyond the stipulated agenda in order to enjoy environs is an added incentive to attend, and generates increased cash flow to the host area. The tourist value of the site is often at least as important as the topic as an influence for attendance. Staff at metropolitan Convention and Visitor Bureaus (CVBs) are usually expert at presenting their community as the hub from which to visit a hinterland with a broad spectrum of varied activities.

Incentive Travel

Incentive travel is a socially important variant of the commercial travel industry. Capitalizing on the motivational power of travel, sales managers in large companies often set promotional sales targets. Individuals who meet or exceed the stipulated goals are rewarded with group tours in lieu of a cash bonus. The travel award is usually preferred in lieu of a cash bonus because it is nondiscretionary income, whereas the family might choose to spend a cash award on utilitarian needs. A farm machinery distributor sold 14 new tractors one winter, at $100,000 each, by offering a free week in Hawaii to each farmer and his wife as a thank you gift for their purchase. The salesman and his wife accompanied the group as a free bonus for his promotional efforts.

Pilgrimage Travel

A pilgrimage is a long journey to a historical place *(Webster's 1988 New World Dictionary of the English Language*, 1988), which could be either sacred or secular. V. Turner and Turner (1978) neatly defined the potential duality of behaviour, noting that "a tourist is half a pilgrim, if a pilgrim is half a tourist. "This theme is rooted in the philosophical context that, a traveler's journey is in part a ritual quest, during which time the individual is (1) separated from his/her past, and distanced or freed from the normal social milieu; the individual then (2) crosses a cognitive threshold, into the period of *liminality* oriented toward a *Center* "in which the structured necessities of ordinary life dissolve into a destructured, non-ordinary state, which can have a sacred aura around it" (D. Nash, 1996, p. 41); and he/she (3) develops a sense of *communitas* with other individuals (tourists or pilgrims) sharing the same process. Returning home following the journey, the individual often perceives him- or herself as "different" or in a new light, somewhat comparable to having experienced a rite of passage. The Finnish tourists exemplify secular pilgrims who, in this instance, have already found their spiritual Center, shared *communitas* with their friends, and annually seek this *liminoid* state through their return pilgrimage to the beach on the Canary Islands.

The differentiation between tourist and pilgrim prompted E. Cohen (1979a) to draft another classificatory system to distinguish between modern pilgrims and pleasure seekers.The former seek values in their journeys, either as (1) *existential pilgrims*, who leave modern life to become absorbed in a new spiritual setting; as (2) *experimental pilgrims,* 'who quest for an alternative lifestyle, especially through engaging in its authenticity; or as (.3) *experiential pilgrims*, who look for meaning in the life of others through an enjoyment of its authenticity. All three variants are prominent in Asia, including Buddhist groups in Japan, the millions of Moslems who journey to Mecca each year, and the throngs who gather at holy sites in India. By contrast, Cohen identifies the mass tourists who have become pleasure seekers either as (1) *diversionary* tourists who seek escape from the route or (2) *recreational* tourists for whom the trip is entertainment. The classification is explanatory but fails to incorporate the duality of sacred-secular behaviour often characteristic of the pilgrim tourist.

The French *Lascaux* Cave was undoubtedly a religious shrine for Paleolithic ancestors 25,000 years ago, and probably constituted a gathering place somewhat like the Inuit rendezvous. Modern visitors were so awed by the religious art work that the government was forced to close the site for preservation, and construct a mediated replica next door. The Mayan temples in Yucatan 1000 years ago were impressive pilgrimage sites for thousands of worshippers, who also shopped in the adjoining markets and gambled at the ball games. Pilgrimage, like tourism, has ancient links with aboriginal people who, probably like modern pilgrims, traveled to sacred sites for religious purposes and for what some scholars term "knowledge-based tourism" (Jackowski & Smith, 1992).

Poland is the most practicing Catholic country of Europe, and the monastery at Czestochowa is the most famous of its 11 shrines. The little town of 250,000 people hosts some 4 million visitors each year, almost one third of whom strive to be on site for the Feast of the Assumption (August 15). In 1989, in the only remaining foot pilgrimage in Europe, 150 groups walked to Czestochowa—some were as much as 20 days en route and covered 600 kilometers (Figure 1.4). The groups formed in their parish (home communities) and, as working people, planned this to be their vacation. Sometimes their pilgrimage was scheduled several years in advance, to ensure leisure and discretionary income. A truck carried camping gear to the selected night stop, and as the "pilgrims" passed farms and villages well-wishers came out to bring fruit, cookies, and juice to cheer them on.

Most Poles make such a trip once in their lifetime (except during World War II occupation when only the daring few attempted it, including Pope John Paul, then not even a seminary student). Singing as they walk, these knowledge-based pilgrims tour their country, bond with their peers (for most will remain friends thereafter), and have a fun-filled holiday under a summer sun. They are the living example of what Vukonic (1996) has termed *Homo Turisticus Religiosus*.

Tourism in Perspective

In the past half-century, tourism has become a way of life for millions of people and a future dream for many more millions. Tourism is essentially a peaceful process that silently and subtly alters public opinion and also coerces behavior. Codes for Travellers are widely published with a central theme such as "Take Only Pictures, Leave Only Memories." As a consequence, the big-game hunters who formerly displayed their mounted trophies on walls are now largely displaced by far greater numbers of travellers who protest killing elephants for ivory and donate funds to wildlife preservation. The generations

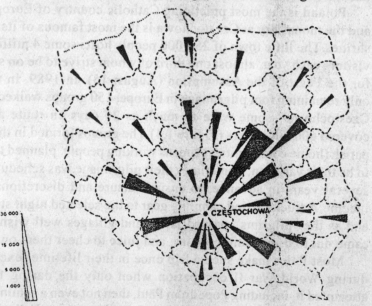

Figure 1.4. Main pilgrimages on foot (over 1000 pilgrims) to Jasna Gora in August 1987 (the triangle surface is proportionate to the pilgrim numbers). (Reprinted from A. Jackowski and V. Smith, 1992, "Polish Pilgrim Tourists," in *Annals of Tourism Research*, p. 100, with permission from Elsevier Science.)

that once mocked tribes who practiced cannibalism and sent out missionaries to "save the savages" are now replaced by a larger generation that condemns "ethnic cleansing" because they have visited African villages or vacationed in the Balkans.

Travellers in the 21 st century have a broader perception of humanity, both from their personal and their media experiences; yet their world becomes ever smaller as transportation speed increases and costs diminish. The prevailing Western philosophy of multiculturalism tends to negate the ethnic categories of "them"or"us" and substitutes the belief that a threat to peace anywhere is a threat to peace everywhere.Taken together, these two concepts support the increased importance of tourism in a plural society, and the power of tourism as a peaceful agent of change within ongoing increased globalization.

2

Tourism on the Maya Periphery

Tourism is not just about escaping work and drizzle; it is about power, increasingly internationalized power.

(Enloe, 1989, p. 40)

Canciin, the resort city on Mexico's Vucatan peninsula, is a location closely identified with the *4 S's* of mass tourism: sun, sex, sea, and sand. It has become a major holiday destination famed for sugar-fine beaches, turquoise seas, and scuba diving along a 280-kilometer coral reef. From the guest's perspective, it offers good and predictable hotels, an exotic ambiance of margaritas and mariachis, lush tropical forests, and Maya ruins. Cancún is composed of two distinct spaces: the hotel zone on what was once an island, and the city proper with a population of more than 310,000 inhabitants, many involved in the tourist trade. This destination is the entry point for more than 2 million visitors annually, an increasing number of which come to stay and play along the coastal strip of the Cancun-Tulum Corridor fronting the Caribbean (Figures 2.1 and 2.2). The "Riviera Maya," as it has now been rebranded, had a 1998 room count of 7600 units, but has attained such popularity with European charter tourists and vacationing Americans that new investment capital plans the construction of an additional 2400 rooms in the course of next 3 years. These developments reflect the 1990's trend towards a tourism oriented to environmental concerns and cultural interests—but without a loss of comfort. A parallel project centers on the transformation of Puerto Morelos, formerly a fishing village, into a major yachting destination with a marina capable of accommodating 300 boats. Other plans include two golf courses and an expansion of soft-adventure activities including scuba diving, sailing, fishing, and outings to archaeological sites. Developers promote a goal of creating attractive resorts in a Quintana.Roo "riviera" that will provide sustainable employment to the people of the area. Whether expansion of this type and magnitude is compatible with the well-being of local populations is a central concern of this chapter.

The indigenous Maya have occupied Mesoamerica for several thousand years, working the land as slash-and-burn

Figure 2.1 Map of the Yucatan Peninsule

(milpa) horticulturists, sustained by a diet of maize, beans, squash, and garden vegetables. The surrounding forest provided them with game animals, and wood and thatch for fuel and housing. The rise of state systems governed by deified kings led to the construction of dramatic ceremonial complexes such as Chichen Itza and Uxmal in Yucatan, Tikal in Guatemala, and Copán in Honduras. Now marketed by the travel industry as Mundo Maya, originally termed "La Ruta Maya CW Garrett 1989), this promotional partnership joins the central American

Tourists at Tulum. (Photo by R. Brooke Thomas and Oriol Pi-Sunyer)

nations from mexico south to Honduras, all of which of which share a Mayan indigenous heritage and archaeological ruins. Most foreign visitors come to quintana Roo as holidays-makers, and are virtually unaware of the consequences for locial inhabitants of the rapid touristic development that has taken place in the past 30 years. The Quintana Roo situation is remarkable because the penetration by a modern tourist industry has not only been fast and recent but also massive in scale. There changes have transformed a territorial periphery of the mexican republic into a First World playround and in the process led to the marginalization of much of the native population.

This case study describes the process of tourism-induced culture change among Mayan villagers in Quintana Roo. Our informants were mostly ordinary people wage workers and peasant farmers—whom we asked to position their lives, hopes, expectations, and fears in the all-too-real world of contemporary mexican politics and development plans. The research describes the specific impacts of tourism penetration on Mayan life, and how this has transformed social organization demography, wage employment, diet, and health we also examined the influence of the media, growing consumerism, and the changing political climate in southern mexico.

The Development of Quintana Roo

A generation ago, Quintana Roo remained one of the most inaccessible locations in mexico, an economic and political frontier where the institutions of the state were minimally represented. From the beginning of our research more than a decade ago, it was clear that local people were reluctant to fill roles designed for tham by the politically powerful (Daltabuit & Pi-Sunyer, 1990). specifically, they recognized that for them the drama of modernization seldom offered more than the lowest paid (and generally uncertain) wage labour. In most instances, there was little choice respecting matters of livelihood, but limited options should not be interpreted as satisfaction with conditions of life and work. Our informants, however, tended to be practical people less concerned with dismantling the structures of state and capital than with working the system to their minimum disadvantage.

In 1939, during an official tour of the then territory of Quintana Roo, President Lázaro Cardenas made it a point to assure the Maya villagers that the government would grant no land concessions to private companies (Quezada, 1940, cited by Villa Rojas, 1945, p. 35). Ten years later, in 1950, the total population of the territory still numbered only 26,967 inhabitants (up from just over 10,000 in 1930), a figure that would increase to 50,169 by 1960 (Villa Rojas, 1969, pp. 247-248), and Cancún was a village of only 600 persons. By 1990, the state's permanent population (i.e., not counting tourists) had risen almost 10-fold to 493,605 (Instituto Nacional de Estadistica, 1991, p. 207).Thus, until the advent of mass tourism in the early 1970s, Quintana Roo (which became a state in 1974) remained pretty much what it had been for centuries: an extensive region with very low population density inhabited by Maya forest dwellers in the interior and small mixed and non-Indian enclaves along the coast.To geographical distance can be added a cultural and conceptual peripherality from the national world.

The Spanish tried to colonize this extensive area, but Quintana Roo proved in hospitable, and as time went on "almost the entire region . . . was deserted by the Spanish, leaving it to those unsubdued and idolatrous' Indians who continued to hold fast to their traditions "(Villa Rojas, 1945, p. 15). Fundamentally, Quintana Roo became what Aguirre Beltran (1979) has so aptly termed a zone of refuge, first for Indians fleeing Spanish control and, following independence, for Maya villagers equally disinclined to come under Mexican rule.The 1847 native uprising in Yucatan known as the Caste War, and the many smaller insurrections that followed, further isolated the region (N. Reed, 1964). Draconian campaigns by federal troops well into the 20th century reinforced the prevailing Mayan belief that the agents of the state were both brutal and untrustworthy. The other side of the coin is that for generations the directing classes of Mexico—to the extent that they gave the matter much thought—regarded Quintana Roo as a worthless and barbarous land that contributed nothing of value to national society.Typical of this perspective is the opinion voiced by a former Mexican army doctor interviewed by the American journalist John Kenneth Turner (1969) in the early 1900s: "Quintana Roo is the most unhealthy part of Mexico. ... . For every soldier killed by a Maya at least one hundred die of starvation or sickness". At issue here is not the accuracy of the statistic, but the sense of the territory as a jungle waste, graveyard for soldiers and would-be settlers.

When did the conquest of Quintana Roo really end? Following their failure to take the city of Merida in the Caste War, the Maya insurgents retreated east and south and established a capital at Chan Santa Cruz (now Felipe Carrillo Puerto), which only fell to the Mexican army in 1901. The Maya, for their part, never conceded defeat. Farriss (1984) offers her consideration that "perhaps the conquest was not complete until 1969, with the death of the ... last of the Caste War leaders" (p. 19). Coincidentally, this date for the end of Maya autonomy is the threshold of the tourist boom.The r gion, and particularly its coast, rapidly became redefined as a tropical paradise and the tourism industry now perceives the natural and archaeological properties of the state to be vital and threatened resources. Both tourism in its more typical sun-and-sea formulation and the new ecological discourse limit the access of local populations to a diminishing stock of natural resources.

Contested control over resources represents a significant part of the broader issues that decide the roles of small-scale agriculturists and similar groups within national and global political and economic structures. When regions such as Quintana, Roo undergo modernization, local populations (still generally perceived by the dominant society as "backward") are assigned subordinate roles in the drama of development—sometimes to the point of invisibility. As Geertz (1994) points out, modernizing states "do not bring all their citizens equally with them when they join the contemporary world of capital flows, technology transfers, trade imbalances, and growth rates" (p. 3) Today, the Quintana Roo Maya find themselves part of a totalizing experience driven by the exigencies of modern tourism. In common with many other previously isolated people, they are marginalized in their own land by a rapid displacement and redefinition that is not only economic and cultural but, in many instances, also demographic. Furthermore, the expansion of tourism has stimulated such an influx of job seekers from other parts of Mexico that the indigenous population now constitutes a minority in its own land. The Maya must compete with more urbane and aggressive employees from the capital and other overcrowded areas.

Under these circumstances, the cultural landscape of the state is not easily defined. Even the use of such conventional terms as "the Maya," which may carry the implication of organic cultures and self-contained communities, has to be used with care. The reality on the ground is complex, fluid, and socially and culturally blurred. Some people are trying to make sense of overwhelming forces by holding on to elements of their past, their language, and their identity. In this dynamic cultural arena, both adaptation and resistance are part of the response. Some villagers live in what are still predominantly Maya-speaking communities heavily dependent on subsistence agriculture; other individuals try to move between several worlds. A growing number of former peasants now inhabit squatter settlements that, in the case of Cancún, are partially screened by trees but begin only a few blocks inland from five-star resort hotels. Many employee communities resemble colonial company towns, created by the demands of the tourist industry. These enclaves of marginality have very little in common with traditional Maya peasant life as conceptualized by Redfield (1947): "folk societies" of small, isolated, homogeneous village dwellers underpinned by a strong sense of group solidarity. Now, in Quintana Roo, factionalism is common and often expressed in the language of religion; there is high physical mobility and many locations, not simply the urban centers, have a heterogeneous population. What is occurring, and with extreme rapidity, is the penetration of a hegemonic order that tries to frame and define social concepts, priorities, and directions.The authority to do this does not go unchallenged, but these forces are backed by the power of the state and by a mystique of development that assumes: (1) the inevitability of economic transformation;

(2) the benefits of this process; and (3) the primacy of national goals over local claims and needs (Escobar, 1995).

To understand how such policies and positions came to impact so strongly, and so suddenly, on Quintana Roo necessitates a brief review of Mexican development policies during recent decades. It illustrates how the "global" and the "local" come together and are reconfigured in this corner of Mexico.

Mexico and the Price of Progress

For all practical purposes, Mexico has been a one-party state since 1928. Every president elected has completed his term of office, then transferred power to his handpicked successor. In terms of political control, state and party are virtually the same. The ruling party, the Partido Revolucionario Institucional (PRI), began as the heir of the Mexican Revolution—the first social revolution of the 20th century. In the 1930s (and to some extent later), the PRI undertook development programmes, not unlike those of the New Deal in the US, with policies crafted to correct social inequities and bring education and health services to the peasantry and the poor. Later, centralized policies and a political culture of authoritarian control became a screen for quick profits and the emergence of a new economic and political elite. The system is esoteric in the extreme, but functions as a mechanism for dispensing favours, grand and petty.

Because of this long history of single-party government, the political and the economic domains are particularly closely linked. Discussing this situation and its relationship to economic liberalization, the opposition presidential candidate Cuauhtemoc Cardenas commented on how the benefits and costs of development should be apportioned. "The issue is not whether the country should be modernized and opened up," he stated, but rather "who should pay the unavoidable costs of restructuring." To date, the Mexican workers—through sharply lower real wages and dramatic cuts in education, health, and housing expenditures—have carried a disproportionate share of the burden. "For Mexico, Freedom Before Free Trade" (Cardenas, 1990). Any political order dominated by centralism, paternalism, and corruption is unlikely to make much headway in reforming itself.

Demographic Pressures

The Mexican economic dilemma is often expressed as a race between development and population, although earlier in the century population grew remarkably slowly.The first modern census (1895) counted only 12.5 million Mexicans, a number that may have approximated the size of the indigenous population at the time of Cortos' conquest (1519). By 1950, the population had doubled to almost 26 million, and had tripled to 77 million by 1984. In 1998 Mexico ranked 11th in population size among world nations, with 98 million people, and is projected to increase another 60% to 154 million people by 2050 (United Nations, 1996).This" surge is most often attributed (sometimes exclusively) to a sharp decline in the mortality rate, but whatever the cause, rapid growth is clearly related to modern social processes and is a pressing issue. In the early 1970s, 2 million Mexicans were born every year, a statistic that would later translate into an enormous gap between a plentiful supply of labour and a lack of jobs.Approaching the millenium, the workforce was still expanding at the rate of 3% per year, and some 35% of Mexicans were under 15 years of age with a full 80% under age 40.

Development Models

In the four decades following World War II, the conventional yardsticks of Mexico's productivity, gross national product (GNP) and gross domestic product (GDP), kept pace with population, rising about 6% per year, which translates to a 10 fold increase. Optimists could argue that growth was winning the race, but these measures are notoriously deceptive. Neither GNP nor GDP measures the welfare of a society or assesses the aims and ultimate uses of goods and services. Similarly, these indices offer no information about environmental and resource issues.To use a local example, the heavy commercial logging and forest clearance in southeastern Mexico, which have devastated the ecology of the region, are included as an added GNP and GDP

In Mexico, even the most favourable growth statistics commonly obscure unresolved problems. The post-World War II development model has minimally improved the living standards for the majority of the population. Its benefits have primarily accrued to the political and economic elite and, to a lesser degree, to the expanding middle sector of society and, of course, to foreign investors. Income distribution is so skewed that the top 10% of the population receives 39.5% of the national income, and the bottom 20% of the population shares a scant 4.1% (World Bank. 1995, p. 221).

Traditional economic plans solicit intensified investment and development with the expectation that these inputs will, in due course, improve the general standard of living and in the process reduce demographic pressure (Rohter, 1990, pp. 1-6). However, it makes a great deal of difference how such investments are allocated. Twenty years ago, the president of the World Bank observed that "if the growth in national income does not result in improvements of the living conditions of the lower income groups, it will not help to reduce fertility throughout the society" (D. Gordon, 1978, p. 3). In general, improvements in the material welfare of poor people lead to important demographic consequences. However, what has occurred in Mexico is that during these decades of industrialization and expanding urbanization, the population has tripled, unemployment has become more acute, and the labour force is increasing more rapidly.There have never been more billionaires in Mexico, but about a third of the population lives in poverty.

Tourism Development in Yucatan

Tourism is a key component in the Mexican development strategy. It is typically presented as a sort of internal export industry; what are sold are the various national "attractions," whether archaeological, natural, or cultural. In the process, a flow of foreign exchange is generated and one can balance the money coming in against the money going.out.The figures are very favourable. In 1990, Mexico hosted 16. million international visitors, ranked eighth in the world for tourist arrivals, and earned US$5,467 million. By 1999, Mexico ranked seventh among all nations with its 20.2 million tourists, and benefited from earnings of US$7.9 billion (WTO, 2000). In global and regional terms, Mexico ranks second only to the US in numbers of international tourists coming to the Americas. Tourism differs from other export sectors in that both production and consumption take place at home, which is another way of saying that it is labour intensive, an attractive feature for a country that suffers high rates of unemployment and underemployment.

Where does Quintana Roo fit into this picture? In many respects, tourism patterns here are similar to those encountered elsewhere in Mexico.Tourism is predominantly a business that takes place in special tourist enclaves, in resorts such as Cancun, and, increasingly, in gated complexes that provide accommodation and recreation within highly controlled, secured, environments. Fundamentally, First World guests are ensconced in what is still very much a Third World country. A middle-class Mexican informant offered his opinion that the lifestyle of Quintana Roo resort dwellers "has more in common with the ways of south Florida than with anything Mexican."

The dominant influence in Quintana Roo tourism remains Cancún, the port of entry for the majority of foreign tourists, of whom 91% are American. Most foreign visitors are relatively young—average age 36 years—with an annual income between US$65,000 and US$75,000 (FONATUR, 1993, p. 12). From its inception, Cancún tourism projects have been large scale, capital intensive, and highly concentrated with respect to ownership. Most are owned by foreign nationals—chiefly in the form of major hotel chains—or Mexican investors. The ability of Mexican national and local elite to exercise substantial influence over Yucatecan tourism has long been noted (R. Lee, 1978). The financial structure dates to a development plan initiated in 1969, ostensibly dependent on a trust fund administered by FONATUR (Fondo Nacional de Fomento al Turismo), the agency charged with planning. In theory, FONATUR was underwritten by the Mexican government, but in reality, of the total initial investment amount of US$70 million, some US$30 million came from the Inter-American Development Bank and a further US$20 million from private, mostly foreign, investors. Fundamentally, this translates into "big tourism" centered on the construction of large first-class facilities, but offering few benefits to small entrepreneurs and local wage earners (L. Turner & Ash, 1976, p. 203).

According to initial plans, Cancún island was to be the primary tourist zone with hotels and guest services. "Ciudad Cancun" was supposed to develop as the secondary tourist zone or service city, and to benefit the locally employed population with utilities, roads, schools, and health facilities. Public assurances promised that strict zoning regulations would be followed and environmental protection diligently enforced. Very early in the building of Cancún, Mexican government officials asserted they had had an anthropological team help lay out the city—its hospitals, its schools and its houses—and were taking pains to avoid social tensions later. Alas, this integrated tourist planning effort was never really put into effect, and FONATUR essentially became a tool of tourism promotion. Cludad Cancún remains woefully short of public services, and environmental safeguards are often disregarded.

To these inadequacies should be added the sense that Cancún is hardly a Mexican city, but one catering to the strange ways of foreigners. Other observers have remarked on this alienness—and the cultural separation that accompanies it: "Begging was banned on the streets of Cancun to minimize tourists' exposure to the poverty of local workers. While wealthy vacationers cruise in taxis to classy restaurants and 'springbreakers' transit to the discos downtown, hotel employees are packed like lemmings into lurching diesel buses that ferry them home to humble colonias north of the city" (Celaya & Owen, 1993, p. 441). In addition, the hours of work are long and hard, wages are poor, and, for the slightest infraction, they may not be paid at all. Many employees work split shifts, with no place to go in the interim; they may not use the hotel-owned beaches or patronize local cafes or shops.

Two further features of Cancún warrant comment. The first is the near-absence of a modern cultural heritage. To fill this void, the individual resorts have concoctd images of faked authenticity, including Caribbean adventure and countless designs vaguely attributable to the ancient Maya. Given this Disneyland-like version of the archaeological past, foreign guests commonly believe that the Maya are "extinct." Second, Cancún reflects the 1960's development concept, with its emphasis on massive investment and huge buildings. The world has changed significantly since Mexican technicians used the magic of the computer to plan the resort. For tourism, probably the most important change is ideological and perceptual, with a much greater interest in, and concern for, the environment. This newfound ecotourism interest has clearly influenced tourism promotion. The following passage from Passport Cancún (1994) is an enticement to experience the natural while it is "still around," and describes the "still crystal-clear waters and virgin beaches" south of Cancún: "This is a land that still belongs to nature, where ocelots, kinkajous and spider monkeys still roam wild in their native habitat, and where giant sea turtles—almost extinct in other parts of the world—still flood the coast each spring to lay their delicate eggs in the moonlit sands.

The Maya and Marginality

Our extensive fieldwork involved four village locations that represented progressive levels of tourism impact: isolated and traditional Punta Laguna; intermediary Cobá (described below); Akumal (destroyed by hurricane in 1995); and Ciudad Chemuyil, the most un-Maya settlement. Daltabuit (1992) had previously conducted extensive research on health and nutrition in the communities of Cobá and Yalcob. The primary research goals were to understand and document (1) the role of tourism as the agent of rapid cultural change and (2) the penetration of state institutions and market forces that were impacting a peasant population.

Cobá seemed a particularly appropriate place to initiate this study. A substantial village of 819 inhabitants (Daltabuit, 1996, p. 21), Cobá has several features that would appear to place it in the category of the quintessential Maya peasant community. It had been settled by a small group of Yucatecan Maya agriculturists some 60 years ago when those living in the Quintana Roo interior were pretty much left to their own devices. Later, the village was granted *ejido* communal tenure to some of the land it worked, but other areas—especially those in and around the extensive archaeological zone—were designated as protected federal lands. All the evidence, both in the literature and from field data, indicates that Cobá was representative of traditional Maya communities that, until recently, had been intimately linked through mechanisms of reciprocity and agricultural practices that reinforced social solidarity. In the 16th century, Diego de Landa (1941) described the Maya as having "the good habit of helping each other in all their labours" (p. 98). Kintz (1990), writing chiefly of the recent past, notes the same spirit of reciprocity:

Collection of goods and the redistribution of items (particularly food) was an economic pattern that enhanced security for all families... . The economic web that collected and centralized goods and redistributed the excess ensured that no one starved.This re—distribution system of economically important goods was formalized under ritual circumstances that traditionally occurred throughout the yearly cycle,

Communal agricultural work, particularly slash-and-burn cultivation *(milpa)*, has been gradually superseded by wage labour jobs that now threaten household co-operation. Individual household plots are still part of the communal land grant *(ejido)* that includes *milpa* and an undivided forest *(monte)* to which villagers have, until recently, enjoyed unhindered access. In Cobá, the minimum land needed to maintain a single family through the slash-and-burn cycle is some 50 hectares of rainforest (about 123 acres), to which should be added space for kitchen gardens and the raising of pigs and chickens. Now many of these holdings are reduced to 20 hectares per household, or even less.The restrictions on forest use are increasingly onerous, and are greatly resented. In Cobá, one must go 4 kilometers into the forest, and it may take up to 50 round-trips to obtain the building materials for a single traditional thatch and hardwood house.

There is a pervasive belief that as each year passes agriculture is becoming more unpredictable. Given the pressure on land and resources, it is not surprising that at least one third of the able-bodied men must now seek employment outside the community. During our stay in 1994, at least 50 Coba men found work helping to excavate and reconstruct an archaeological site inside the extensive Xcaret eco-theme park *(Figure* 2.3).

What is distinctive of Cobá is the location of the village at the very edge of one of the largest archaeological complexes in the Yucatan—a Classic Maya site from which the community takes its name. Since the late 1970s, Cobá has become an important tourist destination. Busloads of tourists, totaling 70,000 annual visitors, arrive daily and make their way to the archaeological remains and the surrounding rainforest. The presence of visitors stimulated the making of handicrafts and the opening of small stores, while the development of the ruins into a destination for adventure tourism led to a greater interest in ethnic tourism. The ecotourism literature promises that tour visits can protect the social, cultural, and psychological characteristics of the local communities, and that in authentic Indian villages everything is as God intended it to be—natural, healthy, away from the stress and the lights and glamour; an area where tourists can relax, be themselves, see the wonders, and help the Indians.

This external modernization has worked to intertwine the world of international tourism (exemplified by the Club Med hotel overlooking Lake Cobá) with the lives of one-time subsistence farmers. Although an estimated 40% of working-age Cobá population derive some income from tourism, this employment pulls the youngest and strongest from the fields. That the people of Cobá are trying to navigate their way through a rapidly changing and contradictor' world is also apparent from the religious-communal dimension. Some 20 years ago, religious

Figure   . Workers reconstructing a Mayan site. (Photo by R. Brooke Thomas and Oriol Pi-Sunyer)

practice in Cobá was a variant of folk syncretism that joined elements of Catholic ritual to a Mayan cosmology in which the *milpa* and the forest represent a model of the universe.The task of the ritual practitioner was to help maintain the various components, and their keepers and spirits, in order and balance. Something of this belief remains, but Cobá is now an arena for competing congregations.There are five—some claim six— different religious groups. Sectarian balkanization has reinforced individualism and tended to deauthorize communal ties and rituals. New belief systems are congruent with a sense of the individual as consumer and autonomous economic agent.

The growing reliance on outside employment and changes in patterns of village reciprocity can be broadly applied to other Quintana Roo communities. Common themes and processes differ in magnitude rather than in subject, and our analysis of ongoing culture change draws on the other three villages as well as on Coba. While tourism has clearly been the engine of economic and social transformation in quintana Roo, from the beginning it was linked to official development plans responding to national, rather than local, initiatives and priorities.

This history, this process, has relevance for our research design and the issues that it addresses. Perhaps even more so than elsewhere, in Quintana Roo one cannot examine "tourism" as something separate from the many other changes that accompany it.To cite a couple of examples, the construction of the highway linking Cobá with the coast not only put this interior village on the tourist itinerary but chiefly responsible for bringing it into the orbit of powerful market forces. The same road that transports busloads of foreign tourists to visit the Maya ruins also carries the trucks that deliver the soft drinks, prepared foods, and other items destined for local consumption. Electrification— another facet of rural modernization—has done much more than improve lighting: in the course of a decade it has helped transform virtually everyone in Cobá into an avid television viewer. In turn, exposure to television entails exposure to the mass-mediated messages of advertising. To interpret changes of this type as simply individual consumer choices misses the consequences they have for an array of communal issues, including social structure, cultural practice, and public health. The decline of kitchen gardens—a general trend to be sure— marks not only a growing dependency on wage labour and commercial foodstuffs but real erosion of local knowledge respecting herbal remedies and their application.

The Elements of Social Change

A major challenge was how to deal systematically with such interlinked processes and influences, and to obtain a sense of the political economy of tourism, especially as it affected: (1) social relations and cultural systems; (2) food consumption; (3) environmental adaptation and resource control; and (4) women's health. A common thread of commodification was apparent in all four settlements, in which most people, in the space of a generation, had been transformed into a class of wage earners. The loss of land instilled a deeper fear of crop failure. Many people felt poor, and spoke of the shortage of cash and the lack of decent jobs.

To assess the broader aspects of these processes, use of a household questionnaire provided information on a range of issues, among them employment, consumption patterns, education, attitudes towards tourism, and cultural identity. A total of 82 households was sampled, with the largest sample (34) from Cobá. We also carried out anthropometric surveys in two schools (most of the elementary school pupils) and a pilot study of food consumption habits. Henry Geddes (1996), a co-investigator, researched the impact of radio and television. The sample—about a quarter of the villagers—is more than sufficient to provide a solid database and suggest trends in social and economic change. For example, the open-ended inquiry, "Who benefits most from tourism?" was often greeted with astonishment (the answer apparently being self-evident) but was followed by a catalogue of such responses as "the hotels," "the bosses," and "the rich." Clearly, the majority of our informants view themselves as exploited, people who receive minimum wages (about $10 a day) for low-skilled tertiary work. Sometimes, this condition is expressed in the most unambiguous terms, as one man described construction work on the coast as "slave work" (Geddes, 1996, p. 5). But this recognition of exploitation does not mean a desire to revert to subsistence agriculture and the old forms of rural life. It is instructive to trace the responses to the question, "Would things be better without tourism?" Seventy-eight percent of the sample responded in the negative. There is clearly a nostalgia for the past, combined with a fear of losing language and identity, but the only alternative to greater poverty is employment in tourism— however badly paid and demeaning.

A particular example may give human shape to the complexity of such attitudes. One of our most articulate respondents is a woman in her middle thirties, a single parent who works in one of the largest new resort complexes on the coast. When we visited her home we were struck by her "modern" appearance and demeanour—crisp white shorts with matching tee shirt, brand-name sneakers, trimmed and styled functional hair. Her house is a *palapa* with wooden walls and palm thatch roof, with a cement floor that keeps it dry and easy to clean. Inside, she had tastefully arranged the spaces and contents, and while hardly lavishly furnished, it was comfortable in all respects. The overall impression of house and owner was of modernity—a traditional structure containing a harmonious mix of old pieces and contemporary appliances.

Born in a Maya village in Chiapas, she described her parents as "good people of the pueblo, of the older generation;" She had married at a young age—"much too young"—to a man who had turned out to be a drunk and a wife-beater. In her own words, she managed to "escape misery and torment." Leaving her children in her parents' care, she headed for the coast and sought work in tourism. A decade later, she had saved enough money to buy a house of her own and regularly sent a third of her wages to support her children and help out her now-aging parents.

   This is a story of liberation—no less than the reconstruction of a life—in the face of adversity and poverty, and our respondent made it abundantly clear that her material and emotional independence, and the well-being of her children, had been achieved as a result of employment in tourism. With the same analytical clarity, however, she detailed the grueling work schedule, the extent of corporate control over the life of workers, a work environment permeated with racism and sexism ("we don't exist as human beings"), and the tremendous disparity between wages received and the wealth of clients. In this resort it was mandatory for workers to carry two types of identification (one pinned to the company uniform), and they were not allowed to stray from strictly designated areas. Her job in the huge laundry, "a place of steam and noise," paid more than chambermaid work, but it left her completely wrung out at the end of the shift. Still, since she needed the money, it was her intention to continue working in this unhealthy and enervating place for as long as she had strength. This biography is not idiosyncratic. The author is remarkably articulate, and her discussion of industrial disciplinary practices echoes Foucault's (1980, p. 39) observation that such power seeks to reach "into the very grain of individuals" She also stands out as a single mother in a rural area where this status is still somewhat uncommon. But what she speaks about, the strategies of making a living, and the pains and opportunities that have accompanied the development of mass tourism, has been related by many other people [see also Madsen Camacho's (1996) discussion of the hotel industry in Huatulco].

Social Relations and Cultural Systems

   Society is undergoing a veritable reordering of cultural meanings and priorities that is externally driven and over which

local people have little control. Quite evidently, much of the
population is becoming wage dependent, and landless Indians
(as well as non-Indians) are moving into the coastal zone in
search of employment.The Maya of the interior, who still control
significant resources, are increasingly pressured to alter their
livelihood and collective identity. As the old structures of
community and subsistence experience increased stress, the
sense of group membership suffers and local discontents mount.
Only a generation ago, property was identified with locality in a
system reinforced by an egalitarian ethos and a sense of justice
that considered exclusive property rights as selfish individualism.
Today, much communal property has been privatized or has come
under government control. This shift is paralleled and reinforced
by the new emphasis on the individual. The government deals in
citizens and voters; for entrepreneurs, Maya villagers are treated
as consumers or would-be consumers, and as a labour supply to
fill servile jobs.

These changes have profound consequences for the fabric
of social life.Thus, in what was once rural Cobá, a new local
bourgeoisie has emerged composed of merchants, shopkeepers,
ranchers, and restaurant owners—stakeholders in tourism and
community leadership. Similar processes of class segmentation
have been documented in several other indigenous
Mesoamerican communities (Annis 1987, pp. 60-74). These
changes are not limited to the material and economic, for
increased social stratification often correlates with cultural
differentiation: the well-to-do are noticeably more comfortable
in the Spanish language and other markers of national culture
than are poor peasant farmers. Religion is not without a cultural
component, and Coba has become a zone of religious conflict.
Evangelical congregations typically conduct their services in
Spanish and host visiting Spanish-speaking preachers and
musical groups. The ideology they espouse stresses the centrality
of individual salvation and the dyadic link of person and God.

The family network is also changing. Young couples were
outspoken in their preference to live separately from their

parents, and nave smaller families. They emphasized the greater freedom (personal and economic) that nucleated arrangements are supposed to facilitate, but it is also possible that such an orientation reflects partly understood metropolitan models, perhaps derived from the media. This apparent trend towards nuclear family structures suggests that support from the extended family in childcare and related activities may become less readily available in the future. Also, we noted that in Coba, some elderly people now live lonely lives of extreme poverty.

Consumerism

Throughout rural Quintana Roo, increased contact with tourism and the national culture correlates with soaring consumption norms. Only money buys the long list of commodities that forms part of the new requirements and aspirations: food and household supplies, agricultural tools and products, building materials, furnishings, and electronic equipment. School children need proper clothes and supplies. Quintana Roo is not a rich agricultural or manufacturing region. Virtually all the staples necessary to feed tourists and resort workers must be shipped in from distant places, at prices high by national, not to mention local, standards. Electricity and butane have to be purchased. Men want new bikes and adolescent boys eye used cars. Younger people are more and more concerned with style and all males now wear some variant of Western casual attire. The *buipil,* the traditional Maya women's dress, is seen much less often, particularly in coastal communities. At times, a substantial portion of household income is spent on medical care and health expenses, especially commercial drugs, a reflection of how drastically the authority of h-men, the Maya curer-priests, has eroded.

The Role of the Media

No single artifact of modernizing society has such far-reaching effects as television, introduced into the villages within the past 15 years or so. According to our household inventory, 67% of Cobá households owned sets, and many families watch TV 6 hours per day. As Kottak (1990) has noted with reference to both Brazil and the 115, "television is one of the most powerful information disseminators, public opinion moulders, and socializing agents in today's world". Television and other mass media exercise their power in diverse ways. They restructure the context of social relations, both public and private; bring about changes in beliefs, values, and types of knowledge; profoundly influence popular culture; impact on political views; and most certainly act as powerful commercial agents (Pace, 1993). Television dominates the mass media environment and plays a critical role in two spheres: the construction of images and symbols of national society, and the propagation of a culture of consumption. Contemporary nation-states use visual mass media to help constitute "imagined communities" in the sense first elaborated byAnderson (1991).Such communities are imagined because even the members of the smallest nation "will never know most of their fellow-members, meet them, or even hear of them, yet in the mind of each lives the image of their communion" (Anderson, 1991, p. 6). In the process of image making (Hamilton, 1990), television functions as a "national imaginary": a mirror of society in which we see ourselves while we think we are seeing others. It matters a good deal what the viewer sees in this mirror.

Television in Mexico is concentrated in ownership, closely linked to the institutions of political power, and homogenous with respect to message— particularly at the level of mass culture. The themes and images to which Maya households are exposed seldom relate to indigenous peoples, or to such pressing social problems as emigration, unemployment, or poverty. Television portrays a national society where everyone speaks Spanish and forms part of a common culture; the message is one of assimilation.This national myth is reinforced through cultural practices that are now highly ritualized (Geddes, 1996), and linked to national stereotypes that celebrate dramatic hypermascufinity and individualism. The principil carriers of these forms are the Mexican-produced soap operas, the telenovelas, which depict a distant fantasy world peopled by men and women engaged in a succession of tragedies, triumphs, and misdeeds. It is a universe that is generally violent and unpredictable, and whose values are often in conflict with the Maya ideals of community, reciprocity, and marital fidelity. Since television is relatively new, the appeal at this juncture is probably as much the medium as the message. But, nevertheless, the message is followed closely. People will discuss at length the plot and subplot of popular telenovelas. Miller (1994), who studied the nearby village of Yalcoba, supports our impression that television makes young people feel impoverished and deprived.

The link between television and the growing acceptance of consumption values is particularly strong. For Maya peasants and unskilled workers, television projects into their lives new forms of being and belonging—metropolitan, competitive, driven'by materialism—that are only being experienced at the edges. As it parades an outside world of wealth and power (the world from which the rich tourists come), some Maya sense their marginality and dissatisfaction with the status quo. However, they generally lack the power to question the contrasts, let alone reject this new materialism.TV sets are expensive and powerful status symbols and commonly the focal point of living spaces; a shrine-like arrangement in which the set is surrounded by family pictures, flowers, stuffed animals, or other mementos is not unusual. And certainly the price of ownership is high. A black-and-white set costs the equivalent of some US$200, with a hook-up fee of US$230 and a monthly charge of US$6-7.

The theme of consumption is implicit in programmes and blatant in commercials. For Mexico as a whole, television has become the major advertising agent, especially for national and international products such as Bimbo bread, Coca-Cola, Nestle, pharmaceutical products, Sabritas snacks (PepsiCo), alcoholic beverages, and cigarettes.The mix of programmes and commercials received in Quintana Roo is similar to the rest of Mexico but the audience is largely unlettered. Products are presented in such a manner as to seem accessible, convenient, not too expensive, and the markers of modernity.

Food Consumption

Both television and tourism are expressions of consumption. Much of what is visibly consumed is various kinds of food and drink.These worlds merge: tourists consume, and consumption is valorized on television. Many products such as Coca-Cola are easily obtained, often within reach of a child with only a few pesos, from a store in an adjoining house. In villages like Cobá, women often operate a refrescos store as a source of supplemental income.

To estimate the degree of dietary change, we used different techniques of measurement, including counting deliveries to town, interviews with storeowners, talking to children, and 24-hour recall.The data are all approximations, but point in much the same direction. A 24-hour recall study in Akumal (McGarty, 1995) found the three most commonly consumed foods at meals to be tortillas, Coca-Cola, and beans. Snacks included white and sweet breads *(pan dulce)* and various types of cookies and potato chips. Combined, they made up a large part of almost a quarter of the meals. Recalled soft-drink consumption (during and in between meals) was on the order of two to three drinks a day, and in actuality may well have been significantly higher.Altogether, this adds up to a lot of sugar, and when cola consumption is combined with coffee for breakfast and a variety of chocolate-flavored snack foods, the amount of caffeine is also quite elevated. The biological consequences of this changing diet, now high in sugars and fat, is a marked increase in dental caries, including secondary dentition erupting with already serious decay. Babies are sometimes given Coke in a feeding bottle after 6 months, and they come to prefer this to mothers' milk. Overall, the pattern is one of dietary deterioration rather than deprivation. Essentially, the shift is not from subsistence farming to a well-stocked supermarket, but from food production to reliance on cheap commercial foods with a long shelf life. Canned Spam-like meat and Vienna sausages, both high in fat and salt, are substitutes for homegrown chicken and pork, and canned tomatoes and tomato paste replace garden produce. These dietary changes are the result of wage employment and diminished resource control.

Environmental Adaptation and Resource Control

Historically, the transformation of peasantry into a proletariat involved the loss of control of the means of subsistence, as was the case in early modern Europe (De Vries, 1976, pp. 30-84) and later in various Latin American societies (Valdez, 1996). In Quintana Roo, however, the situation differed in at least two ways. First, as previously noted, much of the state was a *"zone* of refuge," and inland populations lived in relatively autonomous enclaves; second, the pace of change has been precipitous. Taken together, these two features shed light on some of the stresses that we witnessed.To offset loss of cropland, some Maya agriculturists are turning to cash crops, especially raising cattle. But the meat is sold to urban centers and seldom consumed locally. For dispossessed farmers wage employment is the only solution.

A complex rearrangement of access and rights is under way. Beachfront areas (including reserves and sanctuaries) are essentially under the full control of government agencies and the tourist and recreation industry. Local people have virtually no access. The forests are still very extensive, and 80 miles south of Cancún the Sian Ka'an Biosphere Reserve protects 1.3 million acres of the "ecological cornucopia" (W. Garrett,

1989) that provided' so well for generations of indigenous Maya. Privatization—including changes in agrarian reform legislation—threatens much other federally protected land.

Quintana Roo may, in some respects, be moving in the same direction as Costa Rica, where controls have helped improve environmental protection designated areas—but also profoundly affected local communities. In Tortuguero National Park (Place, 1991) villagers formerly relied heavily on animal protein from the forest, beach, and river. With the advent of tourism, and strict controls on local subsistence, the increase in visitors to Tortuguero has left the local inhabitants with no visible means of subsistence. Likewise in Quintana Roo, beachfront owners have declared themselves protectors of the environment and employed patrols to discourage "poachers." Thus, the specifics of Quintana Roo, as analyzed here, are issues important to regional planning in southern Mexico and Central America, all of which share the mix of cultural tourism and ecotourism. These projects, in particular Mundo Maya and Paseo Pantera, are designed to stimulate regional integration and "soft-path" tourist development. On paper, they call for broad-based community participation, but if the past is any guide, local involvement will be minimal.

Women's Health

Does tourism have an impact on household demography and women's health and diet? The changing diet of the Maya foreshadows serious cardiovascular risks, although high blood pressure does not appear to be a problem at this juncture. Part of the reason may be that pork is still regarded as something of a festive food and that the total consumption of meat is relatively low, even if potted meats and similar products are high in fat and salt, likewise, infant mortality rates arc reported to be low, and young mothers and their babies are not at higher risks according to local nurses and physicians. In all probability, this mixed picture reflects the relative novelty of "convenience foods" and the fact that older people were brought up on a much healthier diet. In keeping with expectations, there is a positive association between a later age of having children and the degree of involvement in wage labour. Thus, in response to the question,"What is the best age to start having children?" the answers clearly reflected the individual's employment status. The link we between wage labour and fertility may be one of the most important changes taking place in the less traditional sectors of Quintana Roo society. Obviously, people living semiurban lives (with little or no possibilities for fanning and gardening) can only make limited use of child labour, and children cease to be an economic asset. Another consideration is the changing employment pattern with its growing emphasis on feminized labour. As tourism shifts from construction to services and maintenance, a greater percentage of jobs is opening up to women—however poorly paid these positions may be.

Conclusions

Our Maya informants were well aware that the benefits of tourism have been very unevenly distributed. They had heard messages of "economic development" and "progress" from the media and visiting politicians, but the language always seemed remote, not really directed at them. Education was deemed an asset, but it spoke more of the outside world, not their own. Nothing in the Mexican system of education reinforces or dignifies the identity of present-day indigenous people. Economically, their stake in tourism is generally limited to the kinds of jobs that they have been allowed to fill, nothing approaching "local involvement in the decision-making process" or "host control or ownership of touristic infrastructure," which Mansperger (1995, p. 93) describes as desirable in effective tourism development in small-scale economies. The full impact of many variables discussed here is difficult to measure, but the evidence indicates that the greater the disruption in land tenure systems and forms of land utilization, the more harmful the impacts of tourism.

How have local people reacted to the advent of tourism? The answer—the only answer that can be given—is that the response has been mixed. There has been accommodation as well as resistance. Some local people have benefited, most obviously the merchants of Cobá, by virtue of proximity to a large-scale tourist attraction. We have tried not to present a picture of a romanticized indigenous society as unitary and in undiluted opposition to the outside world. As Ortner (1995) notes wi:h reference to the colonial Maya, "such groups have their own politics— not just between chiefs and commoners and landlords and peasants but within all the local categories of friction and tension: men and women, parents and children, seniors and juniors . . . and on and on".

Resistance to the dominant order exists, but it is often passive and difficult to interpret. When a poor peasant steals from a rich man, or "poaches" game that the state has defined as protected, is this a form of resistance or simply survival? Many such minor infringements of the law take place. At another level, the vast majority of our informants felt that their culture was being undermined—although what they most feared varied considerably from person to person. There was consensus that education for their children would ultimately improve their income through better jobs, but the school did not teach anything about Mayan culture, even though the villagers of Coba lived adjacent to superb ruins. Our impression, especially in the context of the uprising in Chiapas, is that "Maya" is being generalized to stand for all peasants and workers, all poor people. One of our informants in Ciudad Chenmuyil, whose "European" features and light hair were inherited from Spanish emigrant grandparents, responded to the question of her origin, "I'm not Maya in ancestry, but I understand the condition of the poor and the campesinos; I feel Maya."

Acknowledgments—This chapter is based on two summer field seasons in Quintana Roo (1993, 1994) and a number of other visits. We are very grateful for the support provided by the Wenner-Gren Foundation for Anthropological Research (grant No. 5618) and the University of Massachusetts (Faculty Research Grant, Summer 1994). Our essay is based on data and insights obtained by the whole Yucatan Project team whose other members were MarneT.Ausec, Henry Geddes Gonzáles, Guillermo Iranzo, Catherine McGarty, Markéta Sebelová, and Ellie Zucker. Without the help of many different people in the communities it would have been impossible to piece together this picture of present-day life in Quintana Roo. We are particularly indebted to the Centro Ecológico Akumal for invaluable assistance. Any errors or misperceptions are entirely our responsibility.

3

Power and Ethnicity in "Paradise": Boracay, Philippines

Boracay has often been termed a tropical "paradise"—a beautiful little island with a white beach of "talcum powder" sand fringed by palm trees arching around a crystal blue bay of warm water. This relatively flat island, only 4.5 miles long and 1.7 miles wide, lying on the west coast of the Philippines (Figure 3.1), was a tourist "discovery" 30 years ago. In 1997 it was a crowded Asian "Waikiki" hosting mainland Asians for whom, at present, there is a dearth of inexpensive resorts of this type. The transition from farming community to world-famous resort has been locally painful, resulting in degradation of the physical landscape and marginalization of the indigenous hosts. The demand-supply trend demonstrated here raises important issues concerning power and ethnicity in future Asian tourist areas.

Filipino Heritage

It is important at the outset of this study to understand that although the Philippine islands are geographically positioned off the coast of Asia, the Filipinos do not consider themselves Asian, either genetically or culturally. The Filipino population is descended from several waves of immigrants who peopled the islands over a period of many millennia. They included proto-Malaysians (who probably were also the first settlers in Polynesia), and ultimately Malaysians, Chinese, Indians, Arabs, and Indonesians, all of whom predated Magellan's "discovery" of the islands in 1521 AD. Soon after his report to Spain. Spanish conquistadors and their accompanying friars occupied large tracts of land, and converted the population into the Spanish-Catholic tradition. After nearly 400 years of Spanish influence, educated Filipinos spoke Spanish as well as their native Tagalog. Filipinos looked to Spain as their colonial model during the centuries that China and Japan were closed to outsiders and Manila was a friendly port of call for sailing vessels. The Philippines has long been recognized as the "most Western" country of Asia in language, philosophy, and lifestyle. Following the transfer of the islands to the United States in 1898, English became the dominant language of commerce and government. The tenure of the

Figure 3.1 Map of the Philippines.

United States until World War II continued this Western orientation and intermarriage, and elementary schools were established in rural areas. With the introduction of radio and television in English, most contemporary Filipinos speak Tagalog as a primary language but are equally fluent in English. Their European culture orientation is manifest in their lifestyle and in their arts (as their folk dances include flamenco), and the traditional cuisine is more Continental than Asian. The residents of Boracay share this Euro-American heritage, and as farmers they raise more field crops than rice.

Boracay: The Development of Tourism
The Early Phase: 1970-1984

After supporting a farm population of some 3000 persons until World War II, Boracay was "discovered" as an inexpensive vacation locale in the early 1970s. These first tourists were American and European families from the diplomatic corps stationed in Asia. The hospitable English-speaking Filipino landowners built thatched cottages to house them, provided fresh fish, chickens, and garden vegetables, and pocketed with pleasure this modest cash income. By the mid-1970s, the rustic setting with only kerosene lanterns for light made Boracay a near-ideal family vacation spot at very low cost. Word-of-mouth recommendations about this island paradise—where a cottage was US$5.per night, a main meal cost US$ 1, and a cane of beer only US$0.10—spread to young, single, European backpackers. A few began to drift into Boracay in the late 1970s to spend a few weeks in winter, and more cottage complexes were constructed to house them. By the early 1980s Boracay had attained an international reputation among these dominantly European "drifter" tourists. The salubrious winter climate from November to March brought gentle breezes to warm the fine coral sand beach, and palm trees shaded the thatched cottages.

National Government Interest

The 1970s was the era of World Bank support for tourism development, and the Philippine government eagerly turned to international tourism as a panacea for its sagging unemployment. The Philippine economy had been shattered during World War II by the Japanese occupancy of the archipelago. The fragile postwar independence economy was further shaken by a series of disastrous typhoons that destroyed many coconut plantations and greatly reduced copra production. Copra, or dried coconut meat, had long been an important Philippine agricultural export as a nutritious stock feed. This revenue disappeared when copra was replaced on the world market by other products. Adding to the economic woes, the Huk insurgencies were politically disruptive and discouraged tourism. While continental Asian economies began to blossom, the Philippines was infused by corruption and cronyism.

By 1975, consistent with a national tourism policy (see Richter, Chapter 22), the presence of even these few tourisis prompted then-president Marcos to declare Boracay a Tourist Preserve, and its future development was vested in the Philippines Tourism Authority (PTA). This announcement was a silent signal to some wealthy Manila families that the purchase of land on Boracay would be a good long-term investment, as beach frontage was then selling for only US$I per square meter. With assistance from the PTA, a Cottage Owner's Association was formed in 1979, and the by laws restricted membership to Filipino Cottage Owners (V. Smith, 1992a). This body established development standards, including a 30-foot (Iometer) setback from the beach for all construction to preserve the tropical panorama of palms and sea. All powered vehicles were to be banned. Seemingly, local governance was in place.

Growth and the Quest for Funding

In 1981, the Ministry of Tourism declared the entire island a Tourist Zone and established a Tourist Office (1983) to assist arriving guests and collect statistics (Figure 3.2). By then, enough "backpackers" had targeted Boracay as a destination to support a French-operated sports center, which rented motor scooters (a powered vehicle). To further meet tourist demand, several refreshment stands (nightclubs) installed gasoline-powered generators to refrigerate beer and to provide juke boxes and

neon lights at night. The chickens still crowed at dawn but the
bucolic quietude of Boracay had been shattered.

It is to their great credit that the Philippine Department of
Tourism recognized the uniqueness of Boracay and its tourism
potential in the early 1980s. Based on only visitor statistics of
14,277 annual visitors, the PTA commissioned a well-known
Hawaiian resort development company to determine the resort
capability of this tiny site. Their proposal included construction

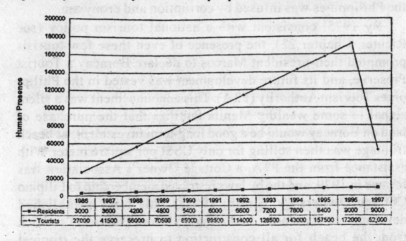

Figure   Growth of permanent residents compared with tourists in Boracay:
1986–1997. Data are averaged. Source: Trousdale (1999).

of a resort with golf course and horse trails but set occupancy
limits of 1700-1900 rooms, a dally employee count of 2400-2600
persons, and a total permanent population of Boracaynons
between 4000 and 4600. However, the report clearly stipulated
the resort required an off-island water source (pipeline), sewage
system and solid waste disposal, and electricity (Helber et al.,
1984).The unstated cost for these services vital to sustainable
tourism implied millions of pesos and the project was not
implemented.

The Philippine government could not support their essential
national social service programmes and also fund tourism projects

on one small island. Rumours spread quickly around the island but no government officials came to explain the project or their inability to implement it. Cottage owners were uncertain what would happen to their business when the big resort was built. Concern about culinary water and sewer did not trickle down to either the tourist market or to the island residents.

The Middle Phase: 1984-1997

The tourist count, initially recorded in 1984 as 14,277, nearly doubled in 2 years to 27,000 in 1986, and doubled again to 56,000 in 1988, and continued to spiral upward. In 1987, Long Beach on Boracay was glowingly described in newspapers as distant and as small as the *Chico Enterprise Record* (March 8,1987, p. 4C) the hometown paper of this volume's editors. An avant-garde travel book, *BMWTropi-calBeach Handbook* (Hanna, 1989), listed Long Beach as "the world's best beach." More tourists arrived!

Officials at the PTA were not unaware of the deteriorating environment and potential health problems on Boracay but lacked funds to remedy them. They also lacked the fortitude to limit tourism to a resident population who were benefiting from the income. For perspective, not far from their Manila office and within daily view (still true in 2000) are the hundreds of "real life" families who literally dwell in the fetid-smelling garbage dumps, which they comb daily for their food and saleable salvage. And on the streets are thousands of young Filipinos who hold bachelor's degrees from one of some 60 colleges in Manila but have no job. By contrast to the urban problems, Boracaynons were well off (and they realized it!). PTA hoped to make of Boracay their "model tourism project" to be replicated for the economic benefit of other islanders in the archipelago. Toward this goal, PTA solicited a 1987 World Tourism Organization (WTO) study to assess the island tourism potential (V Smith, 1992a). Provided with fresh data confirming both the potential and the infrastructure requirements, the government appealed (unsuccessfully) for United Nations Development Project (UNDP) funds. Unfortunately, to UNDP funding agencies Boracay in 1987 seemed inconsequential in the face of pressing urban and agricultural needs throughout Asia. Later, in 1996, the British Department of International Development (DID) also undertook a study (Nicholson, 1997). In 1997, a partnership project of the Philippine Department of Tourism (DOT) with the Canadian Urban Institute (CUI) further confirmed the significant land-use problems in Boracay, related to inadequate culinary water, sewage, garbage, litter, and power for essential services (Trousdale, 1999).

The 1986 visitor count included a high proportion of European and American visitors numbering 8563 (Figure 3.3). It must be

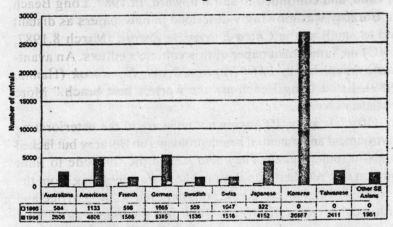

	Australians	Americans	French	German	Swedish	Swiss	Japanese	Koreans	Taiwanese	Other SE Asians
□1986	584	1133	598	1665	569	1047	322	0	0	0
■1996	2806	4806	1586	5395	1536	1516	4152	26587	2411	1961

Figure   International visitor arrivals in Boracay, selected nationalities: 1986 and 1996. Source: Philippine Tourist Authority; 1986 data, V. Smith (1994, p. 145); 1996 data, Nicholson (1997, p. 22).

noted that a high percentage of the nearly 19,000 domestic visitors registered were not tourists but residents and family members going back and forth to adjacent islands on business, to shop in the markets, to visit the hospital, and to see family and friends. It also included outsiders (meaning non-Boracaynons) who were already migrating to the island to build cottages and open businesses. As foreigners they were ineligible for membership in the Cottage Owners Association (COA) nor did any of them follow COA guidelines. Concerned members wrote letters of complaint to the PTA in Manila and locally called meetings to ask,"Why doesn't the government do something? They support tourism, so why don't they help us (with the violations of the setback zoning and the construction of rental units by non-Filipinos)?" No guidance was forthcoming.

Most cottage owners were unaware of the fundamental issues involving waste management and water supply, as the island had never experienced a problem. In 1986 raw sewage drained at one point across the beach walk into the bay. A German visitor engineered a school construction project to bridge this area but it did not abate the contamination. The medical staff at the adjacent island hospital shared my concerns about potential epidemics from mounting piles of garbage and rat infestation.

Tourism continued to expand. In 1988, the DOT in Manila sent in demolition crews to remove buildings that violated the setback (and despoiled the view). The crews were recalled because of protests staged by the in-migrant owners of these offending structures. The increasing community divisiveness prompted the PTA in 1990 to hire consultants to identify new bases for sustainable development but, again, their findings were not publicly shared or implemented.

In 1991, as the prevailing ideas of the 1987 Brundtland Report spread across the world, Philippine national legislation supported the philosophy of administration by local input, or "bottom up' government. The newly passed Local Government Code transferred governance of Boracay from the PTA in Manila to the Municipality of Malay, a small administrative town on adjacent Panay Island. This legislation also voided all *land titles* because the entire island had been declared a tourist zone. In the land rush that followed, as more newcomers arrived to establish businesses, boundary squabbles arose over beach frontage, fence lines, and beach access. Lawsuits and threats of violence followed. (Interested readers may pursue this incredible sequence of events in Trousdale, 1999.)

The Final Phase: 1997 Onward

"On June 30,1997, the people of Boracay were shaken by the news from the Department of Environment and Natural Resources (DENR) that the crystal clear swimming waters off Boracay's internationally renowned Long Beach were contaminated with high levels of coliform blamed on inadequate sewage treatment" (Trousdale, 1999, p. 840).

Tourism dropped 70% almost overnight (Figure 3.3). The decade of neglect crippled local industry and gave Philippine tourism a bad reputation. According to Trousdale (1999), who was in the area at the time, a Boracay Task Force was activated to coordinate the government's "solemn promise of increased spending on much needed physical infrastructure."This Task Force was to oversee the further expansion of tourism, including sewer lines to support three new resorts being developed on the north end of the island, which would double the 1996 capacity to 300,000 tourists (or an average of 25,000 per month).

Trousdale provides an alternative case study of another Philippine island, Kaniki Point, in which the environmental impact studies will (hopefully) avoid the Boracay-type problems, thus demonstrating the advantage of prior planning.

The water pollution edict that dramatically curtailed the tourist influx was, however, only the tip of the iceberg. Common to many areas where "new" tourism is introduced, as at Huatulco (long, 1993b) and Cancún in Mexico, the social problems may be as acute as the physical degradation but remain unresolved because they are not so readily apparent. In Boracay, community divisiveness between the original inhabitants and new business owners shattered social integration and mutual dependence, to breed "them"and "us"as hostile neighbours.The changed guest ethnicity further widened this schism, as foreign capital investment poured into the island and foreigners gained control of the local economy. The bases for widespread Boracaynon discontent are well illustrated by a comparative 10-year assessment.

Boracay Compared: 1986 and 1996
Boracay 1986

The physical assets of Boracay in 1986 were its beautiful beach and the uncluttered beach walk. Cottage units were small, surrounded by gardens, and were almost entirely family owned and operated. Tourism impact was quite limited and the guests were almost exclusively European or American, virtually all of whom spoke English and were friendly. Some stayed for months, others came every year for a few weeks, and others drifted in and went on. In general, life was a pleasant routine.

The elementary school changed class hours so upper grade students were free during lunch hours to work in the family kitchen or wait tables. Some families had small souvenir stands and made T-shirts and shorts, mostly on order. Earned income went directly to the service providers and was commonly used to pay high school tuition so children would have a better life. Above all, residents enjoyed the stability of their land, their community, and their heritage.

Boracay 1996

Nicholson (1997) did field work in three Filipino villages and provides an on--site description of the 1996 transition from the previous pattern of long-stay Europeans to a "mass Asian market for short-stay visitors in high standard facilities" (p. iii).The new, largely foreign-owned and foreign-staffed, hotels opened with 30 or more units and included on-site restaurants, karaokes, bars, gift shops, and for-hire bicycles and sports equipment. They rapidly filled with tour groups who stayed only 3-4 days.and who ate and shopped at the hotel.There was far greater leakage of income and employment to non-Filipinos.

The 1996 visitor arrivals (Figure 3.3) document that of the 52,880 international guests, over half were Korean (26,887), and combining all Asians, the ratio increased to 67%, most of whom did not speak English or patronize local businesses. To cater to this vacation market, the beach walk was soon lined with Asian vendors selling Asian goods from their tricycles, as is customary in crowded Asian markets. This new package tour orientation with its rapid guest turnover changed the leisurely resort pace, and the European and American 'regulars' began to move out, vacating the cottages. The financial security of the cottage owners faded, due to diminished business and an inflationary trend induced by the increased need to import food, water, and other essentials. Even though construction jobs and employment as porters and boatmen increased, wages for unskilled labour were very low, even by Filipino standards. A tourism skills training programme, originally intended to assist Boracaynons, was not implemented. (An economic analysis of the leakage to foreign investors would be very instructive here, to assess the impact of foreign investment in a small indigenous community.)

The Future

The 1997 government promise to build infrastructure and increase the tourist potential to 300,000 visitors offered virtually nothing to the Filipino Boracaynons, for they lacked capital with which to build competing hotels. Families had hand-built their thatched cottages, and they served meals al fresco in a cabana-like structure. Some had lacked money to install electricity when the service was introduced (1991), and most did not have funds to connect their units to the sewer when it was provided. The prospect of a jet runway on Panay Island to provide nonstop charter air service from Seoul, Tokyo, and Taipei would only create more service jobs and the probable in-migration of outsiders from Manila to fill them. To the Boracaynons who had abandoned farming and fishing for the cash income from tourism, the future is discouraging in terms of landlessness and loss of identity.

Power and Ethnicity

This Boracay case study offers an opportunity to consider two significant issues that will arise as globalization increases: namely, *political power* as the controlling force in tourism development, and the *ethnicity of the guests* rather than the hosts.

Political Power

Much of the contemporary literature devoted to tourism development suggests that "good tourism "(sustainable and thus beneficial to all) is rooted in community empowerment. The first decade of tourism in Boracay appears to have successfully followed this pattern and is consistent with the model of small-scale tourism and privatization with tourism under control and profits directly feeding providers (Dahles & Bras, 1999). But the in-migration of outsiders displaced traditional leadership networks. Thus, there appears to be a threshold of locality and size, which, when breached, requires at least some external intervention. By independently commissioning the first resort survey (the Helber project), the national government adopted the "top down" political approach and established the priority that, in tourism, "bigger is better."

Sofield has had extensive administrative experience in community empowerment in the Pacific Rim, as shown in his case study of Nepal. His six-tier multidimensional process offers potential guidelines for fieldwork, to reinforce local participation. However, it is initiated with outside expertise, and thus closely parallels the Appropriate Tourism Impact Assessment (ATIA) described by Trousdale.

The Community Empowerment model (Sofield) provides the following sequence:

1. a consultative process often characterized by the input of outside expertise;
2. the opportunity to learn and to choose;

3. the ability to make decisions;
4. the capacity to implement and apply those decisions;
5. acceptance of responsibility for those decisions and actions and their consequences; and
6. outcomes directly benefiting the community and its members, not diverted or channeled to others.

Tourism brought modernization to Boracay in the form of electricity, television, and a cash economy, but it was purchased at the price of heritage and place. This case study suggests that planning and effective governance could have mitigated many of the existent problems but the greed of numbers dominated the Philippine goals in their role as culture broker. Therein lies an important lesson: the *objectives of governance* (and governments) are crucial to the development of *appropriate tourism*. Confronted with pervasive globalization, privatized small-scale tourism cannot survive but must be shielded by stringent monitoring and aided when necessary by regulatory bodies or it will be displaced.

Once the *imported* infrastructure (water lines, sewer, and electricity) are in place, thereby making Boracay essentially an artificial *built* island platform on which to construct hotels, cafes, and shops, tourism will probably be sustainable but the quality can only be assured by monitoring. The larger process, sustainable tourism development, will have reached a dead end. The island will no longer be Boracay, for its aesthetic essence and physical attractiveness will have been destroyed. This sanitized bit of land could be named "Anyplace .The Philippines gained a client" but lost an asset and, as Trousdale thoughtfully asks: Is Boracay approaching the stagnation phase of the Resort Life Cycle?

Ethnicity.

Ethnicity in Asia has been recently and extensively discussed by Yamashita, Din, and Eades (1997) in *Tourism and Cultural Development in Asia and Oceania,* and by Picard and Wood (1997) in *Tourism, Ethnicity and the State in Asian and Pacific*

Societies. Essentially all the research identified by these authors and their stimuli address only one side of the issue: namely, host ethnicity as it is commoditized, dramatized, or even recreated as a readily marketable, highly profitable guest attraction.The exotic aspects of indigenous cultures provide strong motivations for tourism, and tribal symbols are sources for "market art" in T-shirts and fabrics. If heritage has faded, authenticity can be rec ᵃnst-ucted into "model cultures" such as the new Alaskan Na. ᵛe ʰeritage Center in Anchorage.

The ethnicity of the guests is almost never mentioned— possibly because a hint of discrimination might lurk in the shadows (or some other deviation from political correctness?). More likely the omission reflects the fact that no other case study has as yet demonstrated such a rapid and enveloping community transformation as shown in little Boracay. Indian businesses dominate Nepalese tourism, and the Chinese traders control Tibetan tourism, but these facts are seldom mentioned.

The study of national character has been out of fashion among anthropologists for several decades, yet it is clear from the psychographic profiles that discernible tourism differences occur among people based on the economic and social milieu during their maturation. N. Graburn (1977) observed that different nations take to their countryside differently, and Jafari has noted that in international travel, people take their cultural baggage with them. In confirmation of these generalities, McGahey (1994) analyzed Korean behaviour in 34 countries, in which the data indicate that all local hosts found that Koreans are often rude and discourteous, "more demanding of service staff and less understanding when things go wrong" (cited in Trousdale, 199p, p. 849).

The differences in cultural heritage between the Filipinos and continental Asians are considerable, and ethnic irritation may be dismissed as a phenomenon of tourism but it couid decay into deeper resentment and serious antipathy. There is a clear and pressing need to investigate the relation between ethnic differences and host-guest satisfaction. Ethnicity often lends itself to cartoons, including those created by Africans, who ask, in the book *Touristes-Rois en Afrique* (Dieng, 1982): How are tourists in Senegal viewed by those who serve them?

Research regarding the worlds largest industry serves many masters: scholars, the industry itself, government and its agents, and hosts and guests. The American travel industry has benefited from the studies by Plog and others, which define the five generations of American travellers. Comparable profiles of other nationalities could be of value in alleviating misunderstandings and alicnations involving tourist ethnicity.

Tourist Culture and the Product Life Cycle

When international tourism was introduced into Boracay 30 years ago, the community inherently defined comfortable public and private space. Visitors occupied cottages and beach; the beach walk was common space; and homes, gardens, and inland farms were private. It was the ideal *tourist culture,* destroyed by overloading the carrying capacity of the island. The concept of tourist culture closely parallels the Butler resort life cycle, and Walle (1998) has elaborated it into a marketing model for culture tourist professionals engaged in planning and development. It is instructive to examine Boracay in the light of this model of Classes of the Consuming Public (Figure 3.4).

The five classes of Consuming Public closely parallel the four categories of tourists who have visited Boracay to date:

The Innovators are generally young, upscale, and educated (as was true of the international diplomatic corps families first to visit Boracay). They correspond to the allocentrics defined by Plog. The Early Adoptees are also young, affluent, educated, and near-allocentrics (the "backpackers") who ventured to Boracay with advance knowledge of the tourist amenities, as an alternative to other popular Asian beach resorts such as Goa (India) or Phuket (Thailand).

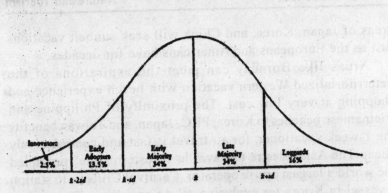

Figure   The classes of consuming public. (Adapted with permission of the Free Press, a division of Simon & Schuster Inc., from *Diffusion of Innovations*, 4th ed., by Everett M. Rogers. Copyright 1962, 1971, 1983 by the Free Press.)

The Early Majority are mid-centrics (the increased European influx from 1987 onwards) who came to Boracay as a "destination," described in guidebooks and by international travel writers.These guests knew in advance which accommodations had concrete "ocean view bungalows" and electricity.

The Late Majority are near-psychocentrics (the Asian visitors) on package tours with bulk airfares and all-inclusive land prices.They are generally a less affluent market who buy into a destination that is possibly declining in quality. The Laggards are the unknown future in Boracay.Will the new resorts rejuvenate the island, or will it become the cheap vacation locale for psychocentric Asian workers?

Conclusions

Boracay is a microcosm, but may be predictive of future Asian travel. Half the world's population lives in Asia, and as their economies rebound from a late 1990's economic crisis, there will be an outpouring of new tourists.This vast population has viewed the world on television; they now want to *experience* it. Many are curious to see snow. Others who live in the northern areas of Japan, Korea, and China will seek sunbelt vacations just as the Europeans and Americans have for decades.

Areas like Boracay can meet the aspirations of the deterritorialized Western vacation with beach experience and shopping at very low cost. The proximity of Philippine and Vietnamese beaches to Korea, PRC, Japan, and Taiwan benefits the 1-week vacationer, for air travel is fast and comparatively cheap. The Asian desire to travel in "Western style" prompted the world's largest cruise operator, Carnival Cruises, to station a vessel in Korea for exclusive all-Asian cruises. The project did not materialize owing to the 1998 financial crisis, but a comparable programme is operating successfully from Singapore. In summary, the changing economic structure of Boracay is not unique. Globalization encourages foreign capital to invest in tourism infrastructure to profitably service their traveling compatriots.

Governments must realistically examine their role, determine the limits of use in conjunction with their residents, and develop effective plans. The Filipino hosts of 30 years ago were proud of their properties and their hospitality, and the income was a positive change in their lives. Trousdale (1999) concluded that the case study of tourism on Boracay Island "supports the assertion that governance is the critical issue in moving development towards sustainability". And the contemporary generation expresses their present dissatisfaction as,"tourists work for dollars and pay in pesos; we work for pesos and pay in dollars (for imported food, water and other essentials)" (Nicholson, 1997, p. 24).

4

Stone Age to Star Trek

Archaeology confirms that Inuit occupied the shores of Kotzebue Sound for several centuries during which time a trading rendezvous became a well-established annual event (Giddings, 1960). The Sound was a rich habitat, flanked by three major river valleys that supported inland Inuit (see Figure 4.1), who came to the coast in late June and stayed until early August. Offshore, the farthest north salmon run in the world easily filled set-nets and baskets every day, and the surplus fillets were dried and stored for winter. Schools of beluga (white whale) and seal augmented the diet, together with tomcod, Arctic char, rabbits, geese, and ducks. Although they were working part-time, sociability overshadowed their labours; the festivities made it seem like a vacation with family and friends. No other site in the Alaskan arctic has a resource base to host such a large seasonal influx, which in 1884 Cantwell (1889) estimated as 1400 Inuit camped together, their skin tents grouped by family and dialect (Figure 4.1).

To go to the rendezvous was everyone's dream;one stayed borne only because of old age or illness. Memories of the six weeks of feasting, competitive sports and story telling for which the Inuit are famous filled ten winter months with a mix of nostalgia, then anticipation while new clothes were made and new songs practiced. The trade itself was a shopping expedition—a trip to an aboriginal mall—for inland Inuit had salmon skin bags and boots, beaver pelts and grey-brown caribou hides, and jade for jewelry and tools. Coastal Inuit had supplies o/muktuk (whale blubber), seal oil, walrus hides and ivory, mammoth ivory, and whale ribs for house supports. The Siberian Inuit brought umiaks laden with sable pelts, black-and-white reindeer hides and, most precious of all, leaf tobacco and *tea*.

The men formed trading partnerships, women gossiped and children played. The social bonding reinforced their kinship networks in the event of failure in the winter food quest, and the need to seek aid beyond the immediate family. (V. Smith, 1966)

Definitions of Tourism

There are as many definitions of tourism as there are disciplines and investigators, but all share commonalties. From an anthropological perspective, a tourist was originally defined as "a temporarily leisured person who travels away from home for the purpose of experiencing a change" (V. Smith, 1977).This

Figure   Summer camp, Hotham Inlet 1884. [Photo by Edward Nelson in *The Eskimo About Bering Strait* 1899. Reprinted by permission of the Smithsonian Institution (SI-6387).]

simple definition has stood the test of time, and remains in wide usage. From the same era but oriented toward the management perspective, R. Mcintosh (1977) defined tourism as an industry catering to tourist needs, or "the science, art and business of attracting and transporting visitors, accommodating them and graciously catering to their needs and wants." Wahab (1975), a professor of law and tourism policy, observes that the "anatomy of tourism is composed of three elements : man the author of the act of tourism; space, the physical element to be covered; and time the temporal element consumed by the trip and the stay". These three social' science definitions of tourism remain academically useful to convey the diversity of tourist motivations and activities. D. Pearce (1992) describes the many organizations including governments, carriers, and industry (termed in this volume the culture brokers) who motivated and manage tourism. He conceptualizes tourism as an'origin-linkage-destination system involving the temporary movement of people from an origin to a destination and usually back home again after at least one overnight stay".

Tourism Elements

All forms of tourism—international, domestic, business related.pilgrimage.or family visits—require participants to have three essential elements, best expressed as an equation: tourism = leisure time + discretionary income + positive social sanctions.

Leisure is the time when an individual is neither employed at gainful work nor attending to essential daily tasks. At leisure, one has a choice to do virtually nothing, such as lie in a hammock and read, or meditate. Or one could participate in recreational activities that are usually close to home, such as dining with friends, playing ball, swimming, or "jamming." Tourism, however, requires money to spend for lodging, meals, entertainment, and shopping Discretionary income refers to those funds not needed for basic survival and available for optional items that are a cultural choice.The individual could buy a car, take a cruise, invest in the stock market, or repaint the house. Leisure and funds are essential prerequisites but the individual choice may be decided at least in part by prevailing local social sanctions. In the pre-World War II era, an American of modest means who travelled overseas for pleasure was subject to community censure for violating the Puritan work ethic that sanctioned "saving for a rainy day." In contemporary America, to stay home because you lack ready cash is "old-fashioned" because travel costs are so easily charged to credit cards.To "fly now, pay later"is the modern philosophy. However, approval for tourism is still sometimes rooted in the appropriateness of the travel activity, considering, among others factors, the age and gender of the travellers, and the social milieu. Examples from the travel industry that might have different sanctions include family travel, singles travel, senior travel, gay and lesbian travel, handicapped (or physically limited) travel, pilgrims, conventioneers, business travel, and youth travel. Sanctions are silent but powerful cultural constructs that vary geographically, temporally, and socially.

Tourism Through Time

A definitive history of tourism is waiting to be written.Towner (1996) has set a high standard for sociopolitical interpretation but the time frame is limited. Sigaux (1966) is difficult to access and lacks the broad perspective. This chapter provides a brief historical analysis of the socioeconomic foundations and the emerging technologies and philosophies that have made tourism a global business leader as well as a dominant recreational mode, and a potential avenue for peace.

Tourism parallels the process of acculturation (culture change and adaptation), particularly in terms of technological innovation. As noted in the Introduction, as speed increases, relative distance is shortened. Dramatic changes in culture and tourism can be directly correlated with the development of new sources of industrial power or energy, including the Industrial Revolution (coal-steam) of the 1790s, the Nuclear-Synthetic Revolution of the 1940s, and the Electronic-Cyberspace Revolution, circa 2000. The travel and tourism activities in each era . can be best defined in terms of the available modes of transportation, and ' us human mobility. Each technological revolution is identified with a progressively larger population, more urbanism, and more stringent education and skill requirements for lucrative jobs, discretionary income, and opportunities for travel.

The Pre-Industrial Era

The limit vignettes describe the travel and tourism of one aboriginal group, with a theme that could be replicated with variations in style for other indigenous tribes. For example, the main trade route of Mayan communities—*a Ruta Maya*—linked Central America from Yucatan south to Honduras (D. Brown, 1999).*d* Religious motivations built the great Mayan ceremonial centers and their shopping plazas to which the devout travelled with gifts and trade goods. For hundreds of years, Mayan market towns were the social hubs and source of regional news. The major Eurasian caravan route, the *Silk Road*, stretched from Rome to Xian (China), along which moved goods (and ideas) to the famous bazaars of Damascus, Samarkand, and Urumchi. African commerce spanned the Sahara for centuries and also dealt in the slave trade, bringing unfortunate victims to coastal markets for sale and export to the New World, in what is now termed the *Slave Route*. These three highways of history, where the traveller once walked, are now promoted by the World Tourism Organization (WTO) as agendas for economic development. Air routes, paved highways, and modern hotels provide 21st century travellers to these destinations with history combined with a standard of comfort unimaginable three centuries ago.

The Industrial Steam Revolution: 1700 AD

The Industrial-Steam Revolution, circa 1700 AD, fathered mines, factories, and the railroad, and introduced the use of nonrenewable resources, especially coal and petroleum. In so doing, it also translated the value of an hour of labour into a monetary unit, based on the worker's skills and expertise. Time literally became money. Men (or women) could sell unlimited weekly hours of labour for whatever wage they could obtain, and keep or spend the earnings as they choose. The concept of "time off," shifts, and workweek crept into vocabulary, as did "paid vacations." Industrialization created new mine and factory towns peopled by in-migrants from rural farmsteads to live in cramped unsanitary housing. The first railroads carried freight but soon these "horseless carriages "were carrying small numbers of passengers, for the new service was cheaper, faster, and more comfortable than stagecoaches.

In 1841, Thomas Cook, a Baptist missionary, persuaded the Midland Counties Railway Company (UK) to operate a special train over a 40-mile distance for a 1-day Temperance meeting. He had no difficulty finding passengers for this Sabbath day, as it was a morally sanctioned cause (and a day of fresh air!). With this initial success, other day trips followed. The rail company agreed to offer tours regularly—if Cook would provide the passengers, which he did. In the 1860s, Cook opened a travel agency, for which he invented the first travel vouchers, so clients could prepay at his office and not have to carry large sums of money to pay on-site for accommodations and meals. He also created Traveller's Checks as a safe means to carry funds, and designed sleeping cars (Wagon-lits Cook) for long-haul passengers. He soon had tours operating to Egypt, Asia, and North America. An ambitious and worldly entrepreneur, he almost single-handedly created the basic operations of today's travel industry. In addition, he became so knowledgeable about world affairs that Queen Victoria once commented that Cook knew more about the colonies than her own Foreign Office.

Rail travel also revolutionized agricultural Europe, whose population lived in dispersed, farm villages, many no more than 1 mile apart. Larger market towns, with churches, shops, and schools, were an hour or two away by foot. With the advent of the train, myriad small rail lines developed throughout Europe, linking farm villages to urbanizing market centers. These lines gradually became the modern network of convenient rail connections that still serve Europe's densely populated countries as well as the mass tourism supported by Eurailpass traffic.

In the US and Canada, a few major rail lines spread westward from their eastern hubs, to service growing cities on the West Coast, and some intermediary centers such as Chicago, St. Louis, Denver, Winnipeg, and Calgary. Distances were great, and the trip was long, tiring, and expensive. Short feeder lines served local coastal and mountain resorts near the populous east. However, even today entire states in the US, and most of Canada, have no rail service (Figure 4.2).

In 1908, Henry Ford introduced his "Tin Lizzie" (the black Model-T Ford), which literally put Americans on the road. Gunn (1995) reports

> To say that the proliferation of Ford cars in the 1920s was the sole cause for the travel boom in American may be taking some license with the truth. But undeniable was the detonation that occurred when the insatiable desire to experience the West fused with the new mass ability to get there. The resulting explosion in tourism had never happened before, and has never been equaled since.

By 1927, 15 million Model-T Ford cars had been built and there were 200 auto factories in 28 Michigan towns involved in automobile production. Despite a "great Depression," in 1935 the American Automobile Association estimated some 40,000,000 Americans (roughly one third of the population) took motor tours each year. They drove to see their national parks, including Yellowstone (established in 1872), Yosemite (1890), Mesa Verde 1906), and Grand Canyon (1908). Americans were soon addicted to their cars and were nostalgic about their highways, including Route 66, which "led from Chicago to LA."

Pioneering airlines had been established during the 1930s, most notable among them was Juan Trippe's Pan American Airways, which was the world's largest mail carrier by 1930. In 1935, the Pan-Am four-engine flying boat, the China Clipper,

departed from San Francisco, where 150,000 people (including
President Roosevelt) gathered to watch the take-off. It
completed the Pacific crossing in a 7-day, 60-hour inaugural
flight, stopping overnight at US naval bases mid-Pacific, and
was greeted in Manila by 200,000 cheering Filipinos, celebrating
a half-holiday. The world audience was ready for air travel but
they lacked the technology, and a war intervened. The first
American architect to design a noteworthy overseas hotel, Frank
Lloyd Wright, was already setting the stage for the new tourism
with the construction (1917-1922) of his Tokyo hotel,
incorporating the stylistic details of Japanese printmakers. It
survived the 1923 earthquake unscathed, giving credence to
American construction, but was razed in 1968 for a high-rise
with more guest capacity.

The Nuclear-Synthetic Revolution: 1940 AD

The military technology, including nuclear firepower
developed to win World War II, spawned many peacetime
innovations in communication, manufacturing, and travel. When
World War II ended, experienced military pilots returned home,
looking for jobs and, finding none, bought surplus war aircraft at
bargain prices and started airlines, including Wien Alaska,
Eastern Airlines, and Flying Tigers (Figure 4.3), the latter destined
to become the world's largest freight carrier and merge into
Federal Express. Underfunded, these neophyte companies
needed revenue, and added charter services to fill passenger
seats For two decades, during the 1950s and 1960s, many
American universities maintained summer programmes in Europe, using cheap charter flights. Their counterpart campuses in
Europe welcomed these visitors, who were an entirely new
element of American tourism. Today many of these youths are
matured "baby boomers," entering senior traveller status, and
are frequent fliers because their overseas college experience
sanctioned travel as a way of life. Commercial jet air service in

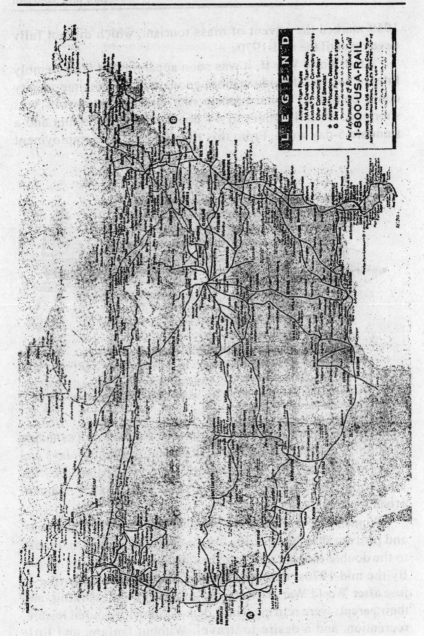

Figure 4.2 Amtrak Route Map

1959 marked the advent of mass tourism, which did not fully develop until the mid-1970s.

After World War II, it was soon apparent that the assembly lines of war could produce more goods than a peacetime society could consume. Consequently, the postwar workweek was shortened from 48 hours to 44 hours, then to 40 hours and a standard 5-day week. From this time forward, the employment

Figure   Flying Tigers Squadron over Salween River Gorge (Burma), May 28, 1942. Returning to Kunming, China, from a strafing over the Burma Road. (© R. N. Smith, courtesy of his family.)

trend has consistently moved to limit the weekly work schedule including "part-time" employment and more paid holidays and 3-day weekends. The Puritan work ethic was replaced by the philosophy that "work is for play," and the seeds for consumerism had been laid.

Women had responded to the wartime demand for labour, and postwar they became the "taste-makers" of tourism, thanks to the double-income families they generated (V. Smith, 1979). By the mid-1970s, the baby boomers (children born during or just after World War II) were out of college and working, and their parents were retiring. Their demographics favoured leisure, recreation, and a desire to .travel. Without fanfare, and little public recognition, travel became essentially a human right.

The Electronic-Cyberspace Revolution: 2000 AD

At the millennium, a new technological revolution is clearly in progress, involving the use of new fuels (fusion), new synthetic materials, and new travel frontiers—in space, in virtual reality, and in a deeper awareness of the need to conserve and protect our planet and our human heritage. If peace—so essential to personal safety and psychological well-being—is preserved, the potential for expanded tourism is vast.

Global Trends

What most Americans did not yet perceive in post-World War II was their new status as a superrich global superpower. The US became the role model of Western industrial society, especially in less developed countries (LDCs), although within the US the shift to a service-oriented economy was already under way. The significance of these impacts on tourism seems to have escaped clear articulation elsewhere, including the scholarly tourism literature. However, to develop tourism policy and management plans for 21st century tourism, it is imperative to understand the newly evolving global philosophies of this post-Industrial era. Three key issues that will dominate the structure and marketing of travel in the next few decades include: consumerism, globalization, and urbanization.

Consumerism

Consumerism is a social and economic outgrowth of World War II, born in the US in an Age of Affluence—in a country that benefited economically from the manufacturing of war materiel and escaped the physical military destruction incurred in Europe and Asia (see Packard, 1960). The war itself displaced millions of residents in Europe and Asia, redrew political boundaries that divided Europe, created two Chinas, and, in spin-off revolutionary wars, divided Korea and splintered Southeast Asia.

In the process, tradition and family ties to ancestral land in much of Europe and Asia were fractured beyond repair. Individuals best identified themselves with their place of origin rather than their homeland, as the latter in many instances no longer existed.Adrift, they sought new bonds in associative organisations in cities, in social and service organisations, and in activist health, political, and human rights groups. Increasingly, these landless migrants travelled in search of a better life, and returned home for family visits.The emerging synthetics industry altered agricultural production, as nylons replaced silk hosiery and polyesters displaced cotton and woolen textiles. Unless they could modernize, old factories closed, people moved, and towns and churches died. Port facilities closed as air cargo replaced shipping. New cities formed, filled with strangers. Megalopolis corridors such as *San-San* sprawled from San Francisco to San Diego, and ethnic enclaves from former colonies formed in many European cities. In eastern Europe and Asia, where land was scarce and valuable, urban housing went skyward in 1000-unit concrete blocks served by school, market, and small shops. Only the world's wealthy could afford a home, a garage, and a garden.

Consumerism has become a major personal identifier in the West (and is a growing trend in the Orient, evident in Japan by the 1990s). Individual worth is measured by possessions, for which one must often work very hard and, if not attainable by work, the alternate avenues are corruption or theft (for which tourists are "soft targets").Although statistics are difficult to establish, it is generally conceded that shopping ranks high if not number one as a travel activity. Within tourism, the trip itself is a consumable to be discussed with all who will listen.The farther one goes and the more frequently one travels, the "best" trip and the "worst experience" are often more important to ego enhancement than the purchase of a new car, new home, or the establishment of a "new relationship." Research probably would establish that the "fashions" in tourism destination develop from consumptive travel. Informal observation reinforces the subjective comment that once several friends have travelled to and returned from a particular "in" destination, individuals are motivated to visit that destination, too. Tourism is often a "keeping up with the Joneses," and the ability to share the chatter of name-dropping about hotels, cafes, handicrafts, and even "experiences." Tourism at the millennium is a prestigious consumable commodity for salaried singles, dinks (double income, no kids), and the upwardly mobile, in all industrial spheres worldwide. The destinations, the duration and frequency of their travel, may be currently restricted among the LDCs but this global behaviour pattern is only latent there.

The Shopping Malls

When customers could not find parking space in the crowded urban core, entrepreneurs moved their shops to new suburban citadels of commerce. Consumerism has turned many shopping malls into mercantile pleasure parks, with food courts and weekly free "shoppertainment". Advertising promotions of "dinertainment" capture evening shoppers, and "edutainment" lure customers to the bookstores (with lecturers offering free advice on "how to write and sell a travel article"). These blandishments are increasingly more important to counter the growing trend to shop on the Internet, to "save time" by catalogne or mail order purchases, and then "spend time" on travel. Millennial consumerism focuses on the acquisition of cars, condos, clothes, and travel that have replaced, for many, the decaying traditions of home, church, and land. Durning (1992, p. 8) observes, "Shopping centers have become the centers of our public life, and consuming has become both our primary means of self-definition and our leading pastime". Malls have matured into international destinations, especially the enclosed Edmonton Mall (Alberta, Canada), noted for its sandy beach, heated water, and a wave machine (Butler, 1991). When February temperatures drop to subzero, a weekend spent there is vastly cheaper and almost as satisfactory as a comparable weekend in Florida, but without the multiple theme parks of Orlando.

The .Mfall of America in Minneapolis is also situated in the winter snow belt of North America, and is more easily accessible by international air carriers than Edmonton. Said to be the largest completely enclosed mall, the three-storied complex surrounds a huge play area complete with roller coaster, Ferris wheel, Camp Snoopy' wild animals show, and Legoland, In 2000, it was the epitome of shoppertainment and, unlike theme parks, admission is free.The annual visitation is consistently 42 million and 1s a mix of domestic tourism plus tour groups from the Orient and Europe who come for a week to shop, to be entertained, and to dine.The economic impact on the surrounding area is impressive. Study estimated the Mall had a US$1.4 billion impact on the Minneapolis-St. Paul (Twin Cities) economy, and that 80% of the impact came from out-of-state tourists. Of that amount, only 20% resulted from shopping. Instead, another 20% was generated by the mall in the form of payroll and taxes.The remaining US$840 million supported the ancillary hotels, restaurants, and transportation *outside* the mall (Simon Property Group, 1995).This impact study attracted international attention and supports the belief that the many small malls already conspicuous in Europe, in major Latin American cities, and in South Africa will expand, diversify, and further serve the objectives of the industries that fuel consumerism. Industrial Japan shunned the malls to conserve farm land, but Shirouzu (1997) predicts malls will "blossom in Japan" in the next 4 to 5 years because of clogged roads, lack of city parking, and the loss of jobs in suburban areas. For the future (both global and interplanetary), Kowinski writing in the *Mailing of America* (quoted in Durning, 1992) predicts:

> Someday it may be possible to be born, go from preschool through college, get a job, date, marry, have children . . . get a divorce, advance through a career or two, receive your medical care, even get arrested, tried and jailed; live a relatively full life of culture and entertainment, and eventually die and be given funeral rites without ever leaving a particular

mall complex—because every one of those possibilities exists now in some shopping center somewhere, (p. 131)

Economic Globalisation

Globalization is described by Short and Kim (1999) as the new meta-narrative for the third millennium. It is a concept with both a process of economic, political, and cultural change, and a discourse of globalism. The upbeat and optimistic view promises "foreign products and investment increased economic efficiency, political transparency and overall competitiveness". The negative interpretation of economic globalization describes the process of change as mechanisms to:

> discipline workers to accept lower wages [NB. sometimes through part-time work], increased workloads and changing labour practices. Globalization, downsizing and restructuring are terms used not only to describe but also to justify and legitimize changes in capital-labour relations. (Short & Kim, 1999, p.5)

Economic globalisation is most immediately apparent in transnational mergers and in the relocation of Western (MDC) manufacturing plants in LDCs to take advantage of cheaper labour. By saving production costs, the product can be competitively marketed at home or abroad. Newly employed LDC workers benefit from discretionary wages to buy their own products and/or to travel. The manufacture of the traditional little Volkswagon "bug," now built only in Mexico for Mexicans, at a 1999 cost per car of US$7000 is a case in point. By intent, as the "have not" nations industrialize and mainstream into consumer behaviour, their labour force will attain both the leisure and the discretionary income to travel. The aspirations and sanctions favouring tourism are already established. The implications of globalisation for increased 21st century travel and tourism are profound.

Cultural Globalisation

The nature of cultural globalisation is important to tourism in relation to the issues of the tourist gase, and to heritage and authenticity. The homogenised global village emerged as the initial specter as the Americanisation of the world spread via CNN and by construction of some 23,000 Golden Arches in 110 countries. Why travel when there is a Benetton in every French village? Subsequent analyses, however, by Appadurai (1990, 1996), suggest that the rampant display of American culture had formed a globalized culture of homogeneity with live dimensions ol flow, including: (1) *etbnoscapes* (the movements of tourists, immigrants, refugees, and guestworkers); (2) *mediascapes* (the worldwide distribution ol information through newspapers, magazines, and TV programmes and films); (3) *Technoscapes* (the distribution of technologies); (4) *financescapes* (global capital flows); and (5) *ideoscapes* (the distribution of political ideas and v. alues, such as the master narrative of the Enlightenment). This is accompanied by a "global babble" of connectedness associated with international organizations, with international spectacles (such as the opening and closing ceremonies of mega-events, like the Olympics, World Cup), and with a rising global consciousness about human rights, the UN Year of the Child, International Day of Tourism, and the important 1992 Rio Conference on Environment and Development. Barnet and Cavanagh (1996) termed this process of homogenization as cultural imperialism.

Deterritorialisation

When popular culture traits spread from their country of origin, changes of *deterritorialisation* occur. As the trait is adopted into a new culture, it changes through a process of *reterritorialisation*. Disneyland is a case in point: the Japanese welcomed it, and many visit several times a year; the French received it, some with visible distaste and refused to visit at all.

In Japan the franchise agreement required Disneyland-Tokyo to be constructed exactly like the Anaheim model but the lease agreement failed to allow for climatic and cultural differences. *C. foruia* enjoys winter rain, and during the busy summer season rainfall almost never oc curs. In Tokyo the busy summer season coincides with almost-daily heavy monsoon rains.The Tokyo property had to renegotiate (i.e.,) reterritorializc) their theme park lease to enclose Main Street with an expensive glass roof and to contruct rain gutters on other buildings Japanese visitors, tired of hamburgers and fries, demanded a Japanese food concession. Another lease negotiation permitted the-addition of a large second-floor restaurant that remained unsigned except for the traditional blue-white curtain at the entry, recognizable to Asians. Warning signs, such as "Watch Your Step" and "Hold Hand Rail," are printed only in English and Chinese and not Japanese. According to Tokyo-Disney public relations personnel, "only Americans and Chinese sue; if a Japanese falls and is injured, he accepts personal responsibility for the accident as a matter of his own clumsiness:" Disneyland was deterritorialized for Japanese to enjoy but reterritorialized to meet Japanese" preferential customs (including a preponderance of "Eastern" toilets in the restrooms). Language similarly adjusts, as Minnie Mouse became Minaku-Mouse.

Cultures are historically resilient, however, and traditions often persist long after the events that initiated them.Their resilience suggests that globalization leads to cultural heterogenizalion, engendering local and regional responses to external stimuli. McDonald's originally enforced rigid franchise stipulations for their Golden Arches but now allows architectural variations to meet local zoning laws. In Austria and Germany, beer is sold to accompany a "Big Mac" and in the new McCafes, the tira misu dessert is advertised as"tira mac su."

A number of governments, prompted in part by segments of the tourism industry, have responded to the challenge of "global Americanisation"by actively stressing a programme of renationalisation, based on traditional values and heritage.

Reterritorialization of immigrant ethnicity is the foundation for many folk festivals that promote multiculturalism and simultaneously involve residents in community activities. Street fairs and cultural shows provide low-cost recreation for the urban poor in the world's mega-cities. This positive trend needs to be nurtured and should figure prominently in future tourism planning and marketing, for it is repeatedly shown that "culture sells"

The Media

The media have played a major role in the development of global tourism, even as Durning notes (1992) "the wildfire spread of the consumer life-style around the world marks the most rapid and fundamental change in day-to-day existence the human species has ever experienced" (p. 36). America started the motion picture industry and made Hollywood glamorous, where tourists could buy a map or take a tour to see where "the stars" lived. Initially, the themes featured lavish living, cops and robbers, and Western gunfights between cowboys and Indians. These movies became the dominant theater fare the world over, including Friday nights in an Inuit village schoolhouse, and established the national character image of "gun-totin" wealthy Americans. Even in the 1960s, these visual images were so real that some educated New Yorkers feared to travel "out West" lest they encounter Indians on the warpath.

"Half the television programmes aired outside the United States are American reruns, so aspirations everywhere are defined by the norm in the United States" (Durning, 1992, p. 127). The effect of American television on global culture has been profound, and although the Westerns, murder mysteries, war films, and musicals are still produced, there has been a perceptible change in Hollywood scenarios in the past three decades. Subsequent to Woodstock '69, the first major televised rock music festival, which proved to be the defining event for the sexual social revolution and "hippie" era of the 1970s, films reflect the use of narcotics, violence, and obscenities as first screened there. Thirty years later, Woodstock "99, advertised as a festival of Peace, Love, and Music, ended in destructive carnage, nudity, and violence. A participant interviewed by a *New York Times* reporter, July 26, 1999, responded to a question, "Violence? That's what my generation is about — violence!" The event raises an important question: if the world's role models—the Americans—smash and burn, what is wrong with hooliganism, or fights at the World Cup? Or violence in a schoolyard? Or randomly shooting tourists in an Egyptian temple to prove a political point? And lead to unprovoked bioterrorism? These are tourism deterrents.

Concurrently the expanding video technology has sharply reduced production costs for films of wilderness travel (such as African safaris and polar bear viewing), participatory adventure tours (including kayaking, river rafting, and scuba diving), and cultural and historical events. TV channels with 24-hour programming of these themes are constant and persuasive incentives to travel, and the accompanying advertising is standardizing consumer tastes, as Pi-Sunyer documents. By this process, English has become the global language and the agent for transmission of American culture. Crystal (1997, p. 61) estimates that at least one fifth of the world population has a working knowledge of English, and 75 countries recognize it as either the primary or secondary language.

Summary

Consumerism and mass tourism are fraternal twins, both born, in the mid-1970s from common parents—the social revolution and the commercial shift from manufacturing to service industries. Americans physically exported their styles of tourism overseas, when Conrad Hilton founded his hotel chain and central reservations system in 1948, and opened the Caribe Hilton in December 1949 as an entrée into a sound business venture in tourism, combining American standards of efficiency and modern comfort with the best traditions of hotel keeping abroad" (Comfort, 1964, p. 219). Pan-American, then the premier round-the-world airline, inaugurated Inter-Continental Hotel chain to house airline crews and passengers The American architect, Pete Wimberly, launched a long and successful career designing overseas hotels to fit local landscapes and incorporate indigenous motifs. In general, these new hostelries were well received in the LDCs for they were visible and validating proof of their progress toward Westernization. Europeans and Japanese whose postwar economies created personal wealth are following the American manufacturing mode and adopting consumption as the organizing principle of their lives. The wealthier citizens of poor nations already emulate this orientation as their status symbol, even as many of their poorer neighbours are already (largely unrecognized) domestic travellers in the patterns of their ancestors, visiting families, going to markets, and making pilgrimages. The major culture brokers clearly recognize these trends, and are designing larger aircraft, longer landing strips, bigger hotels, and more cruise ships to accommodate an ever-expanding travel clientele—and space tourism is plainly on the horizon.

5

The Science and Tourism

Perhaps jew industries have transformed as rapidly as tourism—and all that, despite its age-old origin, mainly during recent decades.As communities and countries discovered its economic prospects and mustered their efforts to tap on its potentials, tourism suddenly evolved into an invigorating business, an international trade, and a global mega-industry. In a short time span. It was first elevated to the rank below that of oil, then at par with it, suddenly above it, and it is now being, positioned as the largest industry in the world. In turn, this impressive growth and transformation stimulated efforts to develop a multidisciplinary body of knowledge that can understand it and guide its planning and development in all phases and spheres: locally, regionally, and internationally. This new field, with its scientification process also in rapid progress, is today recognized as a legitimate and important area of investigation in many scholarly communities worldwide.

The purpose of this chapter is to provide retrospective and prospective views on tourism's scientific journey. More specifically, the aim is to identify some of the past conditions that have helped tourism to assume its present scholarly dimensions and depth; to sketch the formation of this landscape of knowledge, to selectively extract from this context emerging central socioeconomic issues; to suggest research crossroads for advancing to new frontiers; to sample the richness of the state of knowledge—along with challenges and opportunities ahead—that, in turn, can guide present and future planning and operation of this diverse mega-industry. Conceptually informed and practically enriched sustainable strategies, now rooted in this body of knowledge, can and will benefit all those directly and indirectly involved in tourism: the entrepreneurial and public agencies committed to its development; the tourists who invest their leisure time and disposable income to see near and far peoples and places; the host whose communities and resources are mobilized and affected by the needs of tourists and the very industry that accommodates them; and academic institutions involved in research, delivery of education, and advancement of scholarship in this field, now housed on many university campuses worldwide

Evolution of Thought on Tourism

Today, tourism is acclaimed as a major global economic force and a giant industry worldwide. Many publications of the WTO, among others, testify to its steady growth since World War II. For example, in 1950, 25 3 million international tourist arrivals resulted in $2.1 billion receipts. Close to the end of the 20th century, in 1998, 625 million international tourists generated $445 billion receipts. In the same year, worldwide spending on both domestic and international tourism surpassed $3 trillion. The latter is, according to an analyst, several times larger than what the world spends on defense; or said differently, world spending on tourism exceeds the gross national product of any country in the world with the exception of the US and Japan. The estimates on the volume of tourism for the years ahead into the 21 st century remain impressive.

The steady growth of tourism since World War II, and especially during more recent decades, has brought much attention to it. both as an industry and as a phenomenon. A review of the literature sheds light on the growth and popularity of tourism. To reveal this pattern, the writings and insights of the last few decades can be aggregated into four groups, each suggesting a distinctive position or platform of thinking. These, the Advocacy, Cautionary. Adaptancy, and Knowledge-Based Platforms, as will be discussed, have emerged chronologically, with the text and position of one leading to the next, but without being replaced by it; and indeed all four platforms coexist today.

Advocacy Platform: The Good

This first position was formed by those individuals or firms and institutions— including private businesses, public agencies, and trade associations, among others—directly or indirectly concerned with tourism's economic prospects. These "interest" groups often argue that tourism is a labour-intensive industry; that it benefits sectors beyond its operation; that it is a viable economic alternative for many communities or countries; that it generates foreign exchange badly needed to sustain membership in the global community; and more. To place tourism under an even brighter light, these advocates also emphasize other attributes, that tourism preserves the natural and built environments; that it revives traditions of the past; that it actively promotes cultural performances; and that it facilitates cross-cultural communication and the prospects for global peace. These combined socio-economic perspectives (Table 5.1), when placed under such an aggrandized spotlight, have fueled its development and promotion in near and far destinations.

Cautionary Platform: The Bad

With the passage of time, casual observations as well as serious research findings on touristic issues and influences began to challenge the advocacy position. This new voice, barely audible before or during the 1960s, grew to become the Cautionary Platform in the 1970s. Members of the research community, and especially those (private and public) concerned with the protection of culture and nature, contributed to the formation of this cautioning or alerting position. Their message has not been limited to economic disbenefits, arguing that the industry generates mostly seasonal and unskilled jobs; that it benefits only firms and big corporations; that it destroys nature

Table 5.1. Advocacy Platform on Tourism Influences

Economic Benefits	Sociocultural Benefits

• Can be labour intensive, generating:
   Full-time jobs
   Seasonal jobs
   Part-time jobs
   Unskilled jobs
• Can generate foreign exchange
• Can.be built on existing infrastructure
• Can be developed with local products
• Can spread development
• Can complement production of
  of other economic activities
• Can have high multiplier effects
	• Can broaden education
	• Can promote international
	  understanding/peace
	• Can reduce:
	   Language barriers
	   Sociocrultural barriers
	   Racial barriers
	   Political barriers
	   Religious barriers
	• Can reinforce preservation
	  heritage/tradition
	• Can promote worldview and
	  membership in the global
	  community •
	• Can enhance, appreciation
	  of one's own culture

and scenic resources; that it commoditizes people and their cultures; that it disrupts the structure of the host society. Today, as before, this second stand ranges from outright rejection of the earlier position to calculated pronouncements about undesirable consequences of tourism.

As subscribers to these two platforms still express their respective positions (though not in an organized fashion or unified voice), cross-firing between them, which was at its height in the 1970s, has been inevitable. These encounters, often charged with emotion, include exchanges of views and opposing stands as well as sharp criticism of each other's position. For any claim of the Advocacy Platform (Table 5.1), there has been a counterclaim by the Cautionary Platform (Table 5.2), *a* situation potentially not conducive to fruitful dialogues or discourses.

Table 5.2. Cautionary Platform on Tourism Consequences

Economic Costs	Sociocultural Costs
• Can cause inflation • Can result in high leakage • Can have seasonally and contribute to unemployment • Can be susceptible to change, rumor, spread of disease, economic fluctuation • Can result in unbalanced economic development • Can lead to extraneous dependency • Can increase demonstration effects • Can destroy resources and create visual pollution	• Can contribute to misunderstanding • Can generate sterotypes • Can lead to xenophobia • Can result in social pollution • Can commercialize the community and its culture, religion, arts, and more • Can threaten family structure • Can contribute to prostitution • Can increase instance of crime • Can induce conflicts in the host community

Adaptancy Platform: The How

Because the polarized debates between the Advocacy and Cautionary Platforms have been mainly concerned with the *impacts* of the industry, one then could argue that some alternative forms or adapted types of tourism would have lesser or fewer negative consequences than other options. Therefore, attention was gradually drawn to its alternative forms of development. This proposition fostered the formation of a third position in the 1980s: the Adaptancy Platform.

Armed with the earlier separate perspectives, this third position emerged by favouring those forms that are especially responsive to the host communities and their sociocultural, built, and natural environments and, at the same time, that provide tourists with new choices and rewarding experiences. The prescribed strategies have variously been known as agritourism, appropriate tourism, community-based tourism, controlled tourism, cottage tourism, cultural or ethnic tourism, ecotourism, farm tourism, green tourism, indigenous tourism, lifeseeing tourism, nature tourism, paratourism, responsible tourism, rural tourism, sensible tourism, small-scale tourism, soft tourism, and sustainable tourism; the list is still growing, with "no tourism" even named as an alternative by itself.

In general, the Adaptancy Platform argues that these forms are community centered, employ local resources, are relatively easier to manage, are not destructive, benefit host and guest groups alike, and even improve communication between them. Adapted tourism, regardless of its nature or scope, is presented as an informed set of alternative options to the present mass, commercialized, out-of-control, hard forms practiced almost everywhere. One of the latest alternatives, known as ecotourism, has attracted the attention of operators and governments, as well as researchers and academicians, with the former exploiting this for quick profits. However, these and other "alternative" forms, exploited or not, have emerged as partial remedies. But strategies of the Adaptancy Platform cannot accommodate the mass volume of tourists generated globally. While forms and practices can be influenced, the tourist volume can no longer be curtailed.

Knowledge-Based Platform: The Why

The collective positions of the Advocacy, Cautionary, and Adaptancy Platforms were among the main conditions and forces fostering a number of developments in the thinking about tourism. First came a general recognition by all, independent from their positions, that this is a *giant global industry,* that it caters to millions of tourists *daily,* and that both tourism and tourists *are here to stay.* Second, any development, tourism included, generates both desirable changes and unwanted consequences; and it is the *relationship* between the costs and benefits that should matter. Third, the general foci of the Advocacy and Cautionary Platforms on *impacts* and of the Adaptancy Platform on *development forms* represent only a *partial or limited* view. Fourth, therefore, if tourism is taken as a *whole* or a *system*—for an understanding of its underlying structures and functions— this would contribute to the formation of knowledge in this field. In turn, this would aid in further development of theoretical constructs on a phenomenon now evolved into a global institution and on a business turned into a mega-industry. It was due to these interrelated, processual, and assimilating insights that a fourth position, the Knowledge-Based Platform, emerged in the last decade of the 20th century.

This final platform, mostly occupied by members of the academic/research community, has been aiming at positioning itself on a scientific foundation and, at the same time, maintaining bridges with the other three platforms For a balanced view, the resulting knowledge landscape upholds objectivity, with the bridges intended as accesses, not attachments, to other perspectives. Further, it systematically studies tourism's own structure; annexes it to various fields of investigation or disciplines; defines its place in this larger multidisciplinary context that generates and accommodates it; examines its functions at personal, group, business, government, and systems levels; identifies factors that influence and are influenced by it; and more. This all is meant to contribute to a *holistic* treatment of tourism—not just its *impacts or forms. The* main goal is the *forma tion of a scientific body of knowledge on tourism.*

With these processual developments almost simultaneously in progress, the early definitions of tourism, generally concerned with the number of miles travelled, reasons for travel, and money spent (an orientation typical to the Advocacy Platform), have continuously evolved. This shift has been in favour of framing holistic definitions that would include, among other things, the tourist-generating and receiving systems and their inter-dependence and the total text and context that bring them to vitality. For example, tourism may be defined as the study of man away from his/her usual habitat, of the touristic apparatus and networks, and of the ordinary (home) and the nonordinary (touristic) worlds and their dialectic relationship. This, and even more recent articulations, as is the intent, have departed from the earlier notions designed to mainly measure tourism traffic or its economic magnitude, to instead view it as a total system, with economics as only one of its significant constituent dimensions. Such systemic a empts will undoubtedly continue into the next century, aiming for more refined definitions and holistic treatments of tourism as a scholarly field of investigation. Presently, this foundation and orientation is in its solidifying stage: the work of the Knowledge-Based Platform is gradually paying off.

The Scientification of Tourism

The Advocacy, Cautionary, Adaptancy, and Knowledge-Based Platforms, seen together, provide an overview of the formation and transformation of insights on tourism. But hidden in this general sketch are the specific conditions (catalysts, agents of change) that have contributed to this evolution and to the development of tourism knowledge. A review of this scientification process shows that tourism now has almost all properties and tools typically associated with the more established field of investigations.

Tourism as a University Subject

As is apparent from this discussion, the interest of the academic community in research has continued to increase with the passage of time. But research is one valued aspect of the academic world; instruction is another. Many universities have gradually expanded their course offerings to include tourism. In the early part of this century, several European universities had already established professonal chairs in tourism. Universities in the US and elsewhere discovered tourism much later. At the outset, it was the hotel management programmes that added tourism to their curricula. Soon after, it also penetrated such programmes or departments as business, leisure, recreation, and even social sciences.Today's offerings range from a single course/subject to minors and majors in tourism, at both undergraduate and graduate levels. Significantly, the number of universities offering advance degrees is on the rise. For several years now, some universities worldwide have even expanded their existing doctoral programmes in such fields as education, recreation, and urban/regional planning to include tourism, with a few now offering independent doctorate degrees in tourism. Examination of degree programmes and dissertations written on tourism reveals that this truly multidisciplinary field (Figure 5.1) is enjoying a growing rate of popularity on campuses, as both areas of instruction and research. But these developments did not take place in isolation. Other conditions and change agents also have been present.

Research Journals

The scientific role that *research* journals play in their respective fields requires no elaboration. In tourism there are several, of both older and more recent origins: (from North America) *journal of Travel Research, Tourism Analysis, Annals of Tourism Research, Tourism, Culture & Communication;* (from Europe) *The Tourist Review* and *Tourism Management;* (from Asia) *Tourism Recreation Research* and *Asia Pacific journal of Tourism Research;* (from the South Pacific) *The Journal of Tourism Studies* and *Pacific Tourism Review;* and this is only a small sample of English language periodicals. Today the number of English language academic journals in hospitality, tourism, and leisure is about 40. While each, with its wide range of contents and treatments, intends to meet certain objectives, together they structure and are structured by research efforts of a multidisciplinary community of scholars whose contributions can also appear in other forms and places. Their occasional special issues on specific themes provide added focused perspectives, still reinforcing tourism's connection to and dependence on other fields of investigation (Figure 5.1).

Publications

There is certain regularity about journals, assuring a continuous flow of research contributions. Through them, findings appear more frequently and more quickly, and hence contain more up-to-date information: the continuous and cumulative flow of knowledge is reassured. But books, monographs, references, and ether publications serve similar purposes and their contributions to the advancement of knowledge are of paramount importance. The number of such publications was insignificant in the 1960s, more appeared in the 1970s, with still many more published in the 1980s, and the 1990s has already been a decade of abundance. Publishers, some of them among the most prestigious houses internationally, even produce book series committed to tourism. The latter, because of their thematic continuity, also assure the type of regularity inherent with journals' cumulative process. Free-standing books and the series, along with major reference books—such as the *Encyclopedia of Tourism* (Jafari, 2000)—are among significant contributions that collectively advance the scholarly position of tourism worldwide.

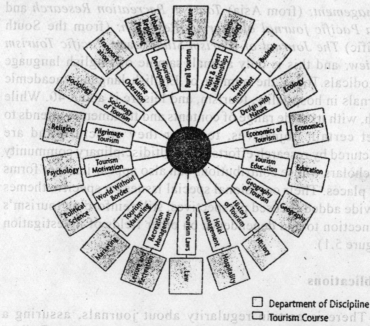

Department of Discipline
Tourism Course

Figure 5.1 The multidisciplinary foundation of tourism studies

Research and Scholarly Groups

Still another structuring and structured force for this scientification process has been the formation of research interest groups, which come in many sizes, with varied systems of operation. In tourism, the number of such groups is not very large, almost all are membership associations, and they have somewhat similar goals and objectives. To build upon the existing efforts and past research accomplishments, such as those started in 1951 by Association Internationale d'Experts Scientifiques du Tourisme and in 1970 by the reorganized Travel and Tourism Research Association, the idea of a tourism academy was materialized with the formation of the International Academy for the Study of Tourism in 1988. The Academy, with its membership coming" from the many fields represented in Figure 5.1, is naturally a body committed to the Knowledge-Based Platform, and hence it directly relates to the theme of this chapter, and therefore another tool and means of scholarship is now in place.

Operational Forces

For decades now, governments have recognized the importance of tourism. Though this has been mainly due to its economic potentials (Advocacy Platform), this stand has nevertheless enhanced its image in circles small and large, private and public. This, in turn, one can argue, has provided some of the impetus at work in the areas already noted. Further, as another set of forces or developments that has helped the scientification of tourism, one should acknowledge the works and functions of those organizations in or closely affiliated with tourism as a business. Such establishments are indeed very large in number and range from local to international levels. Chief among them is the World Tourism Organization, an inter-governmental agency affiliated with the United Nations. While its original raison d'être can be traced to tourism as a trade (and hence its connection to the Advocacy Platform), during recent years it has made giant strides in both recognizing and promoting tourism research and education. Its recent commitment to the latter, including establishment of formal ties with some 15 universities in Europe and elsewhere, speaks to this point.

Tourism Seminars

Still another set of active change agents advancing this scientification course is seminars or symposiums organized by many associations and interest groups, especially those committed to research and scholarship in their respective fields. Thus, the importance of conferences organized by tourism associations or institutions should also be recognized. They bring together researchers and industry experts with diverse disciplinary and professional backgrounds. Their seminar reports, some of which are published in journals, speak to this point, with the resulting proceedings and volumes sustaining the discourse well beyond the conferences themselves. Efforts of anthropology, geography, and sociology associations, as well as the academy, should be acknowledged here.

Training and Education

The scientification process and the use of the resulting body of knowledge directly relate to both of tourism's fields of theory and practice. One of several subjects or themes that concretely connects them together is training/education. At this juncture, it seems appropriate to use this subject to suggest how the knowledge as a whole and its two fields of theory and practice can best guide the present and future human resource development task, which is nowadays more and more assumed by colleges and universities worldwide—the very institutions that in the first place contributed to the development of the knowledge foundation in tourism. Their training aid education mission (on the top of their research and scholarship roles) is not a minor task, as it directly relates to the work/performance of a workforce over 6 million strong in the US alone or over 120 million worldwide. The task does not become any simpler when knowing that this workforce is mostly unskilled and semiskilled, with only a small percentage placed in the management-administration-leadership cadre. Together the workforce forms a pyramid with the latter occupying the top and the former the middle and bottom layers (figure 5.2). In order to make the scope of this discussion manageable, only training and educating of the future generations is kept in mind, but without failing to realize that the same body of knowledge can guide the fine tuning and upgrading/updating of the present workforce at all layers.

In tourism, the training and education terms are used interchangeably, but here "training" covers what is given to those who want to occupy "hands-on" jobs and "education" to those interested in "minds-on" positions. As Figure 5.2 suggests, the top and bottom positions stand in contrast to one another, and thus by commenting on one, the other is also defined. Recognizing the nature of the industry, the top cadre's education must ingrain those multidisciplinary theories and tools that best prepare for the diverse leadership and top-level management tasks in the private and public tourism sectors. Figure 5.2 further suggests that education must provide a "field vision," including a comprehensive understanding of the industry sectors, of their interrelationship, of shifts and trends, of how these all relate to broader sociopolitical systems that shape and control tourism, and more. In contrast, in the bottom, as shown, this vertical bar is narrowed downward to a minimal level; instead these workers (say, those who set tables in the banquet halls of a convention hotel) are expected to simply perform a given task(s) prescribed to them at their "work station."

Moreover, Figure 5.2 shows some other categorically distinctive differences between these two opposite ends. For instance, the curriculum designed for the education" of this upper

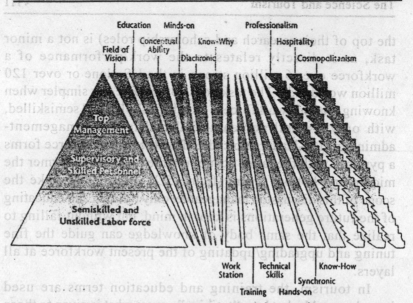

Figure 5.2 Tourism education-training continuum

level must result in "conceptual ability," again nurtured in appropriate multidisciplinary contexts. On the other hand, the bottom layer's "training" would teach "technical skills," whose bar is widest for this group and comes to a point for their counterparts on the top. Other paired bars include "minds-on" vs. "hands-on,"' diachronic" (a vision of the future *á la* present and past) vs. "synchronic"(now and today), and "know-why" vs. "know-how"—a set of bars that, despite their apparent separations, are part and parcel of what constitutes education vs. training and distinguishes them from one another.

The third row of vertical bars relates more closely to whether people are to be placed in front or back positions of the industry, regardless of whether they enter the top or bottom layers Obviously those prepared to deal with tourists need to have added education and training for this not-easy function. That is why the bars do not narrow up or down, but their scope throughout the pyramid reflects the degree of contact with tourists. "Professionalism' is important to the entire workforce, but manifests itself more in contact situations, as does "hospitality." To enlarge on the latter, it must be recognized that the mega-industry of this chapter is an art-and-science field at the same time, with hospitality being its "art" (or soul) and tourism its "science." But regardless of how this distinction between them is argued, still those who are in direct contact with tourists must have mastered the art of hospitality, to appropriately attract, receive, accommodate, and serve their customers coming from many regions, with diverse cultural backgrounds and expectations. Finally,"cosmopolitanism"further defines the concept and practice of hospitality. Education and training of those being prepared for front positions must include an understanding of the cultures of their tourist-generating markets, so that they feel comfortable to operate beyond their own immediate home culture. Cosmopolitanism here also suggests that the front people need to speak at least one of the languages of their main markets, again regardless at which layer of the pyramid they function.

In fact, Figure 5.2 makes more sense when it is viewed in the light of the earlier discussion on the four tourism platforms and the outlined evolutionary process. For instance, typically the advocacy groups show more interest in training and the knowledge-based show more interest in education of the workforce; the trade associations emphasize hands-on and academic circles emphasize minds-on; the industry pushes its trade publications and scholarly circles push their refereed journals, etc. Benefiting from this perspective. Figure 5.2, despite its simplicity, offers insights into curriculum development, range of subjects to be taught, degree of abstractness, techniques of instruction, types of fieldwork, and more. But, even more significantly, this education/training example becomes a commentary on what the new knowledge base is offering to tourism, whether regarded as an industry, as a field of investigation, or both—a distinction that can begin to blend as the landscape of knowledge is being better mapped, marked, and populated. This multidisciplinary foundation provides what is needed to study all tourism aspects, individually yet coherently, including education and training issues that have been discussed for decades. To mention here a newer research theme, the debate on sustainable tourism development is also getting its inspiration, force, and substance from the very evolutionary foundation that can now advance this development theme. Education/training, sustainable development, cultural issues, costs and benefits of tourism, etc., all are becoming even more promising themes as the landscape of knowledge grows in size and sophistication in years ahead, with the old, new, and still unrevealed dimensions of tourism begin to unfold more fully.

The Awaiting Future

The above discussion on the four platforms, the transformative forces or catalysts, the text and context of these in structuring and shaping training and education efforts and outlooks, provide informative retrospective and ongoing insights on tourism-both as a realm of concepts and as a field of operations. This may now be coupled with a prospective view beyond the present scholarly footholds and operational matters, toward scientific and developmental horizons ahead.

Tourism as a Scholarly Field

The cumulative process of building a scientific foundation for tourism—brick by brick, block by block—will continue. As in the past, the social sciences will make substantial contributions to its formation and solidification. Other fields related to the study of tourism will also further define and refine their areas of commonality with tourism. Because it relates to several phenomena and because its study utilizes theories and methods of many disciplines, tourism will assume a truly multidisciplinary position in the academic world. With this foundation in place, its own emerging theories and methods will be borrowed by the same disciplines that earlier on had generously contributed to the formation of its scientific corpus. Furthermore, tourism research will be used at a growing rate in other disciplines' publications and journals in order to illustrate issues native to their own domains. This will be so because tourism has special and unique perspectives to offer, and even more so as it becomes a common phenomenon to which people can readily relate (due to the growing awareness about its place in society and the economy). Moreover, a larger number of Ph.D. dissertations, dealing with old and new dimensions of tourism, will continue to be produced by students majoring in a variety of established fields, as well those doing tourism by itself.

Presently, some disciplinary associations have established tourism interest groups within their formal organizational structures. With the growing importance of tourism, more disciplinary associations will establish bridges with it. These will include formation of additional interest groups by associations dealing with anthropology, ecology, economics, history, leisure, marketing, management, political science, psychology, and more (again, some of these are already in place). As the numbers of these disciplinary interest groups increase, they will begin to sponsor joint seminars or congresses. It is indeed at such gatherings that creative minds will have the opportunity to truly advance this multidisciplinary tourism discourse. With these and other scientific achievements in progress and with sustained growth in tourism jobs, additional universities will commit to offering undergraduate and graduate programmes in this field. Offering doctoral degrees will attract the attention of even more prestigious universities. Many universities will offer their tourism programmes within the presently typical departments/schools, with leisure and recreation departments paying closer attention to tourism for an eventual integration. More university departments, such as those in the social sciences, will first offer tourism courses, then minors, and later majors. This could partly be due to their present lack of ability to attract sufficient numbers of students to their own majors and partly due to the relevancy and attractiveness of tourism to their fields. On the other hand, additional universities will establish free-standing tourism schools or colleges. Their offerings would include general tourism degrees, with specialization options in hospitality management, marketing, planning and development, public administration, tourism in developing countries, and international tourism, to name a few.

The privillege of enlarging the scientific base horizontally and vertically will turn into an obligation—for the tourism faculty to regularly utilize the existing body of knowledge and to productively contribute to its growth. This expectation is already in place in all established fields, and tourism will not be the exception. The present de facto publish or perish rule in tourism will assume a more prominent position among its faculty for retention, promotion, and tenure decisions.

A few universities have already established endowed tourism hospitality chairs. The scientific developments as well as further growth in the industry will increase the prospects of establishing additional chairs in many countries, developed and developing. As in the past, some of the new chairs will be created mostly with direct support from various segments of the industry. Further, as the scientific layers increase and as tourism becomes an even more recognized socioeconomic phenomenon, granting institutions would favourably consider research proposals in tourism, a noticeable shift from the present situation. This change will be both in respect to funding requests for dissertations and for independent research projects. Such favourable developments will be augmented with establishment of prestigious awards recognizing research scholarship in this field. These developments will boost tourism's reaches to a new height, alongside other established fields.

Tourism as an Operation Field

Ironically, the industry itself has not yet fully recognized and supported tourism research and scholarship. This will happen, but more gradually, especially as the number of decision-makers holding tourism degrees increases and as the industry begins to witness more progress through research. As well, responsible governmental bodies and trade associations will not only incorporate more scientific substance and tools in performing their tasks, but will also produce more quality research works with application beyond their immediate parameters. This prospect will be further magnified as they favour hiring employees with advanced training in tourism. Both the industry and public agencies will pay closer attention to the noneconomic dimensions of tourism, with a growing percentage of their research budget set aside for noumarketing studies. In general, the present wide gap between the research and operation camps will be desirably reduced and concretely bridged. The tripartite tourism academic-industry-government relationship will also further solidify.

Collaborative research and action between the operation and concept camps is also one of the desirable and expected outcomes. Many ongoing and emerging themes will be pursued in this joint fashion, including research on and application of, for example, shifting lifestyles and trends. It is often assumed that the future will be a natural extension of the past. But not exactly: people change, societies change, values change, needs and expectations change, and so do lifestyles Such shifts in turn will define and redefine the future of the industry and its many products, as tourism reflects societal shifts.

Another example of joint research/action effort will be in the area of health and tourism. The new and emerging lifestyles encourage people to be, for example, more health conscious. People are exploring various alternatives to extend their lives, to live a healthier life, and to enjoy it fully. Right here an automatic connection between lifestyle à *la* health and tourism is made. Many alternative forms of tourism are favoured because of this "healthy" notion, ns this practice contributes to a healthier mind and body.

Work on the senior citizen market, as still another instance of collaboration, comes to mind. Changes in the lifestyle and the desire for a healthier body and mind are universal trends, cutting across race, class, gender, and age. Dealing with now such an enlarged scope, crowded with many variables, complicates the task of research. Still, lifestyle and health, both boosted with advancements in medicine, technology, and welfare systems, among others, have in turn led to another phenomenon: a sudden increase in the population of the third age, or senior citizens. Today senior citizens are much greater in number, they enjoy an invigorating lifestyle, and they are healthier. Further, many choose to retire at an earlier age in order to move on to the next phase of their lives sooner. With family and professional commitments left behind and prospects of a good life seen ahead, pursuits of a healthy, leisurely life—fueled with saved resources and an "unlimited" supply of just-accessed leisure time—becomes their new profession or religion, with tourism as the main means and end of this living journey. This suggests a massive movement of senior citizens endlessly zigzagging the globe. Studying this ever-increasing population—with its own mindset and philosophy, which "is not willing to die" but is instead-eager to enjoy life," as put in public media, both at home and away for home, at near and far away destinations—would now mean connecting tourism to still other fields such as medicine and gerontology. Significantly, because away from home is where they mostly want to be, as often as possible, with the saved disposable income available to them, challenging, new and creative alternatives emerge, in both fields of theory and practice. Tourism, this convoluted phenomenon, begins to unfold, with often less-than-apparent dimensions brought to new multidisciplinary focus.

To conclude, in a short period of time, the study of tourism has taken several major strides, lifting off from a mainly practical/applied springboard and landing on a small but growing scientific foundation. This transformative process has been benefiting from the insights of four schools of thought: Advocacy, Cautionary, Adaptancy, and Knowledge-Based Platforms. The latter, influenced by several favourable conditions and change agents, armed with multidisciplinary means and tools, has maintained its forward move on a definitive scientific course, now with a rather clearer sense of direction.

Today, as the new century is starting, it is quite evident that tourism is finally assuming its scholarly position among research and academic circles. All signs suggest that this trend will continue, toward new frontiers of knowledge. This development will further enhance tourism's status among formal institutions and in society at large. But attainment of the ultimate scientification goal will depend on the support and the type of influence exerted by the scholarly community itself, grant institutions, government bodies, associations, and the tourism industry. "A journey of a thousand miles," a Chinese proverb says, "begins with a single step "Obviously tourism is already beyond the initial steps, its scientific journey is clearly in progress, aiming at new frontiers, heading to new horizons.The tourism landscape of knowledge is now sketched, as demonstrated by the contents of the 25th anniversary issue of *Annals of Tourism Research* and *Encyclopedia of Tourism,* among others.

The prime beneficiaries of this achievement will be the tourism industry itself and governments who, on behalf of their constituencies, capitalize on it as it utilizes the growing store of basic and applied knowledge to everyone's advantage, especially the total host system. Informed holistic research and operational strategies—which think future, but act today, which project globally but develop locally—provide necessary principles, practices, and philosophies guiding the process. The field, though, is mindful that its scientification course is a journey, not the destination.The goal remains the development of a body of knowledge that is thematically organized and coherently synthesized, which defines and consumes a distinct phenomenon of related concepts and actions, fields of theory and practice, called tourism.

Acknowledgments—This chapter is based on the author's earlier (joint) publications, particularly Jafari (1990, 1994, 1997a, 1997b), Jafari and Aaser (1988),Jafar and Ritchie (1981), and Jafari and Pizam (1996). In particular, in his capacity as Editor-in-Chief (1973-2000) of *Annals of Tourism Research, he* has benefited from the offerings of its past volumes (see *Annals* special 25th anniversary issue 1999). Earlier versions of this chapter have been presented at three international conferences.The author has also benefited from the interactions and comments received at these gatherings.

6

Theory of Tourism

Tourism-defined by the sentence "a tourist is a temporarily leisured person who voluntarily visits a place away from home for the purpose of experiencing a change" (Smith, 1989b, p. 1), may not exist universally, but in many ways it is functionally and symbolically equivalent to other institutions—calendrical festivals, holy days, sports tournaments—that humans use to embellish and *add* meaning to their lives. In its special aspect—travel—tourism has its antecedents in other seemingly more serious institutions such as medieval student travel, the Crusades, and European and Asian pilgrimages.

It is my contention that tourism is best understood as a *kind of ritual,* one in which the special occasions of leisure and travel stand in opposition to everyday life at home and work. This general theory applies to all forms of tourism. Therefore, we have to understand the nature of tourist travel and experience in terms of the *contrasts* between the special period of life spent in tourist travel and the more ordinary parts of life spent at home while working. Tourism experiences are meaningful because of their difference from the ordinary and they reflect the home life from which the tourists stem. Thus, any one kind of tourist experience (e.g., a week in Paris) can mean something very different in the life of tourists from, for example, urban New York, metropolitan Tokyo, or rural California. Indeed, for some people a week in Paris would be too ordinary and boring, whereas for other people, from very different social backgrounds, it might be too daunting and exciting and they would never undertake such a vacation. Thus, we can see that the tourists' gender, class, occupation, and life stage are all significant in determining where tourists choose to go and what they think of the experience when they have been there.

Tourism: Rituals of Reversal

The ritual theory of tourism proposes that the motivations and compensations of tourism involve "push" and "pull" factors. Tourists leave home because there is something that they want to get away from, and they choose to visit a particular place because they believe that they will experience something positive there that they cannot easily experience at home. This kind of explanation involves the "ritual reversal" or "ritual inversion" of some aspects of life. Simple examples would include the winter migrations of Eastern Canadians to the Caribbean and of Scandinavians to the Mediterranean, when these northerners seek some warmth away from home, or when lower middle class Californians go to large hotels in Las Vegas or Reno at any time of the year and "live it up" by occupying large, well-appointed rooms and being served lavish meals (Gottlieb, 1982). Middle class Japanese who vacation in the hotels of Southeast Asia in the wintertime seeks both touristic goals: seasonal warmth and a luxurious style of life (Beer, 1993)—inversions of their cramped lives in cold Tokyo.

The felt needs of tourists, the things that they look for and forward to in their cen travels, are never the complete opposites to their home class position and lifestyle. For instance, erudite people don't want to become ignorant, although they may want a relaxing break, and good athletes don't try to become physically incompetent. The felt needs are indeed the product of, or an inherent part of, the values of the home class and lifestyle. Scandinavians and Canadians value sunshine and warmth; American college professors value culture and history and may seek more of it on their vacations; many obese people value thinness and may visit a special reducing establishment; and gourmets may partake of simple foods in their travels, but never bad foods—not willingly! So the temporary reversal sought is rarely an antithesis of their values but is a product of their cultural background, and the promised reward is supposed to satisfy the need in a direction of further enhancement of these values, not turn the tourist into an entirely different kind of person. The claim that tourism is a secular ritual, embracing goals or activities that have replaced the religious or supernatural experiences of other societies, was strongly suggested by a recent television advertisement in the San Francisco Bay area (1997). It showed exciting scenes of young, fit people diving off cliffs into the sea, skiing down steep slopes, bungee jumping, and so on. At the end of these came a voice-over, "If you want a religious experience, why don't you try a religious experience!" as the scene moved to a shot of the Protestant evangelist the Rev. Billy Graham, who was about to bring his crusade to the area.

Tourism, Ritual, and Time

Tourism in the modal sense emphasized here is but one of a range of choices or styles of recreation or vacation. All of these ritualized breaks in routine define and relieve the ordinary. There is a long tradition in anthropology of the examination of these special events and institutions as markers of the passage of time. Vacations involving travel (i.e., tourism) are the modern equivalent for secular societies to the annual and lifelong sequences of festivals and pilgrimages found in more traditional, God-fearing societies. Fundamental is the contrast between the ordinary/compulsory work state spent "at home" and the extraordinary/voluntary metaphorically "sacred" experience away from home.

The stream of alternating contrasts provides the meaningful events that mark the passage of time. English anthropologist Leach (1961) suggested that celebratory events were the way in which people without clocks and calendars used to measure the passage of time, implying that those who have scientific calendars and other tacit reminders such as newspapers, TV. and radio rely only on the numerical calendar. I believe that even "scientific, secular" Westerners gain greater meaning from the personal rather than the numerical in life. We are more satisfied and better recall loaded symbols marking the passage of time: for example, "that was the year we went to Rome"or "that was the summer our dog drowned at Brighton Beach" rather than "That was 1988," because the former identify the nonordinary, festive or sorrowful, personal events.

Our two lives—the sacred/nonordinary/touristic and the profane/workaday/at-home—customarily alternate for ordinary people, and are marked by rituals or ceremonies, as should be beginnings and ends of lives. For instance, after a period of work we celebrate with TGIF (Thank Goodness Its Friday), "happy hours," and going away parties, to anticipate the future state and to give thanks for the end of the mundane. The passing of each year is marked by the annual vacation (or by Christmas or a birthday); something would be wrong with a year in which these events didn't occur, as though we had been cheated of time! These repetitive events mark the cyclical passage of time just as in traditional Christian societies weeks would be marked by Sundays and church-going and the year would be marked by Easter, Harvest Festival, Advent, Christmas, and so on. These rituals have been called "rites of increase" or "rites of intensification" in agricultural or forager societies (Durkheim, 1912), but are generally better thought of as *annual cycle rites*. The types of holidays and tourism that fill these functions may be family occasions at home but, when they involve travel (e.g., weekends spent skiing or fishing, weeks spent on the beach or even longer trips travelling abroad), they are usually of the seasonal or "annual vacation" type, a form of re-creation, renewing us and making the world go round.

Life is not only cyclical, with the same time-marking events occurring again and again, but it is also progressive or linear, as we all pass through life by a series of changes in status, each of which is marked by different but similarly structured rituals. These life-stage marking events are called *rites of passage* and were first analyzed by French folklorist Arnold Van Gennep (1960); it his model that we shall follow in our analyses of tourism as ritual. Just as rites of passage (e.g., births, graduations, marriages, and funerals) are usually more significant rituals than ordinary cyclical events such as birthdays, Thanksgivings, or *Dias de Los Muertos,* so rites of passage-type tourist experiences may be unusually intense (e.g., semesters abroad, honeymoons, or retirement cruises). But in the relatively individualistic, informal lives of the contemporary Euro-Americans, many rites of passage as kinds of tourism may be purposely self-imposed physical and mental tests (e.g., college-aged people trekking across continents trying to go as far as possible with little expenditure) (Cohen, 1973; Teas, 1988) or when recently broken up, divorced, or laid-off middle-class persons take "time off," for long sailing, walking, or cycling trips or other adventures (Frey, 1998; Hastings, 1988).

The Structure of Ritual and Tourism

For the present discussion our focus is consciously on the prototypical examples of tourism, such as long-distance travel to famous places or to visit exotic peoples, all in unfamiliar environments. However, even the most minimal kinds of tourism, such as a picnic in the garden, contain elements of the "magic of tourism." The food and drink might be identical to that normally eaten indoors, but the magic comes from the movement and the nonordinary setting. Conversely, a very special meal in the usual but specially decorated eating place may also, by contrast with the ordinary, be "magic" enough for a special celebration.

The alternation of sacred and profane states and the importance of the transition between them were first shown by the French sociologists Hubert and Mauss (1898) in their analysis of the almost universal ritual of sacrifice. They emphasized the sequential process of leaving the ordinary, that is, the sacralization that elevates the participants to the nonordinary state where marvelous things happen, and the converse of desacralization and return to ordinary life." Each festival [and each tourist trip, we contend] represents a temporary shift from the Normal-Profane order of existence into the Abnormal-Sacred order and back again"(Leach, 1961, pp. 132-136).The flow of time has a pattern, represented in Figure 6.1.

Each festive or tourist event is a miniature life, with a happy anticipation, A-B, an exciting middle, C-D, and a bittersweet ending, D-F.The periods before A and after F are the mundane, everyday life, expressed in "That's life."The period C-D, the metaphorically "sacred," the "liminal" (see below) out-of-the-ordinary period, is the time of pilgrimage, travel, and tourism.These holidays (formerly "holy days") celebrated in vacations and tourism might be expressed as: "I was living it up, really living . . . I've never felt so alive." These changes in moral and spatial states are usually accompanied by aesthetic changes and markers.This is most obvious in the case of religious rituals and rites of passage, where colorful dresses and strikingly decorated settings are accompanied by chanting, singing, and music. In tourism, too, there may well be aesthetic and sensory changes, in clothing, settings, and foods, and even in touch and smell in the case of tropical beach holidays or Japanese hot springs tourism (Graburn, 1995b).

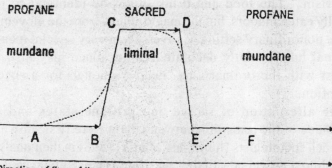

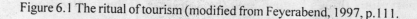

Figure 6.1 The ritual of tourism (modified from Feyerabend, 1997, p.111.

Entries and Exits

The experience of being away on vacation (or going on pilgrimage; has important effects on the life of the traveller outside at the actual time spent travelling. Just as there are rituals of preparation, cleansing oneself, changing garments, perhaps putting on perfumes, or getting into the right frame of mind before undertaking religious rites such as pilgrimages, sacrifices, or Christian communion, so for the tourist and travellers there are rituals of preparation.These routinely involve not only planning, booking, and getting new clothes, gear, or luggage, but also social arrangements such as getting someone to water the garden, to look after the house and pets, to collect the mail, to leave numbers for emergencies, and often having parties for saying goodbye.

All of these necessary actions produce the pleasure of anticipation in the period A-B. the weeks and months before the actual take off B-C, but the feelings are also ambivalent. There may be misgivings about having made the right decisions, having laid out so much money, or having chosen the right travelling companions. There is also the remote possibility that one is saying goodbye forever, especially for long journeys to more distant places for greater lengths of time, as well as for the elderly or infirm either as travellers or those left behind. [For instance, when I went to graduate school in Canada (by ship) my mother at home in England died unexpectedly before I had my first trip home. Nevertheless, this period of anticipation is extremely important: the pleasure being looked forward to itself shines on many of the preparations and is often what people "live for" in their workaday lives.

Going home, the journey D-F, the reentry process coming down from the "high" C-D, is equally important and fraught with ambivalence. Most people are reluctant to end a vacation, to leave the excitement and new friends, and to have to go beck to work, in fact, a desire to get home and end the vacation might be seen as in admission that it didn't turn out to be as good as expected—that the recreation did not re-create. Some travellers even have twinges of sorrow during the period C-D, for instance on reaching the furthest point away from home (Frey, 1998), as they anticipate "the beginning of the end," the loss of new friends, or of the "paradise" visited.

The work of Berkeley undergraduate Amanda Feyerabend (1997) on the rituals and experience of the reentry and the reincorporation into normal society explainss what is called "reverse culture shock." The term is a corollary to the notion of culture shock"—the feeling of strangeness and inability to cope—that travellers feel "hen first in unfamiliar environments, such as tourists at point C in Figure ; The reverse of this is the unhappiness felt when the tourist first gets back into his her home and working environment (the period E-F in Figure 5.1). Feyerabend's informants suggested that while their normal home and work lives might be satisfying most of the time, that life suffered by comparison with the excitement, ...the out ot the ordinary special experiences that they had just left behind; thus, the lowered state of feelings at E-F is a relative measure of happiness.

Feverabend also found that, in general, the length of time this ambivalent reverse culture shock lasted was approximately *half the length of time* the traveller had been away. For instanced after a 2-day weekend of skiing in the nearby Sierra Nevada range, Berkeley students felt the next day (Monday) was a real let down, but they would feel OK by Tuesday. On the other hand, a student who returned from a year abroad in a foreign country might feel ill at case and not quite at home for the whole next semester back in the US.

The Tourist Experience: Liminality and Communitas

Van Gennep (i960), building on the work of Hubert and Mauss, gave us the model commonly used for the analysis of rituals in general. While Hubert and Mauss emphasized the micro-rituals of preparation, separation, and reincorporation in their look at sacrifice, Van Gennep focused on the central period of the ritual, C-D, and the nature of the participants' experience. In his analysis he labeled the "sacred" out-of-the-ordinary period "liminal," meaning "on/over the threshold," following the European custom where a groom has to carry his bride over the threshold of their new home. At this liminal point the participants are neither in nor out, or as V. Turner (1974) put it, they are "betwixt and between." In some societies this special period is likened to a temporary death; the person in their old status dies, then follows the liminal period where they are bracketed off from ordinary time (or their ordinary place in the case of tourism), out of which they are reborn with their new status, e.g.,

Bachelor → [groom @ wedding ceremony] → husband
Single → [bride @ wedding ceremony] → wife

Victor Turner (1974) and his wife Edith Turner (Turner & Turner, 1978) further examined this period of *liminality* in African rituals and Christian pilgrimages, and they noted:"If a pilgrim is half a tourist, then a tourist is half a pilgrim" (p. 20). Turner stressed that for the participants, those to be transformed in the ritual or the travellers as pilgrims and tourists, the normal social structure of life, work, and family roles, age and gender differences, and so on tend to become looser or disappear. This leveling he called "anti-structure" though, of course, these participants are always surrounded by others carrying out their usual structured roles (e.g., priests or shamans at rituals, and guides, hoteliers, and food workers for pilgrims and tourists). Turner suggested that this leveling of statuses ideally sought outside of home and work structures produces a special feeling of excitement and close bonding among the participants, which he called *communitas* . This state is often signaled by a reduction in marked differences, with all pilgrims wearing the same clothes or all Club Med clients in their beach wear, and with people addressing each other as equals, and sharing the same foods, drinks, accommodations, pleasures, and hardships. While consulting for Club Med, I explained this ritual model to a number of *chefs de villages* and *G.O.s (gentils organisateurs)* who replied with a flash of understanding: "Of course, and the hard part of our job is to keep our customers 'up'in the state of communitas for their seven days non-stop!"

This liminal state, this special human feeling of communitas, may be examined and understood in a variety of ways. In lay language "going on a trip" usually refers to a journey but it can refer to a an "altered state of consciousness "(ASC) brought on by drugs or alcohol, and a special religious or magic experience;"trip" literally means away from the ordinary. Such experience may be called "a high"after which there is a "let down'or a "come down" (i.e., period C-D followed by D-F in Figure 3.1), and a "high"is opposed to a feeling of depression or a"low," the negativeASC experienced in period E-E. The special state of consciousness experienced during a "trip ' was illuminated when I was discussing Feyerabend's findings with my undergraduate class on tourism. Some students pointed out that the'reverse culture shock" (E-F), lasting half as long as the period of absence (C), paralleled the students' common belief that the time it takes to get over a serious love affair or a broken friendship is half as long as the relationship lasted, putting the "magic" of tourism .and pilgrimage into the same emotional category as love and friendship!

Variations on a Theme:
Different Strokes for Different Folks

Our analysis of tourism as ritual and the equation of the feelings and meaning of the trip with other human experiences does not mean that all tourism experiences are the same any more than all rituals are the same Turner and others have characterized the state of communitas as being: "high" "liminar" orliminoid when not paist of a truly religious experience,), a state of homogeneity, equality, and humility among the participants, a period of transition, magic, or otherworldliness. For today's tourists, the vacation away from home might be described as above, but may also be described as "away," "timeless," a time of freedom, play, mindless spending, and attention to the past or the future (cf. Dann, 1996).

The range of tourist experiences has best been outlined by Israeli sociologist E. Cohen in his "Phenomenology of Tourist Experiences" (1979a). Here he takes into account the equation I have suggested between today's tourism and more spiritual pursuits such as pilgrimage, by placing such serious pursuits at one end of his continuum.At this serious end, the traveller is seeking a very important or 'sacred" experience or place "out of this world," a sacred center spiritually more important than anything at home. These "existensional" tourists or pilgrims are on a true exploration and many are so moved by the experience attained or the place visited that they stay there and never go home or, in a more practical sense, they never want to go home. Thus, American Jews, having visited Israel, may emigrate there; North American mainlanders may retire to Hawaii or San Franciscans to the Mendocino County coast. The nature of such tourists' experiences may well be spiritual rather than patently religious; one may feel deeply moved by "communing with nature." Others, atheist or agnostic, might follow the old European pilgrimage way through northern Spain, the Camino de Santiago, and have profoundly moving, even life-changing experiences both along the way and on reaching the cathedral in Santiago (Frey, 1998).

At the other end of Cohen's continuum are the mere diversionary or recreational tourists, who never seriously doubt their commitment to their home lifestyle, but just want a simple change—perhaps a change of climate or season, a temporary change of recreation or sports—'and have very little desire to

explore or seek new experiences. And in the middle of the
continuum are the more exploratory tourists, who may make
considerable efforts to go to out-of-the-way places, may try to
learn foreign languages, or may live temporarily like foreign
peoples.These "experiential" and "experimental" tourists are
fascinated by difference, like to get close to others, and like to
immerse themselves in different environments (e.g., jungle
ecotourists, Middle Eastern *souks,* or visitors to remote
Nepalese villages). Such people, often young adults without much
money or work experience, but probably well educated by their
home standards (Cohen, 1973;Teas, 1988), have the exploratory
urge and the *cultural self-confidence* (Graburn, 1983) to get
out of their shell and experiment with different lifestyles.

Plus ca Change, Plus e'est la Méme Chose (The More Things Change, the More It's the Same Thing)

This chapter claims that tourism is a manifestation of a need
for a change, and that the change the tourist seeks depends on
what perceived touristic attractions would satisfy something not
fully met at home. In this concluding section, this general
proposition is explored by some specific cases, pointing in
particular to the social historical contexts.

In the contemporary Western world and in modern Japan,
tourism is the opposite to work; it is one kind of that recent
invention: re-creation. It is a special form of play involving travel
and "getting away from it all" (i.e., from work, including
homework and housework).There is a symbolic link between
work + staying and play + travel. Most people feel they ought
to go away when they have holidays, and never to go on a
vacation might be an indication of sickness or poverty, or extreme
youth or old age. Able-bodied adults who don't take holidays
might be thought of as poor, unimaginative, or the "idle rich."
For the middle classes, this going away on holiday is supposed
to be a worthwhile, even a stimulating, creative, or educational

experience (see below); for such people staying at home can be "morally excused" by participating in some creative activity, such as remodeling the house, redoing the garden, or seriously undertaking painting, writing, or sports.

Sociologist Dean MacCannell (1989) has powerfully expressed another instance of this theory in *The Tourist: A New Theory of the Leisure Class,* claiming that the educated middle classes are the sector of our present population who are the most alienated, contrary to Marx's 19th century assertions. MacCanneil shows that the urban and suburban middle classes feel that their lives are overly artificial and meaningless, lacking deep feelings of belonging and authenticity. These are thought to exist elsewhere, especially in the simpler lives of other peoples such as family farmers, manual workers and craftsmen, and "primitive peoples." This missing authenticity is thought to lie, above all, in the past, as indicated by English geographer David Lowenthal (1985) in *The Past is a Foreign Country.* Thus, historical, cultural, and ethnic forms of tourism have become increasingly popular, all of them catering to one form or another of modernity's nostalgia for the premodern (Graburn, 1995b). MacCannell also shows us that the producers of tourist packages and displays understand these longings and are capable of "manufacturing" authentic Others and Pasts, so that the unfortunate tourists are once more faced with the artificial and commercial in their quest for "reality" and the untouched. One popular arena for getting in touch with the true and the pure is Nature itself, which is often sought in its -vilder forms by Euro-American campers, backpackers, and ecotourists, and in more managed versions by the equally alienated urban Japanese (Graburn, 1995a). The world's tourist industry, in its advertising and its packaged offerings, must paradoxically create the illusion that the tourists are, by purchasing their services, getting satisfaction of their needs.

While MacCannell's work is a brilliant analysis of educated Westerners, it is not a universal theory. Many people in Europe and North America are not necessarily seeking the particular ritual inversion from "fake to authentic culture"; indeed, it has been shown that this "moral" concern with authenticity correlates with years of education.This search for the pure and the Other, which Urry (1990) has called the "Romantic" gaze, is supplemented by a more direct, communal, and, some would say, unsophisticated (perhaps a better term is unpretentious) kind of enjoyment he calls the "Collective"gaze. The latter is typical of the 'working classes," who are more gregarious and derive as much pleasure from the company they keep as the places they visit. Indeed, R. Campbell (1988) has shown that city bus drivers often return to their places of work on their days off, just to socialize with their coworkers. Similarly, Japanese *salarymen* and other groups of male workers often go on trips together, leaving their families at home. Hence, Japanese women often travel in single-sex groups, and children travel in school groups.

The research focus on the "gaze"—the visual practice of sightseeing—has also been challenged by those whose research shows that the changes desired may be sensual or tactile. Selanniemi (1994a) found that Scandinavians wintering in the Mediterranean or elsewhere in the "south" want a thoroughly Scandinavian vacation, but one in which they can soak up the sun, lie on the beach, or play simple sports. Jokinen and Veilola (1994) have criticized tourism theorists in general for overemphasizing the visual, the sightseeing quest, because that is the touristic goal of the educated class to which the tourism theorists themselves belong.

In conclusion, this chapter has taken care in using the ritual model not to see all tourism as one individual might experience it, nor should it be expected that ritual reversals are all-encompassing. In fact, tourists on holiday are seeking specific reversals of a few specific features of their workaday home life, things that they lack or that advertising has pointed they could better find elsewhere. Other than obtaining some straightforward goals, whether they be warmth for northerners, weight loss for the overweight, history for the culturally hungry, or immersion in nature for bored urbanites, tourists generally remain unchanged and demand a lifestyle not too different from that at home. Rarely do the timid become bold, the neat become messy, the educated become dumb, the monolingual become polyglot, the frigid become sexy, or the heterosexual become gay except when these are the specific goals of the trip. Gottlieb (1982) has shown how tourists may play "Queen [or Peasant] for a Day" with temporary changes in life or class style, and E. Cohen (1973, 1979b) and Frey (1998) have described some of the more rigorous touristic choices for the young or the alienated moderns, but most tourists on their seasonal and annual vacations want to enjoy their own chosen pursuits and come back refreshed as better versions of their same old selves.

7

Tourism Into the 21st Century

America is witnessing the most widespread liberalization of casino gaming entertainment in its history. Although permitted in the United States since it was legalized in Nevada in 1931, casino-style gaming is expanding at an unparalleled rate (Satre, 1993, p.5). This chapter addresses the major sources and development of American gaming, and it questions the impact of gaming on society (see Figure 7.1).

Four events contributed to 'his acceleration of gambling in the second half of the 20th century in the US:(1) lotteries became a part of the American scene; (2) the Holiday Inn Corporation, acting on changes made by the Nevada Legislature, made it respectable for average stockholders to be part of the gaming industry; (3) the passage of the Indian Gaming Regulatory Act (IGRA) by the United States Congress caused phenomenal growth in Native American facilities; and (4) human nature.

The British novelist and playwright J.B. Priestly (1894-1984) was noted for his shrewd human characterizations. During his days in England in the 1920s, he wrote book reviews and sold the book afterward. He describes the emotions accompanying the book sales in an essay entitled "Money for Nothing":

At this shop, where human nature was understood, one was always paid at once and always paid in cash, generally in exquisite new pound notes.And of all the money I have ever handled, this gave me the most delight. Money for Jam, Money for Old Rope, Money for nothing. When we receive our wages, salaries or fees, we may be content, for that is what we have earned, but we are a long way from delight. It is money that we have not earned, the windfall, the magical bonus, that starts us capering. *Q*. Priestly, 1951, pp. 349-350)

This "magical bonus" is what drives the guest-as-gambler to take risks at various host destinations that offer this form of entertainment. Anthropologists identify gambling as one of the several forms of redistribution of wealth, together with gift giving, taxation, and theft. Ethnographic research for more than two decades has convinced me not to gamble. Consider the words of Steve Wynn, Chairman of Mirage Resorts Inc. (cited in Spanier, 1992, p. 17) concerning gambling as a way to earn money: "If you wanna make money in a casino, own one."

Figure   The "crazy girls" of the Riviera Hotel and Casino (photo by Charlie Urbanowicz).

Research indicates that individuals go to casinos (1) to gamble (or take risks), (2) to regain some control over their lives, and/ or (3) to feel that they are important! Priestly wrote that he earned a great deal of money elsewhere but that it all was lost in a dreary maze of bank accounts, stocks and shares, tax certificates, cheques and bills and receipts" but, the book sale money, that was something else:

But when I used to hurry out of that shop with five or six new pound notes singing in my pocket, for quarter of an hour or so I felt like a tipsy millionaire or the man who broke the bank at Monte Carlo. Money to Burn! And the only comparable moments I have known since then have been on the certain very rare occasions when I happen to have been fortunate in playing those fruit machines [or slot machines or "one-armed bandits"], which were so popular in the American southwest when we were there. (Priestly, 1951, pp. 349-350)

This unexpected windfall, achieved through a perceived control of the situation, is why people really gamble. Potential guests look to various host destinations to get that adrenal "rush" to remove the boredom from their lives. Romero, an industry consultant, had the following perceptive words about the role that human nature plays in gambling activities:

Why do they come to gaming tournaments? After 15 years of Casino tournaments, I've come to a melancholy conclusion. They come because they're lonely. Sure, price, prize list and free play mean something but those are the intellectual reasons, not emotional reasons. Look carefully at your tournament customers and you'll see most are middle-aged to elderly, living a generally quiet existence (read boring). All this changes at tournaments when they become the center of attention. For brief moments at the slots or tables, they're the stars. It's easy to become addicted to recognition, which is why the best way to keep them as customers is to meet them, learn their names and show them a good time. Did you think they came because of the brochure? Naw. (Romero, 1993, p. 8)

Gambling has evolved into a respectable entertainment industry that is attempting to draw as many new guests as possible to an ever-increasing number of host destinations. On a typical day in the early 1990s, people wagered about

US$627,000 every minute of every day on all types of commercial gambling in the US, and all of these commercial gaming ventures made a profit of about US$57,000 per minute! Data from 1997 indicate that in 1995 the "win" was about US$84,000 per minute in the US (or an increase of US$27,447 per minute from the early 1990s). This revenue underscores the reason big business and corporations are willing to invest a "small fortune" in refurbishing establishments in order to attract consumers for this highly profitable form of entertainment now, and it is predicted to continue into the 21st century. The gaming industry continues to proliferate, adding new sites to compete with the increasing expansion from Indian operations on tribal lands (see Lew & Van Otten, 1998).

Background

We all gamble. The term "gambling" has several definitions, including "to play at any game of chance for stakes" and "to stake or risk money, or anything of value, on the outcome of something involving chance; bet; wager." Ambiguity surrounds the use of the terms "gaming" and "gambling." As someone once remarked, "if you bet on a horse, that's gambling. If you bet you can make three spades, that's entertainment. If you bet cotton will go up three points, that's business. See the difference?"(Orkin, 1991, p. 1). Although the industry executives use the euphemism of *gaming,* our use here is *gambling.* This chapter points out that whereas the outsider (or guest) might think gambling is entertainment, the insider (the hosts, owners, or management) views gambling as a volatile, profitable, competitive enterprise. "Winners" and "losers" exist from the industry or "host" perspective as well as from the perspective of the guests! Not only do "gaming guests" lose money, but certain casinos have also disappeared in past years. For example, in the late 1990s the downtown area of Reno, NV, was literally littered with the "shells" of empty casinos that had prospered when the town was a railhead and served the mining camps at the turn of the last century. These old casinos failed because of their inability to meet market demand for new luxury hotels, big-name entertainers, in-house amusements, and lavish but inexpensive food buffets.

Competition

The competition between the gambling industry casinos to attract guests to their respective locations around the world is multifaceted and occurs as: Nevada vs. New Jersey (and the rest of the nation), northern Nevada Reno) casinos vs. southern Nevada (Las Vegas) casinos; Las Vegas "strip" vs. downtown Las Vegas; the land-based casinos vs. riverboat casinos; and even table games vs. machine games. And in 2000, competition is seen between visiting a casino and Internet gambling (which does not mitigate the loneliness). Technology has allowed various host destinations to change gambling machines from old-fashioned mechanical machines to newer electronic machines with random-number-generated computer chips. These computer-linked machines do pay off and the casinos love the publicity *when* a relatively modest investment hits a jackpot.

Competition also exists between plajers or guests (those seeking entertainment) and casino operators or hosts (who have the statistical advantage). At the end of 1996, the Reno-Sparks Convention and Visitor Authority (RSCVA) made the following statement:

More tourists are visiting Reno this year than last, but more of them are also visiting Indian casinos and Las Vegas—a potentially significant shift, say market analysts. . . "The product in Reno is pleasing a lot more people ... but it's disturbing that we have so much competition," he [Buddy Frank, RSCVA member] said, emphasizing Reno's need to continue improving its product. If it doesn't, he said, "we could lose (business) far more quickly now than we ever could in the past.' Visits to Indian casinos appear to be rising because more casinos are now located in key Reno feeder markets, like the Pacific Northwest and Northern California. (Stearns, 1996, p. IE)

In a hotly contested November 1999 election, California voters affirmed casino-style gambling, with entertainment, on Indian reservations within the state because of the job creation and employment that this tourist industry would provide for native Americans.

Specifics

State and local governments are looking at gambling to pay for social services. Legalized state-authorized gambling began in 1931 in Nevada and was then legalized in Atlantic City, NJ, in 1978, a move to rejuvenate an almost derelict resort. The 20th century legalization of gambling in the US, however, does not mean that gambling was brand new to the continent. Native Americans partook of games of chance long before Europeans arrived in 1492. Patolli was a board game involving competitors throwing dice. In the Yucatan of Mexico (Chitchen Itza), Native Americans made bets at the largest ball court in all of Mesoamerica, measuring some 83 meters in length (272 feet).The following description of the game is interesting:

This game was both a sport and a sacrificial ritual. It was played throughout Mesoamerica, using a large rubber ball that could be hit by the elbows, knees, or hips, but could not be touched by the hands or feet. The game required the players to wear heavy protective equipment, and much paraphernalia was developed during the Classic period. It was often played in masonry courts, and rings or other markers were used for scoring. (Kelly, 1993, p. 4I).

The US has a long and lengthy history of gambling (Findlay, 1986). In a delightful and fascinating book, *Big Deal: A Year*

as a Professional Poker Player. Anthony Holden (1990) made
the following perceptive statement :

> In retrospect, it seems inevitable that games of chance should
> have played so large a role in the development of the
> American character. By the time of the American War of
> Independence, financed in large part by lotteries, public
> auctions had been a routine alternative to taxation since
> Queen Elizabeth I sanctioned England's first raffle in 1566,
> to finance harbour improvements. In the early seventeenth
> century, it was a lottery that funded the first permanent
> English settlement in North America at Jamestown. North
> Virginia.. . . . Risk-taking, by definition, is a fundamental
> aspect of any pioneer or frontier ethic.

During the 18th and 19th centuries, the prevailing American
"Puritan ethic" did not sanction public gambling. It was primarily
identified with pool halls and saloons, especially around the Gold
Rush mining camps, and later with organized crime.The American
musical, *Showboat* (Rogers and Hammerstein, 1927), characterized the gambler as an irresponsible "drifter" and opportunist.

The Effect of Communication Technology

A recent addition to the worldwide accelerating growth of
gambling, however, comes via cyberspace. The gambling industry
is well aware of this cyberspace potential, as one article pointed
out:

> The electronic superhighway now under construction . . .
> has profound implications for USGI [U.S. Gambling, Inc.,
> "a fictional holding company for the nation's casinos and
> slot machines and video poker devices and racetracks and
> lotteries and other gambling businesses"]. How will
> commercial games adapt to the fast approaching interactive
> future? (Christiansen, 1993a, p. 28)

Gamblers no longer need travel but can be entertained in the comfort of their homes.The fiscal effect on the huge casinos is as yet unclear, given the legal issues that have recently been raised. The families of gamblers who "lost" their entire assets have sued the casinos for permitting these individuals to "borrow" money on their credit cards to continue their gambling spree. The courts have yet to decide whether the casino "hosts" have a financial as well as a moral responsibility to monitor guest behaviour. Harrah's, the oldest and largest casino conglomerate, now advertises the motto, "Know when to stop before you start." Large casinos electronically track the wins and losses of their regular clients, using an in-house ID card with an imbedded chip; these data can be then be compared with their personal credit record, as a matter of self-protection. Given this potential liability, even the "Internet gamers" asked for regulations at the March 1998 International Gaming Business Exposition in Las Vegas:

> We believe regulation is needed to legitimize the market and grow the market[5] . . . Internet gambling is here and it is not going to go away, the experts said . . . Three weeks ago, federal prosecutors in New\ York announced indictments against 14 American managers of off-shore companies set up to accept bets over the Internet.

Sources of Gambling

State-sanctioned lotteries began on March 12,1964, when the Governor of New Hampshire purchased the first sweepstakes ticket in New Hampshire. *International Gaming & Wagering Business,* an extremely influential trade publication, had the following statement in 1994:

> It was a simple act, exchanging $3 for ticket number 0000001, but one that would set into motion a juggernaut that, 30 years later, would be a US$25 billion per year

industry comprising 36 states and the District of Columbia. (Dworin, 1994, p. 8)

Corporate America entered the industry in 1978 when the Holiday Inn Corporation made gambling legitimate to stockholders.The following is a dear statement of this aspect:

That [1978] vote [by the Holiday Inn Corporation] marked a significant turning point not just for Holiday, but for the country and the lines that distinguish legitimate business from that which is illegitimate.Throughout history gamblers could earn fortunes, but not much else. If they wanted the status of legitimacy, if they wanted respect, they had to take their money and get themselves or their children out of gambling and into businesses that were respectable because they added some value to society. CD. Johnston, 1992, p. 49)

Prior to corporate America becoming involved in the gaming industry, the expansion of Nevada casinos had come from a questionable source of money:

Throughout the 1960s and well into the 1970s, most of that investment money came from the Teamsters Central States Pension Fund, which provided the money to make Las Vegas the capital of gaming at a time when most financial institutions still steered clear of casino investments. Las Vegas would not be what it is today without the Teamsters Union. ... All the casino loans, however, seemed to come with strings attached. . . . [Eventually] In 1969 the Nevada Legislature passed a corporate gaming control law that permitted corporations to enter Nevada's gaming industry without requiring each shareholder to submit to individual licensing. (S. Lalli, 1997, pp. 14-18)

These cumulative events have been powerful contributors to the acceleration of gambling in the 1990s. Not only can a "guest" be entertained in a gaming establishment, he/she can also "invest" in various industry stocks, such as: Alpha Hospitality Corporation, Aztar Corporation, Circus Circus Enterprises, Inc., Colorado Casino Corporation, Grand Casino Inc., Harvey's Casino Resorts, Harrah's Entertainment Inc., Hilton Hotels Corp., MGM Grand Inc., Mirage Resorts Inc., Station Casinos Inc., and Winner's Entertainment Inc. (just to name a few); one can also invest in various industry suppliers, such as Acres Gaming Inc., International Gaming Technology, Shuffle Master Inc., and Video Lottery Tech, Inc.

Eventually the US Congress passed the 1988 Indian Gaming Regulatory Act (IGRA), and this continued the acceleration. Prior to 1988, federally recognized Native American tribes and individual states had the authority to enter into various agreements dealing with taxes as well as tribal social services. It was the United States Supreme Court decision in *California v. Cabazon Band of Mission Indians* (begun in 1986 and eventually decided in favour of the Cabazon in 1987) that resulted in the passage of IGRA. McKay (1991) pointed out that "the primary issue in Cabazon was whether the State of California had authority to enforce its gambling laws within the reservation occupied by the Cabazon Indians" and the resulting court decision on the Cabazon "allowed unregulated gambling to flourish on Indian reservations" (Weissmann, 1993, p. 124).

Not everyone is pleased with all aspects of Native American involvement in gambling, called the "new Buffalo" by some (Hill, 1993, 1994). In the mid-1990s the following statement was made by a Representative from the state of New Jersey: "We have seen created 296 Indian casinos in a US$7.5 billion industry that is untaxed, unregulated and out of control" ("Lawmakers Aim to Bar Indian Lottery," 1995). The legal situation is so volatile and changing so quickly, one can only cite a 1997 commentator on Native American gambling establishments in North America: "Tribes are groping for ways to deal with immovable state governments" (Connor, 1997, p. 62). According to Connor, IGRA provided "the framework by which games are conducted to protect both the tribes and the general public. Its goals are tribal

economic development, self-sufficiency and strong tribal government" (1993. p. 9). IGRA may have provided a statutory basis
for the creation and operation of Indian gambling establishments
in the US, but the results from IGRA are still evoiving (and for
an excellent short overview, see J. Davis & Otterstrom,
1998).The Mashantucket Pequot Tribal Nation Casino in
Mashantucket, CT, is the most successful casino (Indian Nation
or not) in the Western Hemisphere. An article in the *Pequot
Times* points out:

> Tribal leaders at Taos Pueblo say their gaming operation is
> in "dismal financial condition" and it can afford to pay only
> $4,516 of the $169,000 it owes the state. In Washington,
> one of the 12 tribal casinos was forced to close last summer
> and at least three more have stopped making required
> community-impact contributions. "I don't think anybody
> expected this," said Carrie Tellefson of the state Gambling
> Commission. "We never thought they might be
> unprofitable."Many tribes, with casinos in isolated rural areas,
> are finding that gaming is by no means a sure bet. ("Indian
> Gaming Offers No Assurance of Success," 1998, p. 10)

Symptomatic of the Times

From 1910 to 1931 Americans did without legal gambling,
but that changed because gambling was already such a major
portion of American life and history. Now the availability of
various destinations is getting stronger as marketing becomes
increasingly creative. A new "family" approach (see Figure 7.2)
at destinations makes Las Vegas Americans'destination of choice
(Stearns, 1997a, p. 1).

In addition to getting the "complete family" to the destination
resort, the industry is working on everything to get individuals
to various destinations, including the increasing popularity of
tournament lures by featuring poker, slot machine, Caribbean
Stud. Let-It-Ride, and blackjack tournaments. "High rollers"

have traditionally been rewarded with complimentary items. The industry is also looking at other ways of encouraging gambling, such as discounts, specialized memberships, monthly mailings, and the related electronic tracking of various gamers. Readers of this chapter should consider the words of industry analyst Byron Liggett in *The Reno Gazette-Journal in* the mid-1990s in response to the question "is it true that casinos use certain fragrances to induce customers to gamble more?" The complete answer follows :

> A year-long study at the Las Vegas Hilton in 1992 indicated that certain aromas caused slot players to spend as much as 45 percent more. Since then, numerous casinos have used the science of scents to create a comfortable, conducive environment. Scent manufacturers and casinos consider the use of aromas to be no different than the employment of

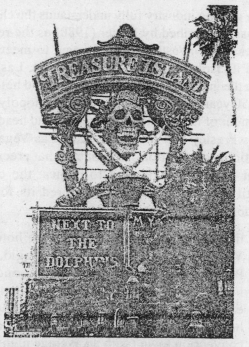

Figure 7.1 Treasure Island Hotel

lighting, sound and decor to create a positive gambling environment. (Liggett, 1995, p. 19)

Gaming guests should be aware that the chemically produced pheromones just might have a greater effect than "lighting, sound and décor" in encouraging gambling. Certain casinos might create a "gaming environment," which is designed to unconsciously manipulate the gambling behaviour of individuals in order to increase their profits: it is a business to the industry and not a game! The "risk-taking" atmosphere is further encouraged when guests are offered "free" drinks by their convivial hosts while being "'entertained"or gambling. The effect of alcohol can lead to fuzzy thinking and increase the risk-taking quotient.

Meeting the Competitive Challenge: Las Vegas

The gaming industry fully understands the changing patterns of tourism, described by Butler (1980) as the resort cycle, and modifies their investment programme to meet new interests. Despite its isolation in the Nevada desert, Las Vegas grew to become the gaming capital of the world, and held that status for almost 50 years. Their long-term legal monopoly, heightened by the glamour of lavish Paris-style revues and headliner stars such as Elvis Presley and Liberace, made Las Vegas an important international destination. To maintain that preeminence, as TV brought more entertainment to homes, the city faced stiff competition and carefully restructured its focus with three innovations:

1. the creation of international "theme'hotels such as New York, Luxor, the Venetian, the Bellagio, Mandalay, and Paris!, with lavish decor, fine dining, and boutiques (see Figure 7.3);

2. extremely high occupancy rates (85.8%) in its 109,365 hotel rooms through promoting Las Vegas as a convention town (with an average nightly room rate of only US$66); and

Luxor Hotel (photo by Charlie Urbanowicz).

3. construction of seven major shopping malls, catering to every purse, to keep visitors occupied and amused.

The city of Greater Las Vegas has a population of 1.2 million (1999) but attracts 31 million visitors per year. The Las Vegas News Bureau (May 1999) tabulates the 1998 economic impact as US$24.6 billion based on 3900 conventions, hosting 3.3 million delegates. The gross gambling revenues for Las Vegas amounted to US$5 billion, which averaged US$469 per person per trip. A serious shortage of air traffic capacity suggests an urgent need to construct a high-speed rail link to southern California to service that large market.

Las Vegas will host the American Society of Travel Agent (ASTA) convention in 2000. With new hotels under construction, there will be 126,000 rooms available, but to maintain the high occupancy level the challenge is to attract an additional 6 million visitors per year. Toward that goal, the casinos seek diversification because only 60% of their revenue is derived from gambling (Much, 1998). The owners of the Bellagio Hotel purchased a small collection of Impressionist paintings by artists such as Degas, Renoir, Cézanne, Manet, and Gauguin for US$260 million, installed as an art gallery exhibit for US$10 admission. The Nevad Division of State Parks is reconstructing the 1855 Old Mormon Fort with Paiute Indian exhibits and re-created pioneer ranch life. Las Vegas has grown into a brand name resort destination with enough attractions to keep guests active for several days, not just the overnight gamblers or conventioneers, and directly supports over 700,000 jobs.

Conclusions

> Security is mostly a superstition. It does not exist in nature, nor do the children of men as a whole experience it. Avoiding danger is no safer in the long run than outright exposure. Life is either a daring adventure, or nothing. Helen Keller (1880-1968)

Living is risky and as social scientists we have the obligation to make others aware of some of the risks involved in various aspects of life. Legalized gambling in the US (1) generates a great deal of revenue, (2) has a great deal of visibility, (3) is creating some interesting partnerships, and (4) is a risky business for both hosts and guests. The visibility and the competition in the industry are obvious. From the bombarding messages of the state lotteries to the development of mega-resorts in Nevada, there is demand for the guest dollar.

From 1931 until 1978, Nevada was alone. Since then, there has been growth and competition; today, Reno/Sparks/Tahoe and Las Vegas must all compete with numerous activities and destinations all across the US (see Meyer-Arendt & Hartmann, 1998). Some establishments will survive and some will fail. In contrast to the fairy tale of Las Vegas (which is not without potential failure at some point), in 1995, Harold's Club closed in downtown Reno, NV, and as of late 1998, six additional casinos in Reno closed their doors since that closing: Holiday-Hotel

Casino, Horseshoe Club, Nevada Club, The Riverboat, Riverside, and The Virginian, while only one new resort "gaming" destination opened.The Silver Legacy (in 1995). The potential guests for all of these destinations (and across the entire US) should realize that gambling is not entertainment. Gambling is a very big business and these hosts always have the advantage! Gambling is very expensive entertainment.

Gambling is here to stay. The long-term future in the US is debatable because there are numerous problems concerning expansion and growth of the gambling industry. Eadington (1992) pointed out that "observers, such as I. Nelson Rose, have argued that the proliferation [of gambling] carries with it the seeds of its own destruction" and this could be true.There is growing concern about "addictive gambling," labeled by the American Psychiatric Association as "an impulse control disorder" said to affect about 11% of all gamblers. Rose (1991) expects that after the boom of the 1990s and the first two decades of the 21st century, gambling will be outlawed again. Whether satiation or legislation ends the current unlimited growth is a question for the future!

8

Finnish Tourists

The Finns have been eager travellers since the emergence of mass tourism in Finland, beginning in the late 1960s and the early 1970s. The Finnish airline, the Kar-Air, opened the first "sunline" from Helsinki via Gothenburg, Luxemburg, and Barcelona to Malaga on April 8, 1961, and the planes were quickly sold out. Since then, there has been a steady increase in the annual number of Finnish tourists traveling abroad. The zenith in Finnish international charter tourism occurred in 1989 when sales topped more than 1 million charter flight package holidays. This statistic is significant for a country with about 5 million inhabitants. A subsequent economic recession in 1993 profoundly reduced the number of sun vacations by half—to 500,000 charter trips. There has been a slow recovery in the number of holidays abroad, again reaching almost 1 million charter trips in 1998 (excluding scheduled flights and boat, train, and auto travel).

This chapter examines tourism from Finland to Playa del Ingles on the island of Gran Canaria. The description and analysis also draw on data from field research in Athens (1991, 1992), Rhodes (1993). Bodrum (1993), and Aqaba (1994) for comparison. Throughout, my role as a tourist among tourists facilitated participant-observation in various touristic activities, from suntanning to barhopping, while recording tourists' behaviour and my own reactions.

Thematic interviews proved to be almost impossible to perform because tourists did not wish to spend valuable holiday time answering research questions. The strategy of "spontaneous chats" with the tourists proved to be a good solution, so I talked with tourists wherever I met them, and made notes afterwards.

I was better accepted by the tourists when I was "one of them," even though all the Finnish tourists who participated were aware of my research.To deepen the introspective view of tourist culture I requested written diaries of their holiday experience. In addition to the qualitative data, notes, diaries, and photographs, statistical data from questionnaires and structured time-use surveys were utilized.

Playa del Ingles

Gran Canaria is an almost circular island of 1532 square kilometers located just 115 kilometers from the Moroccan coast and north of the Tropic of Cancer. Since the early 1970s the island has been one of the most popular winter destinations for Finnish tourists.Tourism was initially directed to the capital city of as Palmas but today Playa del Ingles in the southern part of the island, and nearby Maspalomas and Puerto Rico, host the majority of Finns (Figure 8.1). In 1991, the peak year to date, a total of 283,003 Finnish tourists traveled to the Canary Islands by charter planes.

Playa del Ingles on Gran Canaria is an excellent example of minimal cultural authenticity. It is one of the most popular winter holiday resorts among Finnish tourists. Indigenous habitation never existed in the area of Playa del Ingles or nearby Maspalomas.The hotels and restaurants were constructed on the sand dunes of Maspalomas in the early 1960s, when there was nothing but sand, sea, and a few fishermen's huts. In those early days of tourism, tourists hired a taxi from Las Palmas to Maspalomas to enjoy the natural scenery and privacy. Now 200,000 hotel beds occupy the area.

Today, the town center of Playa del Ingles appears clean, with newly paved streets and bungalows of a very international style, and almost all restaurants and shops are located along its principal streets.The town still has many hotels, but in the more recently developed Maspalomas area, large apartment-hotels dominate. These apartment complexes may feature multiple swimming pools, tennis courts, restaurants, bars, and shops (supermercados) as well as a gym and/or a sauna. Considering the array of services and opportunities for recreation, tourists need not leave the apartment-hotel complex during their vacation, and some tourists never go to a restaurant for dinner. Finnish tourists often make coffee and prepare meals in their apartments. They bring foodstuffs with them, mainly Finnish dark rye bread and, of course, Finnish coffee. Finns are absolutely convinced that nobody can roast and grind coffee beans as well as the

Figure 8.1 Map of Gran Canaria

Finnish companies. One elderly Laestadian man—a member of a conservative Finnish Christian revivalist movement—had elk meat in his luggage. Because these apartment-hotels are self-contained, there is no need to venture beyond them unless one wishes.

The sand dune area of Maspalomas is clearly the most important single attraction in the Playa del Ingles region, where the large sand dunes offer a privacy barrier to nearby nudist beaches. This desert-like environment within a stone's throw from tourist facilities and the Atlantic Ocean also provides opportunities for long strolls or camel "caravan" rides amidst the dunes. Other regional attractions' include two theme parks:

Sioux City and Palmitos Park. Sioux City is a Western theme park located outside the hotel area. Its flyer, available everywhere in Playa del Ingles, uses the following text as a visitor inducement:

> Come on over and visit us! Every boy is a cowboy "Sioux City," the authentic Western Town. Ride back into the days o the 'Roaring West" and find yourself in the middle of a bank holdup or a sudden Shootout between coldblooded cowpokes and the lawman of Six Gun.

It is not difficult to image what a MacCannellian view on authenticity and tourism would have to say about Sioux City. The other theme park, Palmitos Park, is a subtropical oasis with 50 different types of palm trees and 230 species of birds from all over the world. In addition to these, there is a butterfly house and a very popular parrot show. Sioux City and Palmitos Park, as well as Playa del Ingles, entertain and cater to tourists without disturbing elements of locality or reality.

The cleanly paved streets of Playa del Ingles are lined with supermarkets, fast food stalls, pubs, restaurants, and hotels. Several shopping malls exist in the area of Ingles and Maspalomas. The town caters to Finnish tourists by availing them with Finnish shops, bars, restaurants, and nightclubs such as Casa Finlandia with karaoke singing in Finnish. At Tiffany, Finnish popular music artists perform almost every night. These services and the large number of Finnish tourists make Finns very comfortable in Playa del Ingles. One is able to eat Finnish food, drink Finnish coffee and beer, and speak Finnish with neighbours in a very favourable climate compared with winter in Finland! In a way, Playa del Ingles is an extension of the tourists' home culture (see Hanefors & Larsson, 1989, 1993) and could be considered the southernmost province of Finland. Similarly, and contiguous with "little Finland," in Playa del Ingles there are "little" Swedens, Englands, and Germanys.

Alongside "little Finland," comprised mainly of middle-aged and retired Finnish tourists together with other extensions of

the tourists' home cultures, Playa del Ingles accommodates the
touristic subculture of sexual minorities. From a superficial point
of view it is difficult to understand coexistence of "little
Finland"— tourists that are predominantly middle aged to elderly,
relatively uneducated, and apparently conservative—with the
blooming culture of transvestites, transsexuals, and homosexuals
in Playa del Ingles. The big shopping center, Yumbo, frequented
by strolling and shopping tourists during the day, turns into an
archipelago of gay bars and transvestitc clubs at night. The two
worlds meet only occasionally. On several nights I witnessed
the performance of a Finnish male transvestite in the Finnish
karaoke bar, which was very popular among the "typical "Finnish
tourists. Some intermingling of these two worlds occurs even in
"little Finland."

Table 8.1. Age Comparison of Finnish Tourists

Age	Rhodes (n = 150)	Bodrum (n = 58)	Playa del Ingles (n = 118)	Total
16-25	22%	24%	8%	12%
26-35	27%	36%	15%	20%
36-45	17%	17%	15%	20%
46-55	21%	16%	30%	28%
56-65	12%	5%	24%	14%
66-75	1%	2%	6%	5%
76-85			2%	1%

The Southbound Masses

Questionnaires were distributed to Finns arriving in Gran
Canaria on a charter flight for a short-term visit (1-2 weeks) in
January 1994. Longer stays by Finnish tourists are not supported
by my data because those tourists had already arrived before

January. An age comparison (Table 8.1) with two additional holiday destinations (Rhodes, Greece and Bodrum, Turkey) shows that the tourists travelling to Playa del Ingles are clearly older than tourists travelling to Rhodes or Bodrum. These Mediterranean destinations are popular with young Finnish tourists, who party until dawn and live according to this rhythm. In comparison, Playa del Ingles and Maspalomas are rather sleepy bungalow areas where parties occur at concentrated spots while the rest of the tourist community sleeps around them.

A comparison of Finnish tourists who traveled to Athens, Greece, shows that the education level of tourists to Playa del Ingles is distinctively low (Table 8.2). This suggests that there is still a distinction in tourism types by class. The upper levels of the social strata form the typical cultural tourists who travel to authentic historical and cultural sites (see E. Cohen, 1988) while the lower educational levels form the southbound masses. The democratization of tourism has not necessarily led to crowding in the places formerly frequented by the elite but rather in places that were selected for touristification relatively recently—in this case Playa del Ingles (Selänniemi, 1994b).

The level of education among tourists travelling to Athens is very high compared with Playa del Ingles and the general level of education in Finland. The tourists with advance! degrees

Table 6.2. Comparison of the Educational Levels of Finnish Tourists

	Basic School or Equivalent	Upper Secondary Education	Higher Education (MA, Equivalent or Higher)
Athens (n = 127)	15(12%)	40(31%)	72(57%)
Playa del Ingles (n = 118)	59(50%)	54(46%)	5(4%)
Total	168(29%)	284(50%)	122(21%)
Level of education in Finland (as of 12/31/91)	49%	41%	1 0 %

seek destinations that offer more than the sun and the beach, which are the main attractions (sometimes the only ones) of Playa del "Anywhere'around the world. In support, Athens is popular among educated Finish tourists (Selänniemi, 1994a, 1994c).

Despite their low level of education, the Finns who holiday in Playa del Ingles are relatively experienced travellers. Of the sample polled, 51% had made more than 10 holiday trips abroad and only 4% were experiencing their first vacation abroad. In Athens these figures were 70% and 1%, respectively. The statistics are deceiyipg on this point. Of the Finnish tourists who returned the questionnaire, 74% were repeat visitors to the Canary Islands, and many were repeat visitors specifically to Playa del Ingles. What is more significant in comparison with the tourists at the other destinations is the fact that 9% of these tourists had never travelled to a destination other than the Canary Islands (Table 8.3).

A statistical comparison (although samples are small) clearly illustrates travel preferences. Tourists at Playa del Ingles favour Spain as their holiday destination, whereas Finns contacted in Rhodes clearly favour Greece. However, tourists in Athens demonstrated a wide variety of equally favoured destinations with a high percentage of trips to central Europe and long-distance tourism (Asia, Africa, and Oceania).

A Diary: Days in Playa del Ingles

The following diary, written by a Finnish tourist, provides deeper insight into a holiday in Playa del Ingles. The diary was, of course, originally written in Finnish. Translated and shortened here, it is unfortunately bereft of the misspellings and style that contributed to the impression of a happy holiday in Playa del Ingles. Written by a 52-year-old woman who worked in a farmer's locum in a small municipality in central Finland, she was on holiday with her husband. Both were relatively inexperienced tourists (fewer than 10 holiday trips).

Table 8.3. Frequency of Visitation Choices: Athens, Rhodes, and Playa del Ingles

Destination	Athens (n = 49)	Rhodes (n = 150)	Playa del Ingles (n = 118)	Total
Spain	89(7%)	207(14%)	470(31%)	766(18%)
Scandinavia	257(21%)	341(22%)	400(26%)	998(23%)
Greece	125(10%)	339(22%)	105(7%)	569(14%)
Other Southern Europe	175(14%)	155(10%)	94(6%)	424(10%)
Central Europe	218(18%)	150(10%)	151(9%)	519(12%)
East Europe	118(10%)	192(13%)	171(11%)	481(11%)
Great Britain	67(5%)	57(4%)	26(2%)	150(4%)
US/Canada	48 (4%)	27 (2%)	31 (2%) 106 (2%)	
Other long distance	128(11%)	49(3%)	92(6%)	269(6%)
(Asia, Africa, Oceania)				
Total	1225	1517	1540	4282
Trips per person	25	10	13	13

The Chronology

Day 1. We took a bus from Jyvaskyla to Tampere. From there we flew to Las Palmas. We have been here before, so it isn't so strange for us. At the airport girls dressed in green showed us the way to our bus that would takes us to Ingles. We made some coffee and took a shower and went to bed. It is nice to come from the winter to the summer.

Day 2. The morning was warm and sunny. After drinking our morning coffee we went out to take a look at Ingles. We looked for the way to the beach and found it. After 4 hours of sunbathing we came back to our hotel. We sat down in the sun and had a drink. In the evening we just wondered that here we are again.

Day 3. The morning was windy but warm. We have already been on all the daytrips, so we won't go this time. We walked down to the beach to look at the sea. It was impossible to stay there because the wind was blowing so hard. We came back to the pool to sunbathe, and stayed 4 hours sitting and lying and dipping into the pool at times. We got hungry, so we went to Casa Finlandia for a meal. Then we took a nap and in the evening we went to sing karaoke. It was a good day.

Day 4. The morning came windy, but it was nothing compared with the winds of Finland. We strolled in the malls. When the sun rose higher the beach and the sea started to tempt. We walked first to the beach and then to the dunes and to Masapalomas. It was wonderful to walk barefoot in the hot sand just like when I was a child. Tired but happy we returned to the hotel. It feels strange when it is summer and the evening gets dark so quickly.

Day 5- The morning was warm. Today it is going to be a nice weather for sunbathing. Many people came to the pool. We lay down at the pool. The sun warmed nicely. It's wonderful that after a few hours' flight you can be and feel like this. This is a place where all worries disappear. After 4 hours we were "ripe," so we went to make coffee. To celebrate Sunday we went out for dinner. The smorgasbord at Casa Finlandia offered a good meal.

Day 6. The sun kept hiding all day. Still we had lots to do. We walked around and strolled in the mail. We took photos and wondered how many species of plants and cactuses grow here. We looked for our travel agent's office and finally found it. We strolled in the center and shopped a bit. In the evening we went singing karaoke. The Finns were having a party there. It was February when we returned to the hotel.

Day 7. The sun was shining again. We went straight to the pool to sunbathe. The water in the pool was getting warmer. We stayed till afternoon, making coffee in between. In the afternoon we heard that we will have to change hotel tomorrow.

Day 8. Today we moved. It felt a bit sad to leave the places that had already become familiar. We packed our bags and went for our new home. We settled down soon and found a nice sunbathing place on the roof. The travel agent has treated us well. The things happen and they can't help it. After we had finished our taxfree bottle we were ready for bed.

Day 9. The first morning without a cloud in the sky. Today is going to be hot, and it felt wonderful. We started to get to know other Finns. We went to the same restaurant to eat as earlier. At night we walked back to the same place to watch the karaoke contest. We know people there also.

Day 10. Today we went to the sea in the morning. The sun was shining brightly but it was rather windy. We started walking along the beach and there were a lot of people coming and going. My skin started to burn so I took a quick swim in the sea. After 4 km we felt that today's exercise and sun was done. Tomorrow we will go on a sea trip. I hope it will be warm.

Day 11. A bus picked us up at the agreed spot. We didn't understand a word during the whole trip, we were the only Finns. After the return we went to look at the action in town.

Day 12. Sunday came with sun-shine. We got a message that our neighbors from Finland had come here too. We went for a visit. Then we went walking together. They had not seen the camels so we took a look at them. We came back and had coffee together. We decided to go out to dinner together. The food is good here and I eat a lot. We sat chatting together until midnight.

Day 13. I woke up at the same time with the sun. After coffee we went to the roof balcony to sunbathe. We had an invitation to visit our neighbors. We went to the shops before the siesta. We telephoned home, where the freezing cold had not eased yet and had broken the water pipes so the cows had to be watered by carrying the water from the well. This did sink the holiday mood a bit, but you thought that you cannot do anything from here. With our friends we sat in the sun and felt very relaxed.

Day 14. The first thought today was that tomorrow we will return home. The presents and souvenirs had to be bought today. We bought jogging suits. The other one's zipper broke right away. We have kept close contact with our neighbours. We had coffee together and talked about going home. We agreed that one week is too short for a holiday over here. We hope to come back next winter.

Author Interpretation

The writer experiences Playa del Ingles mainly synesthetically with her senses of feeling and sight. The sun is a very central issue in the diary, except for the last day, when thoughts are already directed to the return. Playa del Ingles is sensed mainly as heat on the skin and under the bare feet, warm and beautiful weather, and a cooling sea. Alongside these primarily tactile sensations some visual perceptions also add to the picture of the place visited. Hearing, taste, and smell have been largely filtered out.

The writer's perceptions of Playa del Ingles mainly include things that strike the writer as most different from her home environment—which echoes Urry's (1990) view on tourism resulting from the basis of binary opposition between the ordinary and nonordinary. These observations deal with climate, the sea, the sand dunes, and also the hotel area, which are compared with home. The only places that are named in the diary are shopping centers, hotels, restaurants, and the sand dunes of Maspalomas. With the exception of the sand dunes, the perceptions of Playa del Ingles are interchangeable with any holiday resort in the "south."

The diary implies altered meaning for spatial, temporal, and even social boundaries for tourists in the "south." In some cases they even cease to exist or are at least very ethereal, as in the case of the boundary between inside and outside. The writer does not differentiate between these, even though she refers to the hotel as "home". The ambiguity of these boundaries also affects the experience of the south, as well as culturally determined patterns of perception. This emerges in the sentence where she writes that it feels so strange when nightfall arrives so early in summer. The only time a Finn experiences a warm night is at midsummer, when it is light almost 24 hours a day.

The writer expresses the journey to Gran Canaria as a journey to summertime, away from the arctic winter in Finland. The thought of the south as eternal summer, like the summers of childhood when it was always warm and one seemed to have almost unlimited time, is clearly present in this diary. She expresses her return to childhood memories when she writes about the enjoyable feeling of heat under one?s bare feet, just the way it was when she was a child. These tourist pleasures are derived from tactile stimuli of a very basic nature, to which we do not pay attention in everyday life, nor can we afford the time to stop to enjoy them.As Pasi Falk (1994) has written:

> the human body as a sensory and sensual being presupposes always (already) its counterpart, the 'sensible' body, that is, a body subsumed to a cultural Order—both symbolic and practical—defining its boundaries and its position in the larger whole (community or society), (p. 2)

Perhaps the transition from home to the south in sun tourism can be understood as a crossing of the boundaries of the sensible body.

The diary of the 52-year-old woman from the countryside of central Finland, together with diaries from other destinations (Rhodes and Bodrum) relating to this case study, accentuate the point made by Soile Veijola and Eeva Jokinen that the tourist's physical body is largely absent in tourism research. *The Tourist Gaze* (Urry, 1990) or MacCannell's (1973, 1989a) theories approach tourists' perceptions visually. They become powerful tools for the analysis of sightseeing, cultural tourism, and "secular pilgrimages" to sites like the Acropolis in Athens (cf. Selänniemi, 1994c). However, they are inadequate in the analysis of sun tourism at beach resorts.Tourism research has long focused on one sense—sight—while negating an entire spectrum of human senses, perhaps as a result of the Aristotelian hierarchy of the senses where only sight and hearing were human senses, the rest animal senses. In this sense [sic!] one might see the pleasures of sun Just tourism result from "letting the animal loose" (not necessarily in the stereotypicaily negative meaning) in oneself to enjoy sensual pleasures. Thus, the cultural elite (including many tourism scholars) are given the means by which to create a distinction (cf. Bourdieu, 1989) between the "high" culture/tourism (looking and hearing) and "low" culture/tourism (feeling, tasting, smelling) but they seldom do so. This bias—or even elitism—is apparent in much scholarly work on tourism (Selänniemi, 1996a).

In spite ot the monotonous daily rhythm of this tourist's holiday, she appeared to be very happy. The change from the cold countryside of central Finland with hard agricultural labour seemed to be absolutely wonderful. She did not express any wish to gain contact with local people, or even to see other ways of life. She and her husband even dined either at their apartment or at the Finnish restaurant Casa Finlandia.'This tourist was happy with the "south' where she could do as she pleased at her own rhythm.The diarist expresses almost daily how wonderful the climate and warmth is. Another interesting feature in the diary occurs on day 8 when she implies an attachment to the apartment as a home in "little Finland" with their actual neighbours from central Finland.The recurring social activity of coffee drinking, for example, is very typical of Finns and creates an atmosphere of safety and familiarity by structuring the sojourn and forming a link to the cultural practices of home.The diary quoted above, together with other field material from Playa del Ingles and other holiday destinations, confirms the comment by Richard Butler (1992) that people in fact seem to enjoy being mass tourists:

> They actually like not having to make their own travel arrangements, not having to find accommodations when they arrive at a destination, being able to obtain goods and services without learning a foreign language, being able to stay in

reasonable and sometimes considerable comfort, being able to eat relatively familiar food, and not having to spend vast amounts of money or time to achieve these goals (p. 32)

Ambiguous Places at Curious Times

Playa del Ingles is clearly a holiday destination that is located in the ambiguous zone labeled "the south." Finns often refer to their holiday destinations simply as *etela* (south) without clarifying the exact geographical destination. Common phrases are *kavimme etelassa lomalla* (we went south on our holiday) or *lahden etelanmatkalle* (I will go south). In fact, the term *etelanmatka* cannot be translated into English without losing some connotations. Literally it means a "trip to the south," but the term refers to a specific trait in modern Finnish culture: a charter trip to a holiday destination where the climate is more favourable than arctic Finland.The concept *etela* also is widely used in tourism marketing, especially in newspaper advertisements, sometimes without any identification of where the "south" is. This type of marketing is directed to attract tourists wishing to get away from everyday life for a short time to somewhere where it is "nice and warm"—*Playa del Anywhere*.

The Liminoid South

These southbound Finnish mass tourists do not fit neatly into Valene Smith's (1989b) definition of a tourist: "in general, a tourist is a temporarily leisured person who voluntarily visits a place away from home for the purpose of experiencing a change".

Yes, they are temporarily leisured persons who do voluntarily take a charter flight to a holiday destination in the south. But *do* they really visit a place? The south, the holiday zone, is away from home, but can the tourists be said to *visit* a place if they have no interest in the destination's distinctiveness? They do intend to experience a change, but the change is not extended to the full experience of a place. It is much more a question of *getting away* from work, home, and negative aspects connected with everyday life to a holiday zone with few attributes of a distinctive place. If the holiday destination has too many characteristics of a real place, the tourist will be reminded of everyday life or challenged by the intricacies of cultural difference. Playa del Ingles is a perfect place for tourists who just wish to experience a change, to recuperate, to "charge the batteries," by travelling *from a place to,* in a sense, *nowhere.*

The holiday for the southbound mass tourist is a vacation In *the liminoid zone.* The south is a zone where the sun always shines and produces a nice tan. The climate is warm, and the norms and sanctions are much more relaxed than at home, to the degree that tourists feel "free" to do things or behave in ways that they would not consider when at home. This *antistructure* is to be found in a resort that is often familiar to the tourist in some way. When the principal motive for travel is to get away from everyday life, a destination that has familiar aspects is tempting. In such a familiar, safe place, one can order meals and drinks in Finnish from a Finnish menú. This is especially true for older Finnish tourists, with less education and limited foreign language skills. These extensions of the home culture, the "little Finlands," can be found in many Mediterranean mass tourist destinations as well as in Playa del Ingles.

A re-statement of Graburns model (see Graburn, Chapter 3; cf. Leach, 1982a, p. 134) with a focus on the ritual process (V. Turner, 1978; van Gennep, 1960) allows an analysis of liminoid tourism (Figure 8.2). In contrast to Graburn's and Leach's models, I consider liminal (or sacred) time to be a flow of events, where the ritual subject glides from one condition into the other.

In transition rites, the ritual subjects pass through phases from preliminal (the normal profane state of things), through

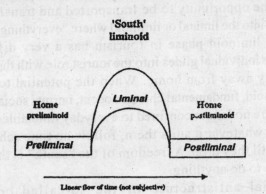

Figure 8.2 The charter trip as a journey to the liminoid

the liminal (the sacred, abnormal, anomalous, dangerous time), then back to the postliminal (normal and profane). Victor and Edith Turner (1978, pp. 249-250) describe the liminal as a state and process in the transition phase, during which the ritual subjects go through a zone, which has few if any attributes of the pre- or postliminal phase. They are *between*. Liminality has often been compared to death, invisibility, darkness, bisexuality, and wilderness (Turner & Turner, 1978, pp. 249-250). The stage in tourism that resembles the liminal phase in rites of passage could be called the liminoid or quasiliminal by Turner's terms.

The liminoid is related to the ritually liminal, but is not identical with it. The liminoid of tourism is *produced and consumed by individuals* while the liminal is believed by the members of society to be of divine origin and by nature anonymous. The liminoid is also fragmentary compared with the liminal. Often elements of the liminal have been separated from the whole to act individually in specialized fields like art (Turner & Turner, 1978, p. 253.) In art, popular culture, entertainment, and tourism products are made for consumption by individuals and groups that promise to remove the consumer away from the everyday experience into a stage that resembles the liminal for a limited time span. The attraction of traveling to the south, "to nowhere," lies in the opportunity to be transported and transformed for a moment into the liminal or liminoid where "everything is possible."

The liminoid phase in tourism has a very diffuse beginning. The individual glides into the tourist role with thoughts about a holiday away from home. When the potential tourist enters the liminoid, fundamental changes occur, normal social time stops. People are no longer confined to everyday timetables; they sleep late, eat whatever it suits them, follow no time schedules, and party until they drop. A freedom of the "south" is that one does not have to do anything.

Social antistructure or the so-called *communitas* (undifferentiated, democratic, direct, and spontaneous social bonds or contacts) is characteristic of liminality. Communitas is a temporary state in which common norms are relaxed and social structure partly loses its significance (Turner & Turner, 1978, pp. 249-250). The communitas-type social contacts become evident when the normally (stereotypically) shy, stiff, and laconic Finns chat eagerly with total strangers, even though these strangers most often are other Finnish tourists. Social bonds are created without obligations. In the holiday resort tourist couples may jointly hire a car and go on excursions, dine together, or invite each other for a drink on the balcony of their apartments, and even exchange driving directions to each other's summer cottages on the plane before landing. But when the plane has landed at Helsinki airport and the "posttourists" have collected their luggage, there is no obligation to contact the people met on holiday, even less to drive up to their summer cottage. It would probably be interpreted as impolite. On another level, it would mix the "south" with "home," that is, the liminoid with the postliminoid.

The liminoid character of the south makes it possible for people to behave in ways they would not consider at home. It is even possible to think that the antistructure of the south entices the *latent other* in the tourist self to come forth. The anti-self (the boozing, destructive, sexual, or adventurous) or the ideal self (social, creative, or sensitive) may take over and even alternate in the same person. In Playa del Ingles I met a person who was happily drunk. At home this person had a rather strict and conservative attitude towards alcohol consumption. And in Rhodes I witnessed a young man become interested in the medieval old town and archeological museum, even though he was supposed to party day and night with a group of pals who had purchased a week in the "party zone "This altered state of mind during liminoidity or fragmental antistructure of the "south" explains why the overt homo- and transsexuality does not raise havoc among the relatively conservative Finnish tourists. In this state, they regard the "south" as a *warm playground* where everything is possible. People are inclined to either accept or close their eyes to normally intolerable behaviour, and also to stretch the limits of their own behaviour.

Conclusions

The Finnish diarist experienced the south mainly synesthetically with her senses of sight and feeling. The trip to Playa del Ingles was a surrogate return to childhood, to pleasures derived from simple but very profound visual and tactile sensations. The "otherness" of the south compared with home was expressed in binary opposites, with only the positive experience actually mentioned and the negative experience implied in the diary. Thus, the recurring mention of the sun implies the lack of sunshine in the winter of arctic Finland; warmth is compared with the extremely cold temperatures, which even broke the water pipes back home; relaxed time use and the easiness of falling asleep implies structured time and even possible insomnia in everyday life; the repeated visits to the Finnish karaoke bar imply the reality of countryside Finland with few leisure opportunities and perhaps even negative sanctions connected with alcohol use.

Location seems to be of little importance to sun tourists as long as the visited resort has all the attributes of the "south," which could be described as liminoid zone or not located exactly anywhere. The attractiveness of sun trips lies partly in the promise of liminoidity; not explicitly, but in the expectation of the freedoms of the south. Playa del Ingles is familiar, either by virtue of prior visit or by word of mouth. The tourists import their cultural habits and practices with them, like the preparation of Finnish coffee, and interact mainly with other Finnish tourists in bars and nightclubs with Finnish hosts and artists. Finns traveling on an *etelanmatka* visit a familiar culture outside time and place, "like fish in water." In essence, the Finns (and probably many others) are psychocentrics who travel *with and in* their culture, but by changing location they leave sanctions behind and gain the freedoms of liminoidity. Thus, cultural authenticity of the destination is of little importance. In this type of tourism *how* you experience is more important than what you experience (Selanniemi, 1996b, 1997). The transition to the liminoid alters our sensual awareness.

In image-oriented sun tourism people buy time as much as they buy a place to visit. In modern society, time is a marketed commodity; to relax from everyday life, a person must "buy time" at ever-increasing cost. It may be one hour in the gym, a season ticket to the hockey matches, or any other preferred activity, including to *be home*. The most conspicuous form of time buying occurs in tourism. Anything from spa daytrips to 24-hour cruises "to nowhere" or charter tourism to the south provides a way of escaping the normal, profane, everyday time to a state of mind where even time loses its importance. The data collected from Finnish tourists indicate that in tourism there are different degrees of the liminoid, which partly supports E. Cohen's (1979a) phenomenology of tourist experiences. However, Cohen uses the degree of alienation from the individual's home society as a measurement of the depth of the tourist experience, and this is open to question (Selänniemi,

1996a). As Tom Selwyn (1996, p. 6) argues, Cohen's classifi-
fication is built on *a priori* grounds and one may doubt its
ethnographic justification.

Sun tourists do not travel with an expectation of something
new or strange. Confrontation with the "other" is not even an
attractive thought to them. They want the same safe and familiar
exterior of home culture with better climate and liminoid
features every year. Even people who can otherwise be termed
cultural tourists may buy a trip to Piaya del anywhere for
relaxation every now and then to avoid the sightseeing obligations
involved in cultural tourism. Individuals who have fulfilled a
secular "pilgrimage" to a place like Athens, Istanbul, Rome, or
Paris know the exhaustion of the touristic rituals of a cultural
liminal "high." In fact, the sun lust tourist may find authentic
pleasure in the inauthenticity of a tourist attraction, or as D.
Brown (1996, p. 38) puts it, "the tourist seeks out the inauthentic.
Other in the quest for the authentic Self".

The key to an emic understanding of Finnish sun lust tourism
lies in seeing the *fourfold transition* that takes place during
the trip. The *spatiatemporal transition* from place to, in a sense,
placelessness (cf. Relph, 1986) and similarly from time to
timelessness are the first two transitions that seem prerequisites
for the following two. The trip from everyday life, home, work—
the profane to the liminoid south—brings with it a *mental
transition* whereby the tourist leaves the everyday Self behind
and becomes the holiday Self. The fourth transition—the *sensory/
sensual transition*—becomes the shift in how we sense our
surroundings.

The critics of mass tourism often say that it cannot provide
personal, unique, and strong experiences. But for the diarist,
the charter flight, package tour, and sightseeing are only a means
to an end. They do not imply superficiality and triviality, as often
stated. The phenomenon called tourism must not be expressed
solely in quantitative terms as one kind of tourism, or as the
largest industry in the world (cf. Davidson, 1994; Theobald,

1998).The qualitative interpretation of Finnish mass tourism to Playa del Ingles (and the other destinations studied) shows that a charter trip to a mass tourist resort in the south can be a very significant experience for the tourist. It is important to know the motives of the tourists who prefer the ready-built resorts of the Mediterranean region and Canary Island as their destinations. Additionally, this type of charter tourism can actually be nonthreatening to the local culture and natural environment. Charter flights transport large numbers of tourists with relatively low environmental impact compared with the same number of "individual tourists" flying to the jungles of Borneo. If the tourists are content with inauthenticity—and many are—they will have minimal contact with local people and a relatively low cultural impact on the host culture (compared with so-called" cannibal tourists"). As soon as tourists step outside the fenced area the trouble begins.

9

Time and Space: Atlantic City in 1886

The board game Monopoly, appearing near the height of Atlantic City's popularity (1930s), revisits the successes and pitfalls of entrepreneurial activity in coastal resort towns. Built uniquely for tourism, the seaside resort of Atlantic City was a genial success while the railroads prospered (1856-1963). Most recent visitors will agree that Atlantic City is no longer a seaside resort. It is a gambling resort by the seaside. This case study converts a selected year of real time into a map of organized space while pursuing two objectives. The first locates a heyday within Atlantic City's evolution. Heyday is defined as the time when essential tourism infrastructure is complete, hosts are prospering, guests are enthusiastic, and the *rate of tourism growth has recently peaked.* The second objective reveals the relationships between selected heyday recreational land uses (transportation, tourist public space, tourist accommodations) and permanent residences. The goal of this exercise is an assessment of the transportation (railroad) impact on resort land use.

Context

Funnell (1975) described Victorian Atlantic City as a Disneyland for adults. This coastal resort town resides on a barrier island belonging to a system of islands and salt marshes on the east coast of New Jersey in the United States. Approximately 10 miles long, it is located in the southern half of a peninsula whose western border is the Delaware Bay and whose eastern border is the Atlantic Ocean. Atlantic City did not emerge from a fishing industry or any industry. It was a planned resort.

In the mid-19th century, Jonathan Pitney, a physician from the mainland town of Absecon, envisioned a health spa for his patients and friends on the neighboring barrier island. Pitney was so convinced of the success of a resort that he persuaded a group of Philadelphia investors to embrace a development plan. The investors constructed a railroad from Philadelphia to Absecon Island and immediately established a land company there. Begun in 1852, Absecon Beach (or Absecon Island) adopted the name of Atlantic City ami was operational by 1856. Investors planned the street grid, transportation access, internal transportation, and a large hotel before any construction occurred. While land company investors and small businesses flourished early on, all of the original railroad investors went bankrupt because they could not combat the political influence and incorporation of the much larger Pennsylvania and Reading railroad companies.

In order to find a year representing heyday, it was useful first to apply the benchmarks of Butler's evolutionary stages to Atlantic City's tourism chronology (Table 9.1). This, exercise located the approximate conclusion of development and the onset of consolidation, which was subsequently compared with data illustrating the resort's cumulative growth and rate of growth. The goal was the creation and analysis of a land-use map of Atlantic City's heyday, marked by the *recent peak of the rate of growth.*

Time: Atlantic City Heyday, 1886
Cyclical Time and Real Time

Urban scholars of various perspectives have described the cyclical nature of cities since the 1920s. The concept of destination evolution most frequently referenced in tourism research bases itself on the product life cycle. British geographer Richard Butler (1980) described the evolution of resort towns in a unique way by proposing that successive phases of a single destination present different "places" during the maturation process. The phases— "places"—range from a total absence of tourist amenities (exploration) to a conspicuous overbuilding (stagnation). Each "place," like sequent occupancy, attracts different types of tourists ranging from explorers to mass tourists. Thus, the phases of a single destination correspond to changes in tourist types and changes in the tourist landscape.

A thorough understanding of Butler's original essay is essential for two important reasons. First, while the article is enjoyable to read, it is conceptually denser than it appears. Butler's findings are based on earlier (1974) work. Second, the "resort cycle," as the concept is informally known, enjoys relationships not only with tourist type, but also with landscape and activity type (Lavery, 1974), resort type (Meyer-Arendt, Sambrook, & Kerrnath, 1992), distance decay (Travis, 1993; G. Wall 1974), cost-distance (Stansfield, 1983), resort morphology (Meyer-Arendt, 1987, R. Smith, 1992), responsible tourism (Wilkinson, 1997), and others. The resort cycle is important in its own right and by its association with other concepts.

The two aspects of growth employed in the resort cycle—cumulative growth and rate of growth—have not always been well understood. Butler's well-known evolutionary chart based on tourist arrival data illustrates cumulative growth (Figure 9.1). The maximum popularity of a destination occurs late in evolution but does not correspond with the highest rate of growth. The highest rate of growth occurs during late development and the beginning of consolidation.

Butler (1980) bases evolutionary progress upon visitor response: the number of tourist visits. When tourist arrival data are not available, it is reasonable to substitute appropriate surrogate data. Because the author could not find dependable visitor arrival data for the closing decades of the 19th century, population census data were substituted. In this particular case study, the substitution is reasonable because Atlantic City's only industry was, and is, tourism. Thus, one can assume that changes in permanent population reflected demand (tourist visits).

Table 7.1. Chronology of Atlantic City's Evolution

1840s	Stage or jersey wagon to Absecon Island; Leed's and Ryan's boarding houses (Wilson, 1953)	Involvement?
1850	Absecon Island inhabited by lighthouse keeper and a few fishermen	
1852	Dr. Pitney secured rail charter for C&A	Development
1854	First train arrives in Atlantic City (Coop & Coxey, 1980); all east-west blocks are the same length (Rose, 1878)	Changes in physical appearance
1856	Regularly scheduled passenger trains to Atlantic City (Stansfield, 1978)	
1863	City ordinance prohibits sand, seaweed, and grass removal to avoid recurrences of beach erosion (Butler, 1954)	
1870	First bridge for horse-drawn vehicles (Stansfield, 1983); first boardwalk along the ocean	Man-made/imported facilities
1877	Original C&A investor, Richards, builds second railway (Cook & Coxey, 1980); significant erosion of north beaches, expansion of south beaches (Rose, 1878)	
1883	C&A and P&AC railroads now controlled by Pennsylvania and Reading Lines, respectively (Cook & Coxey, 1980)	Tourist market open to working classes
1886	Residents plan Chelsea suburb (Funnell, 1975)	Consolidation; Discontent among permanent residents
1887	Iron Pier (later the Heinz Pickle Pier) opened	
1890	Rate of permanent population growth begins to decline	Height of the resort's rate of growth
1920s	Rise of automobile access to Atlantic City (Funnell, 1975)	
1933	All trains owned by the Pennsylvania and Reading Lines merged in South Jersey (Butler, 1954)	
1941-1945	World War II	Stagnation; Economic decline
1963	Passenger train service ends	
1975	Gambling is legalized	Rejuvenation attempt

Cumulative Growth and Rate of Growth

Rate of growth can be derived from cumulative growth. The population data (1860-1990) shown in Table 9.2 portray the cumulative growth of Atlantic City's tourism.

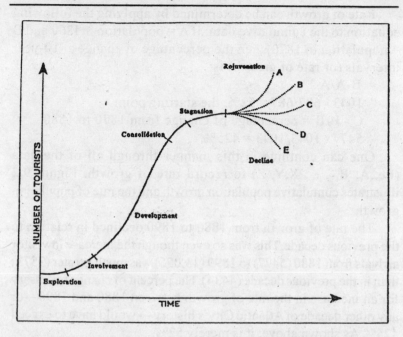

Figure Butler's resort cycle. (Reprinted from Butler, 1980, *The Canadian Geographer, 24*, with permission.)

Table 9.2. Atlantic City population Data

	Year	Resident Population
A	1860	687
B	1870	1,043
C	1880	5,477
D	1890	13,055
E	1900	27,838
F	1910	46,150
G	1920	50,707
H	1930	66,198
I	1940	64,094
J	1950	61,657
K	1960	59,544
L	1970	47,859
M	1980	40,199
N	1990	37,986

Rate of growth can be determined by applying the following equation to the cumulative data: if A = population in 1860 and B = population in 1870, then the percentage of change at 10-year intervals (or rate of growth) is:

B-A/A

1043 - 687/687 = 52%, the starting point

C - B/B = percentage of change from 1870 to 1880

5477 - 1043/1043 = 425%

One can continue in this manner through all of the data (i.e., A, 'B, . . . X,Y, Z) to record rate of growth. Figure 9.2 illustrates cumulative population growth and the rate of population growth.

The rate of growth from 1880 to 1890 declined in relation to the previous decade. This was so even though the increase in visitor arrivals from 1880 (5477) to 1890 (13,055) was much greater (7578) than in the previous decade (4434). The percent of change necessary for an increase in the rate of growth between 1880 and 1890—or any other decade of Atlantic City's history— would have to exceed 425%. As shown above, it is merely 52%.

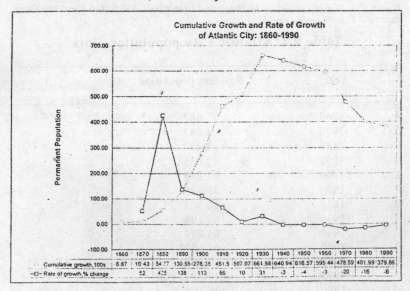

Cumulative growth and rate of growth of Atlantic City: 1860-1990.

The beginning of the consolidation stage corresponds with the height of the rate of growth (Butler, 1980). Figure 9.2 identifies the years between 1880 and 1890 as heyday—just past the peak in the rate of growth. The creation of a land-use map of Atlantic City's heyday required the location of historic records for the period between 1880 and 1890. The discovery of an 1886 Sanborn map of Atlantic City (New Jersey State Library) and Gopsill's 1886 Atlantic City Directory (Atlantic City Free Public Library) proved fortunate in this regard. The map and the city directory complemented each other and permitted the creation of a new land-use map portraying the tourist culture.

Space: Selected Atlantic City Land Uses in 1886
Transportation

Construction of the Camden and Atlantic Railroad (C&A) began in 1852 when the state of New Jersey granted a charter to investors. The right of way followed a straight line from Philadelphia, PA, across the Delaware River and the state of New Jersey to the ocean. In fact, the directness of the route ignored the marshy landscape and attendant engineering problems. When the engineering was resolved, on the other hand, the conservation of time was very fortunate for tourists. In 1879, a second railroad introduced competition for the C&A. After only 5 years (1883), this renegade was taken over by the Reading Railroad, which initiated ticket prices that were lower than those of the C&A. Thus, tourists were lucky to have a very good ticket price—50 cents—and a mere 90-minute ride to the beach from smoky, steamy Philadelphia.

The train tracks for Atlantic City's internal transport spanned the town from east to west, occupying the main street, Atlantic Avenue. Therefore, upon reaching Atlantic City, the C&A continued eastward on Atlantic Avenue toward the Inlet so that wealthier tourists could disembark at the large hotels.

Daytrippers from Philadelphia's factory workforce continued directly to the beach and the boardwalk on the southwest side of town.

Public Space

The dominant public space in 1886 was the beach. Symbolically, the beach represents a buffer zone between culture (human constructions) and wilderness (nature) (Jeans, 1990). Original entrepreneurs envisioned a wealthy clientele who would take elegant carriage rides on the beach, a custom followed in resort towns such as Cape May to the south. However, Philadelphia factory workers delighted in taking donkey rides (Figure 9.3) and wore daring bathing costumes that reached only as far as their knees!

Atlantic City's boardwalk was the second public space and paralleled the beach. It began as an 8-foot-wide path along the beach in 1870 but quickly transformed into commercial space, perfectly representing the classic recreational business district (RBD) (Stansfield, 1971; Stansfield & Rickert, 1970). It was characterized by many mechanical amusement rides (Figure 9.4). Such amusement rides, originating from the great expositions and pleasure parks of North America and Europe, continue their existence in contemporary theme parks and amusement parks. Well-off tourists who became fatigued during boardwalk promenades hired wicker rolling chairs (Figure 9.5). Both amusement rides and boardwalk trams are familiar components of resorts more than 100 years later.

The boardwalk and the beach were separate places. In 1886, the boardwalk was a partially roofed structure that made ocean views difficult or impossible from some locations. More importantly, the boardwalk symbolically turned its back to the water by virtue of its intense commercial nature. Besides mechanical amusements, Atlantic City's boardwalk RBD included food and beverage services, candy-concessions and souvenirs, skating, shooting galleries, water slides, photography

Figure Tourists riding donkeys. (Courtesy of the Atlantic County Historical Society, Scmers Point, NJ.)

Figure Epicycloidal diversion. (Courtesy of the Atlantic County Historical Society, Somers Point, NJ.)

Figure   The boardwalk and rolling chairs. (Courtesy of the Atlantic County Historical Society, Somers Point, NJ.)

stalls, and bowling. At first a novelty that rapidly gained popularity locally, boardwalks contribute to resort landscapes across the United States.

Tourist Accommodations

Accommodations existed south of Atlantic Avenue. The large hotels, served by the first railroad (C&A), catered to upper-middle-class tourists and occupied the eastern side of the resort. The large hotels required spacious grounds because they offered RBD functions immediately on the premises (Brent, 1997). In addition to private room accommodations, the large hotels included a dining room, facilities for entertaining friends, concerts, social functions such as balls and hops, as well as archery, tennis, and quoits outside on the lawn.

Although a great deal of space was required for the hotels, larger profits were gained from the crowded boarding houses and guest houses that clustered south of the second train terminal on the western side of the resort. These accommodations were simpler, more limited in amenities, and much less expensive than the hotels. Although the original investors hoped that the resort would rival other elite resorts on America's east coast, such as Long Branch, Cape May, and Monmouth Park, Atlantic City was favouring lower class mass tourism resort by 1886.

Permanent Residences

Gopsill'sAtlamic City Directory 1886 and the Sanborn Map ofAtlantic City 1886 permitted an understanding of both employment locations and home addresses of Atlantic City's permanent residents. Seventy-five percent of the usual retail goods and services occupied the main street, Atlantic Avenue (Gopsill's Atlantic City Directory, 1886; Sanborn Map & Publishing Ltd., 1886).A node near the original C&A terminal located Atlantic City's Central Business District (CBD). Permanent residents lived on, or north of, Atlantic Avenue, and their demographics reflected the distribution of tourist accommodations south of Atlantic Avenue. Servants and poorly paid workers lived on the west side.These included waiters, wheelwrights, drivers, porters, and other lew-wage workers. However, the northeast was less homogeneous socially and economically. It housed servants as well as professional individuals who lived and worked from the same location.The principal residents listed in the northeast quadrant included engineers, engravers, grocers, oystermen, printers, upholsters, roofers, and real estate agents.Thus, the town was divided on both axes by the railroads (Figure 9.6). East and west generally separated rich and poor while north and south divided residents from the tourists.

It is significant that in 1886 many successful merchants were eager to live in a new residential community in adjacent Chelsea.Atlantic City's business families no longer wished to maintain their homes in the cluttered, noisy, and hectic town that had become a recreational suburb for Philadelphia's factory workers (Funnell, 1975).

Discussion

Historiographical evidence indicates that the dominant class of tourists changed after 1883. The change of tourist type is a direct response to transportation prices, market proximity, and acceptable profit for the railroads, hotels, and small business entrepreneurs. Very simply, transportation was a critical element in the success of Atlantic City's tourism. Further, it has been shown elsewhere (Giuliano, 1986; Hoyt 1939) and reemphasized here that transportation influences urban land-use patterns.

It is reasonable to assume that when one transportation technology is eclipsed by another, former land-use relationships may no longer apply. As a result, the destination can experience crisis. After World War II, railroads encountered a decline as automobile use increased dramatically. Atlantic City's demise followed the disappearance of the trains because it was planned for rail arrivals, not automobiles.

Atlantic City declined as the use of automobiles increased. While there were only two train termini, each automobile required its own individual terminal—a parking space. Besides parking spaces, maintenance, repair, and fuel services were required for automobiles, which crowded out residents and even tourists and the land use created for their enjoyment. There was no means of isolating Atlantic City from the predominant transportation technology apart from going back in time and disallowing the automobile bridges constructed from 1870 onward. While the physical tourism infrastructure remained, the merchant population finally closed their businesses in the 1950s and 1960s. Without an active merchant population and enough tourist parking, the original resort died.

From the example of Atlantic City, one can consider rate of growth as a series of points, each calculated from the previous point. Cumulative growth, on the other hand, reflects change occurring between the initial and concluding points of data. Cumulative growth data are more compelling in later stages of evolution than those from the rate of growth. For this reason,

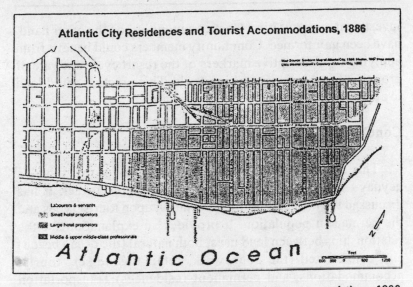

Figure   Map of Atlantic City residences and tourist accommodations, 1886.
(©1997 M. T. Brent and the University of Waterloo.)

marketers often promote cumulative growth when the rate of
growth is slowing down or declining. It is important for both the
community and industry to understand the implications of slowed
rate of growth. While large corporations use growth concepts
routinely for marketing, tourism communities normally understand
little about it and are thus vulnerable to negative consequences
when their destination is no longer the "in" tourist location.

Understanding evolutionary stages is significant for the
economic survival of resort towns. Tourist destinations are
vulnerable to a cyclical nature attributable to all cities. In addition,
they are often subject to a seasonal nature. They are ex-
ceptionally responsive to external events such as terrorism,
economic recession, and crime. While a given destination may
appear to be robust, the link between appearance and reality
might in fact be fragile. Host communities, local entrepreneurs,
and large hospitality corporations all benefit from recognizing
the current evolutionary phase at their destinations. The tourism
industry is skillful at determining when to enter and retreat from

investment opportunities. Host communities, on the other hand, have been uninformed. Community members could benefit from applying the descriptive markers of the resort cycle and rate of growth information as tracking tools. This practice could lead to appropriate planning at their destination.

Conclusion

This chapter study has identified a stretch of real time—a heyday—and converted it to a land-use map. Further, it has discussed the influence of transportation upon tourist types and the permanent population. It provides an explanation for the relationships between land uses, both natural (the ocean beach) and constructed (the boardwalk, retail businesses, tourist accommodations, and permanent residences).Transportation technology determined the location of the tourist BBD (Stansfield, 1978) and changed the nature of beach activities.Transportation infrastructure physically divided permanent residences from tourist functions from north to south.At the same time, it bisected the town with an invisible class barrier on the east—west axis.This research has demonstrated the powerful influence of transportation technology in determining land-use borders, shapes, and relationships at tourism destinations. It has also shown that the resort cycle has become integrated into many aspects of tourism theory and has the potential of contributing practical applications in tourism communities.

10

Tourism Change and Influence

"There she blows.. ."came the cry from the crow's nest, as the first whaling bark, Superior, ventured into the Arctic Ocean (1848) in search of a new harvest, and took so many bowhead whale that the following year, 154 whaling vessels cruised north of the Bering Strait (Oswalt, 1979, p. 206). These sailor guests bartered for Inuit services with sugar, cloth, kettles, rifles and, ominously, with rum. Whaling crews needed manpower, warm clothing and food. Inuit men were hired as sailors (or 'shanghaied') aboard the whaling ships, or they hunted for game. Inuit women sewed skin clothing, dried fish and meat, and also became "seasonal wives"for men aboard vessels that over-wintered. The sailors taught Inuit to distill liquor from the potatoes and molasses brought as trade goods. The effects of culture change were immediate and major, especially the introduction of tuberculosis, that spread as the ravages of liquor sometimes reduced subsistence hunting to near starvation levels. The subsequent purchase of Alaska (1867) introduced government officials. The gold-miners of 1898 were another intrusion of exploitative newcomers, who often turned to Inuit hosts for food and clothing. The influence of the Friends' Mission (1898) was predominantly positive, and provided elementary schooling in English, and became a much-needed new surrogate social network in a rapidly changing world. Four distinct types of foreigners: whalers, government officials, miners, and missionaries had significantly changed aboriginal culture in the hundred years before tourism began in 1948.

More than 50 countries attained independence after World War II (Table 10.1), a list that spans all but two continents (Australia and Antarctica).Their colonial history and subsequent acculturation all bear resemblance to the Alaskan Inuit example.

Table 10.1. Independence of Former Colonial Possessions:
Post-World War II

Europe		Africa	
1949	Ireland	1951	Libya
1960	Cyprus	1953	Egypt
1964	Malta	1956	Morocco
1990	Lithuania	1956	Sudan
		1956	Tunisia
North America		1957	Ghana
1961	Jamaica	1958	Madagascar
1966	Barbados	1958/9	French West and Equatorial Africa
1968	Bermuda	1959	Zaire
1973	Bahamas	1960	Chad
		1960	Mali
South America		1960	Mauritania
1966	Guyana	1960	Nigeria
		1960	Somalia
Asia		1961	South Africa
1945	Indonesia	1961	Sierra Leone
1946	Jordan	1962	Algeria
1947	India	1962	Burundi
1948	Sri Lanfia	1962	Uganda
1948	Burma	1964	Tanzania
1948	Israel	1964	Zambia
1953	Cambodia	1964	Kenya
1956	Pakistan	1965	Gambia
1957	Penang	1966	Botswana
1957	Molucca	1966	Lesotho
1958	Iraq	1974	Guinea-Bissau
1963	Malaysia	1975	Angola
1965	Singapore	1975	Mozambique
		1980	Zimbabwe

Oceania
1970 Fiji

Source: Wetterau (1990).

Explorers charted their shores, alien governments accessed their lands, and colonial managers exploited their resources with extractive industries. The Victorian mind-set often deemed the lifestyle of the indigenous people "primitive" and they introduced elementary schools and clinics from the outside, industrial world. Some of these newly independent nations have prospered as important tourist destinations, either as sunbelt centers (Bahamas and Cyprus), wildlife safaris (Kenya/Tanzania), or historical and cultural treasures (Israel, Egypt). By contrast, Libya. Angola, and Guyana have languished for political reasons.The list is instructive because it recognizes the role of governments as culture brokers in tourism development and culture change .The influences of colonialism and the subsequent importance of the media have usually far outweighed the role of tourism in effecting economic and social change. McElroy and de Albuquerque (1998) astutely summarize this process of economic development,

> The post-1960 restructuring . . . from colonial export staples to tourism has been facilitated by a confluence of forces: metropolitan affluence, multinational investment by invitation, aid-financed infrastructure, and the advent of low-cost jet travel. (p. 145).

Additional factors important to post-Industrial tourism include the progressive sophistication of communication technology and marketing, with a shortened workweek and a changing work ethic.

Tourism: Blessing or Blight?

In the 1980s, individuals questioned whether tourism was a blessing or Wight, but the issue is now essentially academic, given the value of tourism as the world's largest industry and its role as a global employer and customer. However, stresses are still evident in the interface between the *supply* and *demand* sides of tourism. The *supply* side of tourism becomes the assets of the culture brokers and also provides service employment.

Modern consumer society creates many "aspiralional wants" in contrast to "needs" and, for the unemployed, these "wants" may become incentives for crime: car theft, shoplifting, and mugging. Unemployed youths in crowded cities are a frequently untouched labour pool, overshadowed by aggressive in-migrants.An important activity of the World Tourism Organization (WTO) is the impetus to establish training programmes to assist young people, especially in Less Developed Countries, to qualify for tourist industry jobs. The *demand* side of tourism reflects contemporary travel motivations, which in 2000 presses for great travel diversity, including a search for knowledge, for self-identify, and *for fun*. Given the 21st century lifestjie of "hyperculture "(Bertman, 1998), in the Westernizing world the speed of cyberspace has changed the work place, altered family life, and induced greater bodily stress. We work harder, longer (Lardner, 1999), and the pace is quickly absorbed by children born into the microwave culture. Vacations become an essential therapy beyond reach of a cell phone to restore personal equilibrium.

The impacts of tourism reflect incompatible philosophies between demand and supply. On the demand side, the tourist who wants a private beach and the amenities of a fully staffed five-star hotel is unrealistic, because she/he disregards the basic economics of hotel keeping. From the supply side, residents in some rural or suburban communities prefer to limit tourism yet their municipal leaders may be committed to the growth machine philosophy that "bigger is better." Disney Corporation wished to establish a war-related theme park, somewhat in competition with Gettysburg National Cemetery. Supporters included real estate brokers and concessionaires who would benefit financially from this new virtual reality attraction. When the contentious issue was finally brought to a vote, residents overwhelmingly rejected the Disney plan.Their action clearly showed the importance of community input in tourism planning.

The role of tourism as blessing or blight may be assessed by a consideration of its costs and benefits. Table-10.2 summarizes the most basic economic, sociocullturai, and environmental influences (or impacts) of tourism, all of which are subject to extensive elaboration.

Tourism income usually benefits a community economically but the associated development often serves as a magnet that attracts labour from outside the area. When Cancún was developed, individuals with greater sophistication and travel industry skills quickly recognized the opportunity for new jobs, and they moved to Cancún.Too much tourism, or the wrong type of tourism, can despoil a community and marginalize the

Table 10.2.Selected Cost-Benefit Factors of Tourism

Positive Aspects

Economic

    Influx of "hard" currency

    Multiplier effect

    Labour-intensive service industries

    Better infrastructure: roads, water, sewage, airports, recreation opportunities Income from residents' use of amenities

Sociocultural

    Widening of social perspective

    Preservation of family ties

    Upward mobility

    Appreciation of heritage and ethnic identity

    Folklore stimulation (or stimulus?); creation of museums

Environmental

    Awareness of conservation needs

    Establishment of eco-labels

    Awareness of global resource limits

    Establishment of land use limits

Negative Aspects

Economic

    Seasonality

    Economic leakage

    In-migration of outsiders as managers/labour

    Cost of security to offset crime
    Loss of receipts owing to external economic crises/terrorism
Sociocultural
    Coca-colaization
    Loss of culutral identity in the Global Village
    Commodificatin of tourists as "things"
    Deterioration of histori sites owing to overuse
    Fearfulness from terrorism and crime
    Commodification of culture
    Misuse of intellectual property rights
Environmental
    Preservation costs
    Transformation of national parks and zoos
    Loss of wilderness
    Pollution
    Overuse of habitat from the ecotourist fad

---

residents.The case studies in this section detail some of these issues.'the Norwegian resorts still fight "turf wars" to attract and maintain their tourist influx but elsewhere, as in the beach resorts of Cancún and Boracay, communities are overwhelmed by mass tourism. However, even a cost-benefit analysis can mask fundamental societal issues including the self-enhancement and greed of individuals who, like Philippine president Marcos, identified the development of tourism as a contribution of his/her leadership.

Tourist Culture: Bridging the Gap Between Resource and Consumer

Our accumulated knowledge of culture change can facilitate two important goals in the decades ahead: finding the "best use" of the tourism resource for consumers and creating proactive tourism management policies. Best use of resources and good policies can "bridge the implementation gap' (Pigram, 1993).

The intent of tourism development will achieve what Selwyn (1996, p. 249) terms *tourist culture*. Ideally this local hegemony over economic and political institutions would permit hosts to cope with tourism by "providing some cultural space for tourists while simultaneously preserving other, more private space for themselves." The significance of this space dimension was defined by Goffman (1967) as the *front* and *back* stages of communal life. The front is the meeting place between hosts and guests, including main streets, plaza, and beach; the back region is the private zone such as the little stores where locals shop and eat. Puijk describes the problems of violated space in Norwegian life. Each tourist community could develop a unique tourist culture that reflects the ethnographic portrait it wishes to display, including public festivals. Some communities in Europe have long-standing traditions for wine festivals, Christmas markets, and other events that are openly advertised. The sites may not be much visited at other seasons except as place markers (an Olympic host city, or a former World's Fair location).

An alternative approach to tourist culture might also be viewed in terms of effective management of the local carrying capacity (P.Williams of Gill, 1998). Investigation of carrying capacity became fashionable in tourism research a decade or more ago, when carrying capacity was defined as "the level of visitor use an area can accommodate" (WTO/UNEP, 1992). The criteria included statistical data about the volume of tourists (bed nights, visitor days, etc.), their density (numbers of persons per unit of space or activity), and the market mix (the ratio of visitor to resident use of a facility). Farrell and Runyan (1991) note, "the concept is attractive in its simplicity, yet difficult to employ as a basis for a management system" (p. 31) because of the complexity in trying to quantify social and environmental quality. Acknowledging that it is a neat sounding phrase, Lindberg, McCool, and Stankey (1997) echo many of the criticisms directed against carrying capacity and suggest that the concept is inadequate to measure the complexities of tourism.

Many social scientists share skepticism about digitizing human behaviour as "garbage in, garbage out."

Greater scientification of community ability to better cope with mass tourism depends upon increased sophistication in assessing the host resources and the guest preferences and linking them more carefully through *place marketing*. Cities (and many towns) are becoming particularly adept at creating distinctive self-images, as Las Vegas proclaims it is "the entertainment capital of the world,"Vienna is the "city of Strauss," and Manchester, England is "the gay village" (Short & Kim, 1999). The creation of a public culture, by designing open space with artwork, attracts tourists and simultaneously invisibly defines the "front stage" boundaries.

Ethnography of Tourism

The identification of culture change, the management of impacts, and the development of a tourist culture requires breadth and depth of data, best accomplished by envisioning the "big picture" or an ethnography of tourism. Van den Berghe (1994) has provided a rare model in *The Quest for the Other: Ethnic Tourism in San Cristobal. The* case studies in this volume are mini-ethnographies descriptive of one major facet of a larger whole. Ideally/every community should draft its own tourism ethnography, as a description of the lifestyle and values of a group of people'united by a culture. If done as a self-analysis, the ethnography elicits knowledge of local strengths and weaknesses in their tourism programme, and identifies strategies for development of their tourist culture.Toward that goal, the 4 H's of tourism, are outlined here as a field technique for gathering, organizing, and analyzing the essential data for a local tourist ethnography.The 4 H's provide a time-depth, cross-cultural methodological tool that fills a gap in tourism research.

They can be effectively used at various levels, including: (1) introductory workshops to solicit *local input* from residents concerning their tourist resources, and their interest and ability to participate in tourism; (2) an *assessment* mechanism that identifies new opportunities to refocus existing tourism that is approaching decline (on the Butler model); (3) *analysis* of potential sociocultural conflicts in the existing programme that may require remediation; (4) provision of a *database* in association with other contiguous destinations to form a regional tourism programme and (5) identification of *potential tourist market(s)* in terms of existing psychographic guest profiles (see Table 10.4).

The 4 H's of Tourism:
Habitat, History, Heritage, and Handicrafts

The 4 H's of tourism—habitat, history, heritage, and handicrafts—pinpoint host assets and liabilities in the market mix for initial tourism development (Table 10.3). The same method can also be employed to examine new strategies related to psychographic profiles among the guests, and may reveal previously unrecognized but usable resource assets.

Habitat

Habitat refers to the physical landscabe and its tourist attractions: the Great Barrier Reef of Australia, the beaches of the Philippines, or the marshes of Lake Balaton. Critical questions pertinent to habitat areas include: (1) access of the area to tourist markets by reasonable (inexpensive) transportation (this may be a limiting issue for remote islands and for many communities in the sparsely settled exotic locations such as northern Canada and Greenland); (2) visitor seasonality due to climate; and (3) recreational and participatory activities available for the visitor.

Table 10.3. Analysis of the 4 H's for Tourism

Habitat	Heritage	History	Handicrafts
Access	Museums	Decision-makers	Heritage crafts
Appeal	Ceremonials	Conflict resolution	Innovations
Climate	Experiential	Modern showcase	Authenticity?
Landscape	Ethnnic centers	Marginal man	Miniaturize?
Resources	Folk villages	Honorifics	Artisans

History

History, as used here, is delimited to the record of prior contact with *outsiders*. Exploration and colonialism differ in their degree of cultural disruption, but the nature of those early contacts may predispose an interest in, or success with, modern tourism. For Kotzebue Inuit, most early contacts were relatively benign and hosting outsiders had historically been profitable. By contrast, farther south, the Russian invaders and settlers all but annihilated the Aleuts, and residual resistance to outsiders is still evident in a disinterest in tourism. In 1993, an east Greenland village, Scoresby Sound, refused landing permission to a Russian icebreaker with more than 100 American and German tourists aboard, fearing their presence might endanger local wildlife (as had earlier nontourist vessels, intent on trophy hunting). Hours later, and too late for the icebreaker to return, the decision was reversed when Inuit learned by phone that passengers on this cruise had purchased more than US$10,000 in handicrafts the preceding day, at the neighbouring village of Angmagssalik. Both craftsmen and tourists were disappointed at this lost opportunity for sales. Here the roles of decision-makers and marginal men (who may be bilingual and function as cultural intermediaries) are often of critical importance.

The history function provides insight in assessing potential conflicts between government and individuals in decision-making. Some cultures have successfully sustained leadership roles and authority even within a colonial structure. The Maharajahs of India retained most of their lands and privileges intact for nearly a century under British rule. Today many of their palaces are still privately owned and operated as hotels for the benefit of their original owner families. Other groups, such as Aboriginals in Australia, have successfully reasserted tribal authority in conjunction with a supportive government, and are making their culture an integral part of the Australia travel experience atAlice Springs, the Atherton Tableland, and Kakadu National Park (Zeppel, 1998).

Heritage

Heritage refers to the analysis *by the resident population* of the traditional culture in terms of appropriateness for display and manner of display. Museums, folk villages, ceremonial events, and festivals are among the options. Such decisions are often rooted in cultural sanctions, as the Amish have tried to preserve their traditions in private, despite the external commercial interests that commodify their religion. In the American Southwest, the Indian pueblo of Acoma has a history of visitor hospitality, and now welcomes Western guests to their annual festivals (V. Smith, 1996b). Potters display their wares on stands outside their homes, and purchasers may photograph artisans with their work. The adjacent Zuni have strong religious sanctions that ban outsiders, and their pueblo is closed to tourists (Mallari & Enote, 1996). The Zuni are world-renowned silversmiths, but sales of their jewelry are handled by a tribal Co-op at the entry to the pueblo and by retail jewelry and curio stores throughout the region. Such decisions regarding tourist access are politically sensitive and reflect a growing awareness of indigenous autonomy and identity.

Elements of cultural heritage, including traditional knowledge, when commodified and publicly shared, have an obvious monetary value to the host culture, but there are few mechanisms to realize payment and equitably distribute the income. Acoma charges an admission fee, provides trained guides for a short tour of the pueblo, and the earned income is used for community projects and social services. Zuni forego the tourist income for high moral purpose, remain poor, and face increasing internal disruption from consumer-oriented youth who value money more than philosophy. The Amish case study (see Fagence, Chapter 15) highlights the fact that Amish culture is the tourist attraction but non-Amish entrepreneurs reap the benefits. The Chinese government has recognized the importance of their minority peoples and encourages the creation of folk villages and folk arts to augment the national treasures, including the Great Wall.

Heritage, as history, language, and custom, is a powerful culture marker that differentiates and unites nations, tribes, ethnic enclaves, or even neighbourhoods. The travel industry recognizes and markets heritage tourism as niche travel. The identification and development of heritage assets is crucial to sustainable tourism.

Handicrafts

The production and sale of handicrafts depend on the availability of raw materials and a craft tradition. The aboriginal Inuit in Kotzebue Sound worked well with skins and sinew and wove willow baskets but seldom carved ivory, which was only available through trade with Bering Straits people. The Canadian Inuit are now widely identified on the world art market with stone carvings and block prints. Neither craft is aboriginal in origin but was introduced into the Arctic villages at mid-20th century by Canadian artisans and representatives of the national government, to create a source of wage employment. The introduction of new art forms to create income and serve the tourist market, as was true in this Canadian example, now raises questions of ethics and authenticity. Native images, when screened onto a T-shirt, usually do not protect the owner-rights or provide income to the designer. The development of marketing cooperatives, with logos that guarantee authenticity and quality, protects the integrity of artisans as well as the purchaser.

The manufacture of artifacts is one issue, while their safe to tourists is another. Many world cultures are noted for their aesthetic creativity in fine pottery and porcelains, large stone carvings, and well-designed furniture, but massive or heavy items are difficult to transport, especially for air travellers. Market demand commonly generates heterogenization of tourist art including miniaturization of traditional forms and proliferation of new styles (well illustrated by the Acoma potters who created small animal figures—including penguins!—decorated with age-old Mimbres designs). Over time, these innovations may achieve a status of "assumed authenticity." E. Cohen (1993c, p. 160) carefully notes that authenticity is not a theoretical concept by which the status of a craft article can be "objectively "evaluated but rather depends on the criteria by which authenticity is conceived. When tourists choose to purchase modern innovations for reasons of size, price, or style, they have stimulated the market and become "culture brokers". In the American Southwest, traditional Indian designs that originally decorated large pottery vessels now appear on pottery earrings and necklaces. Large (and expensive) Navajo wedding baskets have been miniaturized to wearable brooches and earrings. The bulky and fragile spirit figures, or *kacbinas* of the Hopi Indians, are now available as refrigerator door magnets or even earrings.

The Kotzebue Inuit: A 4-H's Assessment

The introduction to each section in this volume incorporates a mini-ethnography of Kotzebue Inuit. Using the Inuit example, the 4.H's assessment illustrates the claim that this is the "most successful tourism programme in the (North American) North".

Habitat

The Arctic and its indigenous Eskimo sparked curiosity and admiration for several centuries among early European and American explorers. The lure of the "midnight sun' and the hardy fur-clad dwellers, made famous in Flaherty's documentary film *Nanook of the North*, were reasons enough for many travellers in the 1950s and 1960s to venture North. In 2000, a two-day excursion to Kotzebue cost only $ 500 for airfare, hotel, and guided sightseeing. The trip was highlighted by regional diversity. The hour-long jet flight from Anchorage to Kotzebue passes close to Denali, the highest peak in North America, with a dramatic view of the glaciated. Alaska Range. The routing then descends to the Bering Sea coast over the bruad treeless tundra dotted with lakes and meandering streams. The summer days are warm and the tundra is a "Persian carpet" of wildflower blossoms. Tourists are thrilled to watch the sun circle the horizon at midnight, so light they can be photographed reading a paper with their watch showing the hour. NANA's Musuem of the North, generally listed as one of the four leading Alaskan museums, provides an interesting educational display of landscape and resources. The addition of a sightseeing stop in Nome, to visit the 1898 Gold Rush town, adds further regional interest as tourists pan for gold. Nome is the terminus of the famous Iditarod sledge race and tourists are treated to a sled ride (on wheels), pulled by a team of Huskies or malemutes. The afternoon return flight to Anchorage often affords a final photo op, in a sunset view of Denali. Only one other North American location, Iqaluit (the capital of Nunavut, on Baffin Island, eastern Canada), offers access to comparable scenery but at far greater cost and with less historical interest. On a grading scale of +, 0, -, *Kotzebue rates a + in Habitat, for access, interest, climate.*

History

Details of local history have already shown that the Inuit of this area have had a long exposure through the intercontinental trade with Siberia, as a source of tea (termed *chai* from its Chinese origins) and tobacco, glass beads, and iron knives, the latter fabricated from Ural Mountain ore and associated with the 1000-year old Ipiutak site at Point Hope, north of Kotzebue (Rainey, 1947). Using Kotzebue Sound as the hub, local Inuit traders profitably exchanged goods far upcountry. Kotzebue Inuit history reflects an openness in dealing with outsiders, in contrast to the frightened Canadian Inuit who saw the beleaguered and starving sailors of the ill-fated Franklin Expedition but failed to approach or assist them. *The history of Kotzebue tourism merits an analytical +.*

Heritage

Cultural traditions may be suppressed by outside influences but they can survive and resurface, within a generation or two.The Friends Mission in Kotzebue in 1898 banned native dancing, shamanism, and use of the Inupiaq language in school Much Inuit lore gave way to the modernization of airplanes, snow machines, and supermarkets in lieu of dog teams and subsistence food. Following the 1971 Alaska Land Claims Settlement Act, which awarded to indigenous tribes their aboriginal lands and some money, Inuit leaders expressed the view that the claims were awarded in recognition of their traditional culture (of which the younger generations knew very little). NANA hoped to restore pride in heritage to offset welfare dependency and alcoholism (and to expand tourism for its job benefits). In 1976, NANA leaders obtained a matching State grant, and with US$60,000 brought together into their Nullukvik Hotel all NANA Inuit above age 65, for a 2-week *Inupiat Paitot* or Elder's Workshop (V Smith, 1976). Of the 80 original participants only two dropped out, for reasons of health. Numerous youth participated as recorders and became deeply involved in cultural revitalization. Subsequent small workshops followed for two additional years. Combined, the data generated three published volumes (Lore of the Inupiat, 1989/ 1990/1992) of historical and educational value. The 2 weeks of social networking renewed group solidarity and restored the summer games, once an important part of the aboriginal trading rendezvous. Significantly, it was the Inuit who initiated this recovery of their cultural traditions, and hired their ethnographer to organize the workshop and elicit the information. Subsequently, NANA received a US$ 150,000 Ford Foundation award for this innovative effort, which has subsequently encouraged other Northern peoples to look more closely at their heritage. *For Heritage, Kotzebue clearly deserves a +.*

Handicrafts

Handicrafts virtually disappeared in the Kotzebue Sound area after World War II, with the subsequent importation of sneakers, then Nikes and Eddie Bauer parkas. The brackish waters of the Sound do not support a walrus population and thus there was no aboriginal source of ivory, except by trade. A few older Kotzebue Inuit women made small fur items—pins of Inuit faces surrounded by a fur ruff or pairs of Eskimo yo-yos. Eskimo dolls by Ethel Washington became the only collector items of note. *Inupiat Paitot* influenced other women to again make, for the tourist trade, traditional-style willow baskets, wolf-roarers, and wooden snow goggles.The Visitor Center at the US National Park Headquarters has encouraged their production and proudly markets such items in their gift shop. *Kotzebue handicrafts merit a + for cultural revitalization.*

The 4 H's as a field tool are equally applicable to rural tourism, to enclave and ghetto tourism, and to the analysis of special interests such as sport tourism, historic homes, or ethnic festivals,The 4 H's provide information to identify impacts, and can suggest avenues to effect change in the tourism product. However, the analysis is best utilized when matched with the appropriate tourist market(s).

Psychographics: The Five Generations

From the anthropological perspective, tourism involves transactional relations between hosts and guests. Tourism's success can be enhanced when hosts use the 4 H's to fully understand their assets and form partnerships with the culture brokers to market their product to the clientele who will most enjoy it. American travel suppliers, especially tour operators and experienced travel agents, recognize psychographics as an important tourism marketing tool. The research has been largely undertaken in the last decade by several firms including Plog Research of Redondo Beach, CA, and API Travel Consultants of Seattle.WA, to name two of the best known American firms, and whose data appear occasionally in trade journals. Until recently, quantitative questionnaires and surveys have provided data about styles of travel (Taylor, 1998). Psychological "ladders" have defined motivations, but tourism is experiential and involves individual thoughts and emotions (A. McIntosh, 1998) These psychographic perceptions are not solely demographic, expressed in age or gender, but reflect aspects of the culture and time frame in which individuals were reared, schooled, and employed. In the year 2001, there are five age levels of travelers whose life experiences and education have differed quite markedly, with a consequent effect on their destination choices and their styles of travel. The data presented here are taken from US sources but seem to have some parallels among other travellers. Elderly (senior citizen) American women, mostly widows, travel on motorcoach tours, Elder Hostel, or on cruise vessels (especially those that employ male "social hosts" as dancing partners). Many German and Japanese women of the same age group never married due to high male mortality rates during World War II, or are now widowed. These women all share similar travel requirements, of "safety in numbers" and companionship.

Psychographic Evaluation: The Five Generations

The widening tourist market, created by population growth and supported by increased global affluence and heightened consumer orientation for travel, now includes multigenerational travel. Gebhart (1999) identifies five distinct American generations whose lifestyles are based 'mostly on what they experienced during their formative years into high school" (pp. 9-10) (Table 10.4). These market segments are well described in American travel industry literature, have quite different tourist profiles, and make different demands on the same destination or attraction. K.Jones (1999) observes, "an old Arab proverb states "Men resemble their times more than they resemble their fathers.' "The five generations include the following:

The Depression Kids were the first generation of jet setters. Born in the late teens and 1920s, they lived through the "Great Depression," were proud they finished high school, served in the military or worked in defense plants during World War II, and established most of the post-World War II traditions in travel (V Smith, 1998).

The Swing Generation, born in the 1930s to 1945, was strongly influenced by the frugality of their parents and the rationing of food and gasoline during the war. They now tend to follow the travel patterns of their parents. For the decades of the 1950s to 1980s, most visitors to Kotzebue were Depression Kids and the Swing Generation, who drove their RVs to Alaska (because they remember the construction of the Alaska Highway as an "engineering marvel" during World War II) and wanted to "experience" both it and the "North". When the cruise industry to Alaska expanded in the 1980s, more Depression Kid travellers came in increased numbers.

Table 10.4. Five Generations of US Travelers

Generation Name	Birth Years	Economic Profile	Travel Style
Depression Kids (now mature seniors)	1915-1930	25% of total population; 50% of US discretionary income	30% of omestic travel; 80% of RV travel; 65% of cruise travel
Swing or Silent Generation	1931-1945	Inherited money and substantial incomes	Moving into travel patterns of parents and elder siblings
Baby Boomer Generation	1946-1964	Indulged by parents; Vietnam and dissent; Woodstock '69 is the defining event of sexual revolution	Self-indulgent, want luxury; now middleaged; seek nonstressful vacations and sports
Generation X	1965-1980	Fewer in numbers; from broken homes; seeking personal identity	Self-testing sports: surfing, skiing, trekking; "backpackers"; sanctions gay and lesbian travel
Echo Boomers	1981-present	Children of the Baby Boom; torn between doting parents and a soulless society; Woodstock '99 is defining symbol of violence	Dreaming of travel, not yet independent travellers; a few are "protestors" wearing chic T-shirts of the riot city origins

Source: Gebhart (1999), K. Jones (1999), and S. Mitchelf (199S).

These mature travellers now represents a little over 1/4 of the population . . . make up more than half of all discretionary spending and account for well over a third of all domestic travel. People above age 50 account for 4/5 of all RV trips, 65% of all cruise trips, spent 74% more on a typical vacation, more nights away from home and travel farther distances on every trip than any other age group" (Ahlsmith, 1999). However, they are aging and progressively moving into nursing homes.

The Baby Boomers, born between 1946 and 1964 and now aged 35-54, were the dominant travel market in the 1990s and

2000, and are the largest travel market in history. According to K.Jones (1999), in North America (and also in select areas of Western Europe),

> Boomers are the most educated generation ever—a third of the men and a quarter of the women have college degrees; nearly 20 percent of the 45-54 year olds households have incomes in excess of US$ 100.000.Women are the primary decision-makers . . . and make 80 percent of the leisure travel decisions. By 2007 Boomers will control US$ 12 trillion in assets, fully half of the wealth of the USA. (pp. 9-10)

Boomers consider travel an entitlement and their largest stress reliever. Many live in a centrifugal family (Bertman, 1998), and "it's not uncommon for Boomers on their second or third marriage to have children the same age as grandchildren from their first marriage" (Mancini, 1999, p. 16). Boomers have seen Alaska on TV documentaries. They will take their children or grandchildren on Inside Passage cruises to Alaska to introduce them to shipboard life. As individuals they are more interested in "experiencing the North" by an adventure icebreaker cruise in the Canadian High Arctic, or kayaking the rivers in the new Arctic Alaska national parks.

The American Association of Retired Persons (AARP),in a recent poll (Ahlsmith, 1999, p. 38), found that 80% of the Baby Boomers plan to continue working beyond the normal retirement age of 65 (compared with only 12% of people over 65 who are currently employed).These "extended careers" mean more frequent and shorter vacations, more luxury vacation travel, and will extend the Boomer travel market for at least another decade.

Generation X, born 1965 to 1980, were children during the Sexual Revolution that followed the first Rock festival, *Woodstock* '69, and the "hippie era." Often a product of dysfunctional families and poorly defined life values, they seek persona! identity and are drawn to social experimentation in the "backpacker" lifestyle or to physical self-testing in sports.Those who can afford it (and many Americans and Europeans can) fashionably trek in Nepal, bicycle in New Zealand, or become active "danger tourists" in war zones.

Echo Boomers, children of the Baby Boomers, were born since 1981. They are generally in school but a significant number have generous allowances from parents or inheritances from grandparents, which provide funds for vacation travel. Many are already frequent travellers, as young as age 5, shuttling airborne between divorced parents on custodial visits. Rock music and the violence of the media, motion pictures, and video games influence this high school age group. Two hundred thousand music lovers gathered at *Woodstock '99,* which ended in a fiery riot "while naked men and women danced around and jumped through the flames" (Strauss, 1999). The *New York Times* reported on July 27, 1999 that "Mark Szcerbiak, 20, a body piercer from New Hampshire, walked away from the flaming trucks in a gas mask he had brought to the festival: 'Our generation isn't about peace and love anymore; they're all about destruction and hostility. This is to show everybody that we're young and we don't care, just burn everything.'"

These comments must not be taken lightly by tourism planners, especially the convention and visitor sector, given the mobility of jet travel and youthful incentives to be "where the action is." Many Echo Boomers have money to quickly join political protests in Indonesia or Timor, Seattle or Vienna, and proudly wear riot-theme T-shirts as trophies to impress and inspire their peers. In balance, their forebears joined the French Foreign Legion, rioted against the Shah of Iran, or fought in the Spanish Civil War, but that commitment was longer term, not the "smash and grab" philosophy of some Echo Boomers.

Looking Ahead

The progressive increase in Western affluence in the past 50 years has given millions of people the opportunity to travel who, as Depression Kids, never expected to leave their farm, their town, or their country. The media and tourism have made us all world minded, even as the television sequence of the December 31, 1999 Millennial celebrations demonstrated the universal human desires for peace, goodwill, and prosperity.

The supply-demand disparities and the impacts of tourism will take new directions in the decades to come—first as the present LDCs attain new status based on higher standards of living for their citizens, second as the Asian economic "tigers" rebound and provide more discretionary income for their citizens, and third as space tourism moves from dream and drawing board to eventual reality. Each new stage will require increased sophistication in tourism assessment, implementation of programme, and mitigation. It will also necessitate renewed

Figure   New Guinea native with a ballpoint pen through his septum. (Photo by
V. Smith)

effort to develop psychographic profiles of new travellers from different cultural backgrounds.

In 1963, at the Sing-Sing (Highland Show) in Goroka, New Guinea, a tribesman pointed to my ballpoint pen. When I handed it to him, he removed a boar's tusk from his nose and substituted the pen (Figure 10.1). When I pointed to a landing helicopter, I was told, "him big mixmaster belong Jesus Christ now." What is his psychographic profile?

The stereotypes of host-guest impacts that have dominated academic analysis for a quarter century, starting with *demonstration effect,* the *tourist bubble,* and classifications of tourists as *ethnic; cultural,* or *historical,* must now be cojoined with both the host ethnography and the psychographic guest profile. Multidisciplinary research has advanced the scientification of tourism, even as case studies continue to illustrate the importance of the historical sequences of culture and their varying effects on tourism.

11

Sustainability in the Accommodation Sector

Since 1990, in common with leading players in other sectors of the world economy ... Inter-Continental Hotels and Resorts has positioned itself with WTTC at the forefront of implementing the principles of sustainable development (Robert Collier, see Foreword).

Apart from same-day visitors, tourists by definition stay one or more nights in the places they visit. Accommodation is, therefore, one of the five integral components of tourism products. This holds good whether the accommodation is commercial—such as hotels or holiday villages—quasi-commercial—such as youth hostels or university accommodation operated on a non-profit basis, or noncommercial—for example, when visitors stay overnight with friends and relatives. There is a very wide range of both serviced and self-catering commercial accommodation types available around the world.

It is important to make a distinction between holiday accommodation provided essentially to give tourist access to the resource attractions of a destination, and accommodation provided for other reasons. Historically, inns and the fore-runners of modern hotels were not provided for leisure but for business travel purposes at ports, towns and cities and at staging locations on the main road network. The railway and steamship era in the nineteenth century promoted extensive hotel development, first at stations and ports and then in purpose-built resorts, for exactly the same reasons that airline expansion in the twentieth century has produced its own parallel developments. Around the world, business travel was and still is a vital element of the accommodation business in many destinations, and for mam' hotels the per-capita revenue contribution of non-leisure travel far exceeds that of leisure travel. Outside purpose-built resorts, relatively low-yielding leisure products are often built onto the back of higher-yielding business visitors, utilizing the space available at times when it cannot more profitably be sold for business and other non-leisure uses. In the 1990s, conferences, seminars, training and business meetings are increasingly targeted by leisure hotels and resorts for the higher yield they provide.

In many countries accommodation businesses are by far the largest group of employers in the tourism industry. Not surprisingly, large accommodation businesses and trade associations representing them together with smaller businesses often play a major rile in tourism destination politics and wield important influence over tourist board and local government decisions. In the UK, for example, many locally elected poli-ticians in tourist destinations are hoteliers, and most businesses in membership of area tourist boards are drawn from the accommodation sector.

Overall role of accommodation in the environment of the destination

Decisions taken by commercially provided accommodation critically influence the practice of sustainable development at any destination. *Collectively,* at the end of the twentieth century, including the decision whether or not and to what extent to put destination marketing in the hands of tour operators, accommodation businesses have perhaps the major influence over two key factors:

• Volume and type (segments) of staying visitors that any given destination attracts.
• Quality of the destination environment as perceived by visitors, especially its physical appearance and image.

Decisions to build particular categories of accommodation, such as five-star or two-star ir. serviced or self-serviced units, together with the related marketing decisions, means accommodation businesses directly influence and in many cases effectively decide the profile of staying visitors. They largely determine the type of products visitors buy, their behaviour patterns at the destination, how long they stay, the amount of money they spend, and the season-ality of visitor flows. Because each customer segment has a different level *of* economic and social impact, the characteristics of the accommodation provided for them directly influences local environmental impact.'

In other words, the design of accommodation and its marketing may largely determine not only the profile and characteristics of the visitors attracted to it but also the whole character and image of a destination. The bed capacity provided (mainly a commercial decision) is usually the principal determinant of the volume of tourists. This is easy to see in the case of new hotels or time-share properties which are purpose-built to supply products closely matching the researched needs of an identified group of target market segments. The position is less obvious for an established hotel if it has to adjust its marketing to new types of clients, but the principle of targeting market segments is the same. In all cases, the role of accommodation, and the mix and price range of serviced and unserviced accommodation at any particular location, are crucial to the achievement or failure of sustainability locally.

Although accommodation is, by definition, always part of the tourism product, it may not necessarily be part of the environmental attractions or quality of the places in which it is located. Accommodation often plays just a facilitating role which makes it possible for visitors living beyond a convenient day-visit return distance to gain access to a destination's attractions or to do their business. A growing sector of modern accommodation is provided on or adjacent to airports or along major motor routes for use *en-route* to the primary attractions of a chosen destination. This functional role raditionally has not involved either environmental or aesthetic considerations. Many modern accommodation blocks for tourism constructed since the 1960s are downright ugly from the-outside, having all the architectural charms of high-rise blocks of municipal housing or car parks. This is true from the Gold Coast in Australia, through Florida, Hawaii and the coastal resorts in Spain, and it can be seen also in the emerging destinations in the Pacific Rim. Thus far, developers have been able to build and sellugly functional hotels because it was usually cheaper (more profitable) to do so, and for decades tourists showed no signs of caring if the price v ` right. In response to the growing influence and changing attitudes of better-educated, more experienced and more demanding customers of the late 1990s, this now appears to be changing.

In the short run at least, ugly structures, even blots on the landscape, are able to perform an adequate role in the functional provision of accommodation and food and beverage, and they can be sold. The authors of this book do not believe this will be a sustainable position, however, looking ahead to the next century. The architecture of a hotel makes the most highly visible statement about its owners' environmental awareness and commitment, especially if it is located in an area of high environmental quality. It is interesting to see the very different new approaches to hotel and resort architecture being pursued since the 1990s.

The size of business influences environmental impact

The section above notes the overall or *collective* influence of accommodation on the environment. In practice, accommodation provision and marketing decisions are made not collectively but separately by hundreds or even thou sands of mostly small and medium sized enterprises, with no collective vision. To under stand the impact of accommodation on sustainability it is vital to draw distinctions by size of operation.

First, for large businesses in the international holiday market, where a self-contained integrated resort hotel is built on its own island or in an area surrounded by its own grounds and a with its own leisure facilities on site, the destinastion, the attraction, the environment, and the accommodation provided may coincide within one enterprise. This is clearly the case with large hotel resorts such as the Sheraton on Maui (Hawaii), with Center Pares in Europe, and with Club Mediterranee villages and with most time-share resorts. It is true of many island resorts in the South Pacific and the Caribbean where environmental quality is under direct private sector control. At this level, the resort effectively is the destination. It is also designed to be an attractive product in its own right and it may matter little to many customers where it is actually located geographically. Such resorts are typically operated by international corporations providing products at premium prices and they have a heavy investment in the quality of the environment as the core asset of their business. They are committed to it. Market forces and commercial self-interest are likely to encourage such corporations to develop sustainable policiese specially if their customers expect high standards and active pressure groups with easy media access are monitoring developments and seeking to expose any perceived transgression. Increasingly, in the future all such large new developments are likely to have to undergo an environmental impact assessment study (EIA) before construction and to modify their building designs and EMS to enhance as well as to protect the environmental resources at the destination.

Second, among the thousands of medium and smaller accommodation businesses, such as those to be found in the large resorts around the coasts of the Mediterranean, different considerations apply. Most such businesses are independently owned and many have become wholly or largely dependent on international tour operators and retail travel agents for their marketing in the last two decades. These resorts are an important phenomenon in the international tourism industry at the close of the twentieth century, although measured in global terms they comprise only a minor part of commercially provided accommodation in the travel and tourism industry. Allowing corporate responsibility for marketing to be divided from corporate responsibility for designing and providing accommodation facilities, especially when the marketers have no vested interest in the environment of the places they include in their brochures, has been a recipe for environmental degradation in many places. It has led to reckless short-term attitudes to profit and overcapacity of beds. and it is potentially disastrous in environmentally sensitive areas.

Such a division of responsibility is not an inherent characteristic of the tourism industry, however, merely a reflection of business opportunities in tourism resorts in a particular era of tourism development. The division represents a failure in tourism to comprehend the nature of modern marketing and we believe it reflects a temporary phase in the progress of the world's largest industry.

Third, at the small and very small end of the accommodation scale the direct links between accommodation and environment appear to be rather more clear, at least in principle. Most farmhouse accommodation, many bed-and-breakfast establishments in rural areas of high scenic quality, and holiday cottages in rural areas such as national parks combine environmental resource, attraction and accommodation in the same accommodation product offer. In this case the operators appear to be providing on a micro scale exactly what the large resort corporations provide on a much bigger scale. But in doing it the small businesses do not take responsibility for the resource; they draw on, one might say feed off, the environment and other local visitor facilities and attraction:" in the same location. They are typically part of a 'local community' but they make their profits by trading on an attractive environment to which many make no direct contribution.

The operations of a few dozen bed-and-break-fast places, even a few hundred holiday cottages, may have only a very minor impact on a scenically attractive area such as a national park. They can easily be absorbed by the environment and the visitors they attract are part of the tourism economy and may help to provide economic uses that sustain traditional buildings in good repair and provide much-needed local employment. But when dozens become hundreds, and hundreds become thousands, and they are concentrated in areas which are the most scenically attractive and environmentally fragile, the issue looks different. The authors believe that for many countries it is at this scale of operation, where very few official regulations can be effectively enforced and monitored, and where individuals make decisions on how to make short-run profit from a 'freely' available resource base, that collectively the worst excesses of environmental damage are likely to occur.

It would be naive indeed to suppose that such decisions, taken individually by esns of thousands of small businesses or *micro-operators*, ever considered environmental sustaina-bility as part of the process. But the impact collectively is massive. In many of the attractive villages in the Lake District National Park of England, for example, much of what is now holiday accommodation was bought by people who live elsewhere as an investment and is rented out for holiday purposes. The families of many local residents cannot afford the prices that properties fetch on an open property market; many incoming visitors with cars have no obvious reason to respect the social and cultural environment of the remaining residents; they have paid for a holiday home providing 'free' and unrestricted access to the environment; and the scene is set for resentment of tourists by a local community. It was not planned as such. It was not a commercial conspiracy. It is not an inevitable consequence of tourism. It was simply the working of opportunism in a free society with consequences which none could foresee. To place the blame for this on 'tourism' or to see it as an unalterable characteristic of the accommodation industry is foolish and impedes the sensible route to finding solutions.

Formulating the accommodation product for environmental purposes

From a marketing standpoint, the simplest way to understand the formulation of any commercial product, including accommodation, is to 'deconstruct' it into its component parts. Environmental considerations can be built into each element of the product as indicated in the two case studies in this chapter. The quality of the resources at a destination is frequently the most important element of the core product or *promise* which accommodation providers make to holiday visitors in their advertising and promotional work. It is the promise which influences the expectations of first-time buyers and strongly influences their perceptions of satisfaction and value for money. We have argued throughout this book that environmental qualities - although not using those words - are increasingly the element: that determines customer satisfaction, repeat visits and competitive advantage.

For hotels and other forms of holiday accommodation a key issue for designing and landscaping buildings is the extent to which they blend into and respect the local environment and minimize environmental impact. Apart from the capacity of the chosen location to absorb the number of people to be provided for, this includes technology for the efficient use of energy and water, and control of waste. Safari Parks are a good example of sensitive product formulation because the over-intrusive participation of visitors into a natural environment may bring about changes in the behaviour of animals and alter the habitat. It could destroy the resource. Bed capacity is the key judgement reflected in the product formulation decisions taken at Kruger National Park, for example, where the Park authorities have successfully restricted accommodation capacity, contained it within enclosed camps, and managed visitor flows for over sixty years in accordance with their judgement of how many visitors the Park can sustainably absorb.

Sustainability for accommodation purposes—the environmental management perspective

Reflecting the issues, and the overall approach to environmental management programmes, the main environmental impacts to which the sector has responded include the following.

Specific environmental impacts
Resource depletion:
- Use of energy generated from fossil fuels.
- Use of non-renewable natural resources such as oil, coal, and natural gas for heating or the production of manufactured goods.
- Consumption of fresh water, especially con spicuous consumption in areas of water shortage for swimming pools and golf course irrigation.

Pollution:
- Contribution to global warming and add rain through the consumption of energy.
- Contribution to global warming, acid rain, low-level smog, and potentially ozone depletion through the use of transport both directly and by visitors travelling to destinations, and the import of goods to service visitors' needs.
- Pollution of watercourses through the discharge of sewage, untreated waste water from laundries, kitchens, guest rooms, swimming pools, and run-off from chemi cally treated golf courses.
- Production of solid wastes for landfill sites, and sometimes landscape deterioration from illegal dumping.

- Contribution to ozone depletion through the use of CFCs, lulons, etc.
- Of local footpaths, heritage sites or cultures caused by a large number of people visiting sensitive areas.
- Reduction in species diversity as a result of infrastructure development, building, or landscaping work such as golf courses, plus direct interference by visitors as on coral reefs.
- Reduction in landscape quality as a result of ? creeping urbanization associated with in-fill development which has characterized many large tourist resort areas.
- Of local cultures in economically developing countries through disruption of traditional male/female employment modes and commercialization of traditional ceremonies as visitor entertainment.

Regulatory background

Environmental regulations have not been developed specifically for the accommodation sector. It is instead subject to the wide range of more general environmental and environmental health and safety regulations that exist in all countries. For larger establishments in developed countries, the regulations which impact on the accommodation sector include:

- *Planning and building regulations.* These regulations encompass the broad range of planning and building issues from the need to gain planning permission to extend or change the use of a building for small hotels, to the requirement that large hotel developers go through a full environmental impact assessment (EIA) prior to gaining permission to go ahead.
- *Environmental health and safety regulations* which encompass all aspects of the safety of employees while at work and guests while on the premises.
- *Regulations governing the use and disposal of potentially hazardons materials.* Like any other

business, hotels are obliged to ensure that potentially
hazardous materials are stored and disposed of
appropriately after use. When detected, discharges to
landfill or watercourses are penalized by heavy
fines, or in some countries, gaol sentences.

• *Regulations governing the responsible disposal of
wastes.* Failure to dispose of wastes appropriately is
increasingly penalized by regulators and many countries
have now introduced a 'duty of care' system whereby
the originator of the waste is liable for its responsible
disposal, even if this final disposal is undertaken by a
contractor. Increasingly in the EU, accommodation
establishments are subject to a range of regulations that
require waste separation and recycling. The Packaging
Waste Directive due to come into force in the UK in
1997 requires that a high percentage of packaging waste
is recycled, which will necessitate increased levels of
waste separation by accommodation establishments.

Self-regulation in the sector

Beyond the normal processes of compliance with the law,
self-regulation initiatives are more responsible for shaping the
environmental credentials of the hotel industry than regulation
and the sector has already achieved some progress. The
International Hotels Environment Initiative (IHEI) has been
particularly successful at driving the agenda forward with
membership and funding from eleven of the world's leading hotel
chains. Regional hotel associations such as the Finnish Hotel
and Restaurant Council, the Thai Hotel Association, and the
Caribbean Hotels Association have also been successful at
encouraging hotels—especially larger ones—to adopt
environmental programmes. A 1996 report from the International
Hotel & Restaurant Association with UNEP (Green Hotelier)
lists fifteen good practice case studies from eleven countries
around the world and includes reference to environmental

programmes developed by fourteen "different national hotel associations. None of these were in place before the early 1990s. Specific issues which have been covered by voluntary programmes include :

- Purchasing policies, especially as regards favouring locally produced products, selecting non-chemical cleaners wherever possible and the use of organically grown agricultural produce.
- Use and disposal of potentially hazardous materials, such as chlorine bleaches, PCBs and CFCs.
- Use of transport for company purposes.
- Development of alternative cycle routes, etc. for visitors.
- Integration of the community into the com pany's environmental programme, through local educational initiatives, donations to local charities, or initiatives to clean up local landscape areas
- Cost saving areas of energy, waste, and water management.

A number of guidelines and manuals have been developed in different parts of the world to help accommodation establishments improve their environmental performance and good practice examples have been widely publicized, in some cases by the government department responsible for environmental issues. Some of the 'green' labels which have been developed for the tourism industry are applicable to the accommodation sector and these include WTTC's Green Globe and PATA's Green Leaf.

Summarizing the environmental issues for accommodation businesses—the way ahead

The key issue for accommodation businesses, even though comparatively few have formally recognized it at the present time, is that the future value of their capital assets as well as their earning potential is at risk in a deteriorating environment. Since 1991, through the International Hotels Environmental Initiative and WTTC, the large international corporations have begun to demonstrate their awareness through mission statements, environmental audits of operations and implementation of environmental programmes (EMS) as noted above. EMS procedures are still rare in this sector, however, has only evolved since 1990 and are still typically focused only on cost savings. Most accommodation businesses have been reluctant to involve clients in their environmental programmes, fearful that guests may perceive they are being offered a reduced level of service. Apart from marketing approaches, four primary avenues of development for sustainnbility are open to accommodation businesses at local level:

- A programmed approach to the *Ten Rs,* which is a logical extension of traditional controls of waste and costs and leads into a formal purchasing or procurement policy to deal as far as possible with suppliers who operate on environmentally sustainable principles.

- Design and building of new accommodation units which are environmentally sensitive in the obvious dimensions of architectural features and visual impact technological efficiency, attractive and locally relevant landscaping; "and regard for the recognised capacity limits at a destination. Although new buildings are easier to handle from the design point of view, the same principles apply to modification and refurbishment of existing buildings - especially where there are important heritage features of structures that merit preservation.

- Proactive use of the time that visitors, espedally holiday visitors, spend in their accommodation, 'to communicate environmentally interesting as well as functional messages ranging from appreciating something of the history of the local culture and natural resources at the destination, to encouraging a more economical approach to the use of fresh water and bath towels.

- Participating in destination partnerships to formulate goals and objectives in the long- run interests of all the stakeholders in the destination's environment and collaborating on mutual marketing and development objectives with tour operators. This partnership process is likely to include both the negotiation and application of any regulatory agreements, merits, and forms of trade association and marketing consortia to influence, monitor and self-regulate the activities of smaller and medium sized enterprises which will othere wise tend to slip through the established networks of environmental control.

Accommodation business examples

Inter-Continental Hotels and Resorts

Led by a small number of international hotelchains, there are now several sectoral guides that help companies to address many of the major environmental impacts associated with their business activities. Taking a leading role within this group, with more than 200 hotels in overseventy countries around the world and some 71,000 bedrooms, Inter-Continental Hotels and Resorts is one of the longest-established international hotel companies. Of the total, 124 hotels are first-class Inter-Continental properties, twenty-six are mid-market Forum hotels, and some fifty-five are affiliated hotels designated as Global Partners. The hotels cater for the needs of both business and leisure travellers. The company employs in the region of 40 000 personnel and had an annual turnover approaching US$2 billion in the late 1990s,

Environmental improvement is a core tenet of the company's overall mission:

To establish Inter-Continental as the leading and preferred hospitality outlet by the year 2000. This will be achieved through consistent improvements in the commercial and leisure services that we provide to the global business traveller. We aim to achieve our goal while consistently enhancing returns for our stakeholders and preserving our ethic of being an environmentally conscious corporation and a responsible employer.

To fulfil this mission, the company was the first international hotel company to develop a comprehensive approach to environmental management and this programme was fundamental to the subsequent creation of the International Hotels Environment Initiative (IHE1).

Rationale for a Sustainable Strategy

Inter-Continental Hotels and Resorts' environmental programme was developed from both a business and an ethical standpoint. On the one hand, in line with the aims of AGENDA 21, the company recognized that 'real improvements in the global environment will only be realized when all stakeholders take steps to improve their environmental performance'. On the other hand, the company was aware that significant cost savings could be made through the adoption of a systematic environmental programme.

Partnerships involved

Partnerships have been essential to the programme, both internally to motivate staff and externally to pass on the message of sustainable development to the other companies with which Inter-Continental Hotels and Resorts interacts. Partnerships have been formed between individual hotels, between hotel employees and community groups, with financial institutions such as the World Bank, with conservation groups, with local

authorities, and with competing international hotel chains. Within
its environmental programme, the company is one of the few in
the travel and tourism industry to make information available to
its competitors which can actually help them to cut costs and
gain market advantage.

Environmental programmes
(a) Environmental management

Flexibility has been essential to the establishment of a
programme which can be adapted and implemented by a
committed staff throughout hotels in vastly different cultural,
physical, and political environments around the world, and at
the same time be monitored at head office level. Head office
commitment has been essential and a General Manager has been
designated with responsibility for environmental issues. The
General Manager chairs a world-wide Environmental Committee
that coordinates regional programmes through ten Regional
Environmental Chairmen (one for each of the global regions
into which the company's operations are divided). Each individual
hotel has an environmental chairman who is responsible for
convening an environmental committee. Individual hotels can
then report progress or problems to this Chairman, who either
provides answers, or passes them to the World-wide Environmental Committee for solutions. Good practice examples,
or solutions to problems, are regularly published and distributed
to staff and clients through the environmental news bulletin,
The Daily Planet.

This environmental management process has been extremely
effective in facilitating the monitoring achievement of the six
point environmental commitment described below, which lays
out the company's aims and objectives concerning overall
environmental improvement. The commitment is supported by
annual improvement targets which provide short-term objectives

company-wide. Compliance with these targets is carefully monitored and reported.

Individual hotels are provided with an environmental reference manual and a 134-point environmental checklist which helps them to monitor compliance with the environmental commitment, achieve targets, and ensure that they address the range of environmental impacts generated by a major international hotel company.

(b) Inter-Continental Hotels and Resorts enviornmenial programme goals for 1997

1. *Energy conservation.* Inter-Continental is committed to reduce global energy costs by 2 per cent over 1996 actual costs: Base: 1996 Actual $79, 500 million 1997 Goal $77 900 million

2. *Refrigerant management.* Inter-Continental will implement refrigerant containment techniques for existing equipment operating with CFCs:

   (i) Wherever low-pressure chillers are installed, the purge units are to be replaced with high-efficiency units.

   (ii) Install centralized leak monitoring and detection equipment in mechanical rooms where CTC plant and equipment is located.

Environmental audit/review. Inter-Continental will improve its environmental audit rating world-wide by 2 percentage points.

Base 1996-actual average rating world wide 77 per cent

Target	From	To
UK/Scandinavia	73.0%	76.0%
France/Mediterranean	57.5%	62.5%
Forum/Benelux	64.8%	68.0%
Germany	82.4%	84.4%

Austria/Eastern Europe	94.5%	95.0%
North America	78.1%	81.0%
Latin America	84.6%	86.6%
Middle East	75.9%	78.5%
Africa	64.0%	67.0%
Asia/Pacific	83.3%	85.5%

Inter-Continental Hotels and Resorts six-point environment commitment and how it is implmenting action

1.*Conservation of natural resources and energy in its hotels without sacrificing safety standards or jeopardising guest satisfaction* Progress in implementing this area of the mission statement has been outstanding. By adopting a comprehensive approach to management and measurement of resource use, and by allocating resource costs to individual department heads, inter-Continental Hotels and Resorts have significantly cut overall energy' and water costs over a seven-year period.

2. *select only product and materials from environmentally responsible sources whose use - wherever possible - has positive and beneficial effects.* Many products have been replaced as a result of initiatives to seek benign alternatives for potentially damaging materials. Wherever possible, for example, individually packaged food items have been replaced and paper products are recycled and recyclable. German hotels have led the field in developing a product and Purchase List and have identified more than 5001 products which are regularly used and targeted 100 of these for phase-out and replacement.

3. To *minimize and efficiently manner waste production, ensuring the least possible negative impact on the environment.* Measurement of waste throughout the chain has proved problematic with currently available methods, but some hotels have managed significantly to reduce their total waste output.

4. To acknowledge regional differences in environmental needs and practices by- establishing adapt able local programmes designed to improve the performance of each individual hotel. The key to the success of the Inter-Continental environmental approach has been flexibility and a number of hotels, have adopted particularly innovative approaches to environmental management. The Regional Chief Engineer at the Nairobi Inter-Continental, Kenya, has been particularly innovative, producing an environmental management guide and supporting video to help other hotels in developing countries to adopt suitable environmental programmes.

5. To identify ways to participate in local community action on the environment world-wide A hotel cannot operate sustainably in isolation from the community in which it is based; to do so is to risk the quality of the product. Community programmes have been a great motivator in the Inter-Continental approach and more than twenty-eight new programmes were initiated in 1995 alone, ranging from a community-based waste composting programme in Bali, Indonesia, and an Environmental Olympiad for schoolchildren in Abu Dhabi, to support for a homeless shelter in the centre of London.

6. To develop awareness of environmental initiatives internally and externally through a variety of education and training initiatives There can be no doubt that the environmental programme has been very successful in raising awareness and shifting attitudes. Within the company, all staff now have access to environmental information and are given some form of relevant training. Externally, significant media coverage and PR benefits have been achieved through the leading role the company has played in IHEI, through the specific publicity achieved by the programme locally and internationally, and through the outreach activities undertake by individual hotel managers.

In support of its six commitments, Inter-Continental Hotels and Resorts has developed a comprehensive monitoring system to measure achievement and ensure that progress is quantified where possible.

Summary—Inter-Continental Hotels and Reports

The approach to environmental management taken by Inter-Continental has been innovative and successful, reflecting management commitment to the programmes at all levels, starting at the top. The company has invested in financial and personnel terms to develop the programmes and this has resulted in pay-back in terms of improvement in overall staff morale, cost savings working through to the bottom line, partnerships with local authorities in the destinations where the hotels are located, and partnership with the World Bank. It has also generated valuable positive PR.

Although there is no solid evidence that the programme is of itself generating new customers, it is now part of the product quality approach the company adopts. The company sees potential growth in niche markets such as the increasing international environment conference circuit and, as many more companies develop the relevant technology and good practice, business clients whose companies have established their own environmental programmes prefer to deal with like-minded companies. The Olympic Games Committee, for example, is incorporating environmental criteria into its location decision processes.

The company remains aware that the full benefits of its programme will only be achieved as more travel and tourism companies participate in programmes such as IHEI and Green Globe, as part of the drive to improve the environmental performance of the whole accommodation sector. In early 1997, the company announced that it would invest US$1 million over the next five years in the development and implementation of travel and tourism environmental programmes generally, responding to the challenge of the Earth Council which called on the industry to implement AGENDA 21. All the company's hotels are now Green Globe members.

Grecotel SA

Catering mainly for holiday travellers who select their accommodation as a part of a package tour, Grecotel offers a quite different product from Inter-Continental Hotels and Resorts. It has also fully incorporated environmental management into its corporate philosophy, however, and has pioneered a very comprehensive and successful environmental programme. Grecote! is the leading hotel chain in Greece. It owns fifteen luxury and four-star hotels and manages six other units under different corporate labels, comprising a total of over 10000 bed spaces based mainly in the Greek islands. In 1995 Grecotel recorded some 1.3 million guest nights and had over 3000 employees. Grecotel drew up an environmental policy statement in November 1992, staring the company's intention to develop comprehensive environmental programmes with the aim of becoming the 'environmental champion' of the hotel industry, and to act as an example for resort hotel groups throughout the Mediterranean. European Commission funding was sought by the company for these initiatives and a grant was provided for environmental improvements within the hotels themselves, within the local communities in which they operate, and for developing an awareness of environmental issues among other tourism managers.

Rationale for a sustainable strategy

Primarily attracting holiday markets, Grecotel's management were well aware that deterioration age their business interests. With ownership the company also felt a strong moral responsibility towards environmental protection and enhancement of the communities in which it operates. In 1996 the company stated:

'Environment is one of Grecotels most determinant factors in all its activities, including renovations and new building standards, applied technology, fixtures and fittings, food and beverage material and... guest entertainment programes.' (Grecotel Environment Progress Report, 1996).

Partnership Involved

Partnership have been the key to the success of the Grecotel strategy. At one end of the scale the partnership achieved EC funding, which was fundamental to the establishment of a professional programme and at the other partnership with suppliers have been essential in reducing the resource impacts of the operation.

Partnership with tour operators have also been important. Both Thomson (UK) and TUI (Germany) have been involved in the programme and have great potential to influence other hotels in the region to adopt similar programmes as well as communicating with tourists prior to their holidays. TUI is partowner of Grecotel but the group was dealing with some sixty different tour operators in the late 1990s.

Local autorities in the Mediterranean area have been stimulated into action by the programme and the partnerships have not ended once the programme has demonstrated its success. Through the link with the IHEI, Grecotel will continue to champion to help the resort hotel sector improve its environmental performance.

Environmental programme
(a) Environmental management

Environmental initiatives are managed within individual hotels by an environment coordinator who reports to the Environmental and Cultural Department at head office first established in 1990 and the first such departmant for mediterranean hotel groups. Hotel staff are fully involved in the programme and as of 1993, Grecotal's management consultancy, all hotel personnel job descriptions. This ensures that central policy is implemented in each hotel unit. An environmental manual was developed and provided to all staff, explaining the importance of the environment to the industry and indicating ways in which staff could become good enviromental citizens.

The enviromental programme aims to achieve gradual improvement for the hotels and areas affected by them resulting in a lowcost basic programme which can also be implemented by other hoteliers without specialist expertise. The company aims to share the experience it has gained from developing its programme with other hotel compames.

(b) Staff and guest awareness

Initiatives currently under way include internal ecoaudits, staff and guest awareness programmes, aducational seminars with local schools and colleges, provision of information to potential empoyees, improved purchasing policy and pressure on suppliers, close cooperation with major tour operators in Europe, and sponsorship of non-profit organizations affected by tourism.

(c) Improvemenst in operational areas

By 1996, eco-audits under the EC (EMAR) regulation had been completed in six of the hotels and were being extended. The steps taken to manage day-to-day business operations are extensive and include measures to conserve and manage water now implemented in all hotels including a scheme to change guest linen on request; recue of water from biological waste water plants for garden irrigation wherever possible; metering of water use and analysis of usage for inage for individual depatrments; weekly analysis of the quality of pool, sea, and drinking water instructions issued to all staff about water saving; use of throughput regulators wherever practical and use of throughput regulators wherever practical; and use of environmentally friendly cleaners in all hotels where possible to minimize water pollution. All hotels also use commercial water sottening plants there by reducing the amount of defergent neccessary for washing and cleaning.

Sewage treatment is an important part of the programme. All Grecotels operate biological waste-water treatment plants and the company has worked Closely with the municipality in its head office town of Rethymnon in crete to assist in the construction of a waste-water treatment and refuse landfill plant.

Despite the fact that most Greek islands do not have a municipal recycling programme or facilities, the group has made considerable progress in waste managemant: bottled water is now provided in glass rather than plastic bottles; individually wrapped catering supplies have been replaced by reusables, where possible, and manufacturers pressured to find alternatives; all cocktail decorations have been replaced with or flowers; recycling boxes have been provided for aluminium cans; guest soaps are issued without packaging and dispensers are increasingly used; paper is always used on both sides for photocopying and waste peper is re-used as memo pads; Kitchen waste is separated into organic and nonorganic categories and waste food is donated to local farmers as animal feed. Recycled paper is not widely available in Greece but is used whenever possible-recycled photocopier paper has now been introduced into all head office departments and some hotel units. In addition, the group is supporting the establishment of a private glass recycling plant for the island of Crete, thus encouraging the development of appropriate infrastructure for use by other industries.

Energy conservation has been a prioroty in all hotel and an investment of some 10 million drachmas has replaced all incandescent lamps with energy saving units; water is now heated by solar panels (accounting for 70 per cent of all hot water in the group); gas appliances are purchased in favour of solid fuel, thus minimizing atmospheric pollution, In addition, all new facilities are designed to be fuel efficint and use double-glazing and thermal insulation; bedrooms have master switch has which automatically turn power on and off as guests arrive and leave; condensers are used in electric circuits for the efficient use of energy; air conditioning and heating is controlled by thermostats and all bedrooms have shutters or heat insulation curtains.

Landscape and outdoor facilities are important to the tourism product and environmental quality. Wherever possible, local materials are used in hotel construction and renovation; larger hotels are built in a style reflecting that of traditional Greek villages; environmentally friendly materials are used throughout; gardens use local species of flora and fauna and areas have been allocated for apecial endemic species; synthetic fertilizers and pesticides have been replaced by environmentally friendly products and organic fertilizers. In addition, local arts and crafts are used extensively in the interior of all hotels.

(d) Programmes to involve local people and support the local economy

Efforts are made to sustain the local economy and minimize the transport of goods; fruit and vegetables are brought freshly from local producers; most wines, soft drinks and beers are local, and fresh bread is baked daily; all produce is preferred in returnable wooden crates; Greek specialities are always available in the restaurants and locally produced foodstuffs are sold in hotel shops.

Cultural and environmental activities are also a part of the programme and the hotel chain actively encourages enviromental conservation. For example, Grecotel has sponsored a major archaeological exhibition which is now promoted through tour operators and has also supported the Sea Turtle protection society of Grecce since 1991. Guests are encouraged to visit small vill?ges and staff have been trained in flora, fauna and cultural inte est. Local crafts are actively supported and increased awareness of the environmental quality of the islands is encouraged in local people by the development of posters and visits to local schools.

(e) Spreading the sustainable message

The group has a commitment to encourage environmental awareness among other Mediterranean tourism businesses. It hosted a seminar highlighting the need for private sector Greek companies to solve environmental problems which affect tourism. Staff and local people are involved in programmes promoting the economic value of green tourism. Guests are invited to slide shows of local flora and fauna and provided with copies of Grecotel news with details of the environment programme.

Summary — Grecotel

The comprehensive approach adopted by Grecotel has brought promising results, including an increase in awareness of environmental issues among local people, increased environmental activity with some local authorities, an effective partnership between tour operators and the hotel chain, an improvement in; guest communication, and an improvement in the local cultural and physical environment. Through its communication programme, the hotel chain hopes to be able to encourage other hotel companies in the region to adopt sustainable methods which will help to preserve the attraction and viability of the Mediterranean coastline as a tourism destination.

In recognition of its achievements, Grecotel has been awarded over forty-five international awards by guests, tourism organizations, tour operators and international associations, for the quality of its hotels, its contribution to upgrading the Greek tourism product, and for its initiatives in the environmental and cultural field.

Sustainability—the marketing perspective

Figure 11.1 summarizes in note form the extensive role and the massive power of marketing influences which accommodation businesses are in a position to bring to bear on achieving a more sustainable approach to tourism at any destination. As with tour operators the leverage of accommodation businesses is still mostly potential rather actual; partly because most are not yet organizad to orchestrate their efforts within a partnership approach partly because the larger players and trade bodies have also to accept and exercise collective responsible and influence over the smaller players who are quite capable of frustrating local environmental initiatives for their own reasons. As always, the development of proactive partnership organizations point the way to a more sustainble future.

By the nature of their operations, especially where hotels and other accommodation structures are built in environmentally sensitive areas, accommodation supplier are generally the most powerful players in the overall quality of the environment at destinations, as it is perceived and experienced by visitors.

Their marketing decisions strongly influence and in some cases directly control:

- Customer segments targeted for promotion and distribution io optimize yield.
- Product design and quality of the accommodation provided.

- Price levels to be charged for the accommodation on offer, including promotional tar iffs and discounts (approximate price bands are also established by design decisions, such as five-star or two-star accommodation).
- The capacity to be offered at a destination (a function of bedspaces available).
- Architectural/visual impact (for good or ill) on destinations including the architectural styles adopted and their 'fit' with a destination's cultural/physical environment— influencing a tourism destination's image.
- The quality of the building and design and i the landscaping quality around aceommodation.
- The distribution process, including the decision to market direct or with selected partner organizations, for example in transport, or to pass the marketing task over to tour operators.
- The information flow to customers on the premises about the destination and its special environmental/cultural qualities, including the opportunities it affords to visitors and their responsibilities in the way they treat it.
- A major part of what most visitors experience of host-guest encounters at destina tions.
- The level of repeat customers, reflecting satisfaction and perceived value for money.
- Customer knowledge through profiles held on databases for analysis and future marketing.
- Marketing objectives, budgets and programmes.

Accommodation suppliers in particular have a vital role for the environment in that most visitors spend more hours within and around their holiday accommodation than in any other tourism facility. They could use this power to better effect than at present by working more closely with their logical destination partners such as tourist boards, tour operators, transport operators and the larger visitor attractions.

12

Sustainability in the visitor attractions sector

Although we tend to be obsessed with the environmental issue of our own time, one should not forget the long-established recognition of intrinsic values. Such recognition can be traced back in modern times to the eighteenth century and the development of cultural tourism in Europe, the so-called Grand Tour. By the latenineteenth century, travel motivated by what we would now call environmental purposes was well established, ranging from cities and the Alps to antiquities in the Middle East. In America and Britain the origins of national parks can be traced to conservation movements in the late nineteenth century and to farsighted thinkers such as Ruskin. Even in South Africa, where one might have supposed the environment would be taken for granted given the size of the land and the smallness of the population, the origins of the Kruger National Park can be traced to z. nineteenth-century concern for the protection of wildlife from indiscriminate hunting.

In the late 1990s, although not recognized as such by most tourists, the perceived quality of the environment is the primary rationale for most forms of holiday tourism. Resource qualities, perceived and used as visitor attractions, are the basis for much of the 'world's largest industry'. It is one of the many paradoxes of modern travel and tourism that the environment is at the same time the victim of tourism through overexploitation of access, and its major beneficiary. Reducing the negative effects and increasing the benefits of tourism through systematic management action is the principal concern of this book. It is especially relevant to managing resource-based visitor attractions.

The tourism role of resource-based visitor attractions at destinations

Visitors need to be transported and accommodated, with or without the intermediary role of tour operators and travel agents, but it is their awareness and perception of a destination's attractions on which the other components of leisure tourism are based. The fact that visitor attractions and environmental resources tend to coincide in practice led one leading contributor to conclude that tourism is a *resource industry* (Murphy, 1985, p. 12). 'Resource' is a very broad term in this context, howeveer, and it covers the widely disparate resources that reflect society and culture, ranging from geographically extensive areas of natural environment, cultivated sites such as parks and gardens, heritage areas such historic cities and villages, to specific buildings and collections including palaces, local museums, and zoos. It also covers a wide range of cultural provision. Figure 12.1 notes twenty types of resource-based visitor attractions grouped in four categories.

The first three categories in 12.1 are resourcebased attractions with intrinsic values specifically related to the communities in which they are located. They typically serve an important role, acting as guardians and communicators of what exists of a sense of place and history, and they are managed as much for the benefit of residents as for visitors. This distinguishes resource-based attractions from accommodation, tour operators and much of the transport sector, which are essentially facilities provided solely for the benefit of tourism. The management and marketing decisions for sustainable development noted in this chapter typically have to balance the needs of the resource with the demands and usage patterns of residents and visitors, as in Florence or Venice (see the quote introducing this chapter). Many tourism destinations also have other attractions such as amusement parks and theme parks, constructed primarily to appeal to day-and staying-visitor markets, but many of them are economically viable only because they are built in or adjacent to areas with intrinsic environmental values.

Reasons for growth in the provision of resource-based visitor attractions

Around the world, throughout the 1980s and 1990s, there has been what amounts to an explosive growth in the provision of resource-related visitor attractions of all the types noted in Figure 12.1. This development appears certain to continue well into the twenty-first century. Not only is the number of managed visitor attractions increasing, but the great majority of them are seeking mere visitors and, crucially, more revenue. Most cannot survive without visitor expenditure. The reasons for the growth of resource-based attractions are not hard to discern. Briefly they are as follows:

- The economic role of the natural and cultural environment in securing sustainable growth and jobs in both developed and developing countries.
- The strong association of an attractive natural, built and cultural environment with quality of life for residents.
- The powerful role of heritage and culture in motivating tourism - perceived as a growth sector in all parts of the world.
- The perceived, relevance of cultural/entertain ment provision in helping to break down barriers in multi-cultural societies.
- The need to preserve important buildings and town-scapes for which tourism uses are often the only economically viable options.
- The need to foster a sense and pride of place for local communities.
- The acknowledged role of managed attractions based on environment, heritage and culture as lead sectors in urban regeneration schemes.

Heritage-related retail parks

Although not part of natural, built or cultural resources there has been a remarkable growth of retailing centres utilizing heritage themes in North America, Europe, Australia and New Zealand. City examples are: Baltimore and Boston (USA); Covent Garden and Nottingham lace market (UK); and Darling Harbour, Sydney (Australia). Such 'Retail Parks' are developed specifically for visitor use and they represent an important form of modern tourism in which heritage themes are likely to become more important because they signify 'Place' and provide the distinctiveness and image appeal which the operators need to achieve their retail marketing goals

attractions and provide a powerful economic and social rationale (especially where subsidies are involved) for creating more. As with the accomodation sector, a country's resource based attractions usually comprise a wide variety of types and sizes and ownership patterns. An important destination management problem arises however, because the individual organization in the *spectrum of provision* set out in Figure 12.1 are mostly in competition with each other and seldom perceive mutual goals or act in collaboration Each player within the spectrum decisions about its own development and marketing usually with only the most limited knowledge about its competitors. Typically in the late 1990s there are no effective area or destination strategies for the sustainable development of resource-based visitor attractions across the spectrum.

For most of the twenty or so main types of visitor attraction shown in figure 12.1 it is possible to control visitor access to their areas/sites and some charge the public for admission. But controlled access and pricing are not defining characteristics of resource-based attractions. The principal characteristic which links and moves them inevitably in the direction of more effective environmental policies and action is the fact that they are designated and managed for visitor-related purposes and ultimately survive or fail according to the relative quality of the experience and satisfaction they provide.

Management and control of resource based attractions

With a few significant exceptions such as national parks, most of the natural or built resources attracting day- and staying-visitors could be enjoyed until recent times without much intervention or need for management. It is only as the number of visitors increases, and other pressures of modern living are exerted as in Florence, that it becomes increasingly necessary to control and manage resources so that their qualities and values are not eroded by overuse. Intervention justified initially to control visitors (essentially negative and reactive) translates into management to sustain and enhance resources (essentially positive and proactive). The shift towards management is increasing in the 1990s because the better the perceived quality of the environmental resources, the greater the prospect of generating and retaining visitor expenditure in an ever more competitive world. The greater the level of expenditure by visitors, the better the prospect of managing and sustaining the quality of the environmental resource - if part of the expenditure is used for resource conservation purposes. Management and sustainable goals may be linked in a virtuous circle. *Management* in this context means that a body, whether it be public sector, commercial, trust or an individual, has accepted responsibility and statutory obligations for the resource. That body typically makes decisions that influence directly the key aspects of visitor capacity/volume, price, and products to be provided, and determines which groups or segments of the public are to be encouraged or discouraged. The particular combination of these elements achieved in practice, which readers should recognize as the primary responsibility of marketing management ultimately determines whether or not any given attraction is sustainable in terms of its visitor use.

In the negative/reactive control phase for resource attractions, attention focuses primarily on estimates of the capacity of supply. In other words, assuming existing visitor uses, what is the perceived visitor capacity at the busiest times? That appears to be the position in Florence and Venice in the late 1990s. In the positive/ proactive management phase, much more important is the knowledge, vigour and professionalism with which the resource is actively managed and marketed to the visitor groups it aims to attract. That requires research knowledge of visitors.

From ancient monuments to zoos the need to draw in more visitors and the income they generate has become the dominant agenda for competition in the 1990s and it has created a revolution in management terms. For example, historic royal palaces and the royal parks in the UK, a highly significant element of London's heritage, were relatively passive state-owned and controlled resources for most of the twentieth century. Not any more. There is no new capacity in the palaces or parks but, under the stimulus of their new management arrangements created at the end of the 1980s, they are creating and staging events, refurbishing and interpreting their attractions, and vigorously exploring new ways to attract more visitors and generate more revenue. With their massive intrinsic appeal, the flexing of the management and marketing muscles of London's royal parks and palaces is capable of doubling visitor numbers and tripling visitor revenue within *existing* notions of capacity. Their core mission to protect and sustain vital heritage resources remains pre-eminent.

Product formulation and design for visitor attractions

Biologists, archaeologists, anthropologists, sociologists, planners and geographers apply their science or methodology to define and measure the values of environmental resources. Scientifically defined criteria are usually essential for the systematic evaluation of resource quality, but such criteria do not explain the appeal or attractiveness of a resource as a tourism product.

Tourism products can only be understood in terms of the experiences they provide for visitors.

A mountain range in a national park, for example may provide the benefit of spectacular views amounting to an uplifting spiritual experience for those who contemplate them with an artist's eye. The hills may provide a precious and disappearing habitaf for wildlife such as eagles and other birds of prey. For others the visitor benefits afforded by the same mountains could include an excoting lication for rock climbing, for hang-gliding, for mountain biking or walking, or in winter for sking. The same range may serve as the visual backdrop and a unique selling propositions a gourmet weekend, or others visition a health resort to relax and recuperate their energy. It may serve as a routine, daily recreational tacility for the residents of an area within say 30 miles—for them a good place for walking dogs riding horses, using cycles of motor cycles shooting, golfing and fishing.

- Begins with images and anticipation of an experience, stimulated by effective advertising and promotion, especially printed materials to capture and communicate the benefit which users can expect to find.
- Commences formally through the quality of signposting and the initial physical impact and attractiveness of the entrance to the site.
- Continues through the ambience and layout of the point of entry to a site or building where visitors are especially open to influence by being introduced to or reminded of what is available. For example, why a temple is important, its history, any dress codes which should be observed by visitors, and so on.
- Includes the process of paving if appropriate and the provision of any information to read and take away, or audio equipment to carry within a building or site.
- Proceeds with the interpretation of the re source, explanations and any routes designed for visitors, and includes displays and the appearance, knowledge and friendliness of guides, if they are provided. It also

includes the cleanliness of the building, state of repair of the fabric and any objects, use of music and lighting and other influences on a visitor's appreciation and satisfaction.

- Comprises also the range of ancillary facilities which support the basic satisfaction or experience being sought, including toilets, refreshments, and shopping facilities.

It is always helpful to view these product elements both separately for management purposes and as part of a bundle or an 'engineered package' of components marketed as an overall experience for visitors. Every element in the package noted above is capable of development and change by management decisions.

Sustainability for attractions the environmental perspective

The environmental impacts, responsibilities and opportunities for visitor attractions cannot be compared directly with those for accommodation, transport and tour operation. Essentially most resource-based attractions are established to protect and interpret natural, built and cultural resources and to provide and manage public access. In that sense they are already part of the visitor management solution to environmental impact at destinations and have a special role to play in communications, interpretation and influencing visitors' behaviour. On the other hand, many attractions are also very large businesses, typically established in sensitive environmental areas, operating on commercial principles with some of them attracting over a million visitors a year. They are, 'therefore, also part of the problem and require .environmental management programmes in the same way that any other business operating in fragile areas does. This point applies especially to large commercial theme parks such as Disneyland Paris or Alton Towers in the UK.

Because attractions are such a disparate group (see Figure 12.1), as well as a special case, there is no international trade association forum equivalent to the IHEI for accommodation, or IATA for air transport, to drive the environmental agenda forward in this sector. With the major exception of national parks, seme of which are managed as visitor attractions as in the USA, and all of which have special planning status (see the Kruger Park case in Part Four) specific visitor-related environmental regulations only affect most attraction operations at the fringe. The main environmental impacts which the sector generates are broadly similar to those for the accommodation sector and include the following.

Specific environmental impacts
Resource depletion:

- Use of energy generated from fossil fuels involved in bringing visitors to sites.
- Use of non-renewable natural resources such as oil, natural gas, and coal for heating and lighting, and the production of manufactured goods needed at attractions and for sale.
- Consumption of fresh water, especially for large landscaped attractions.
- Consumption of natural resources, such as coral reef systems, in the conduct of their operations.

Pollution:

- Contribution to global warming, acid rain, low-level smog, and potentially to ozone depletion through the use of transport by visitors travelling to the area.
- Contribution to global warming and acid rain through the consumption of energy.
- Pollution of watercourses through the production of

untreated sewage, waste water from kitchens, guest facilities, run-off from chemically treated landscapes, and in the case of aquariums, from fish tanks which may have specific consequences for local marine ecology.
- Production of solid wastes for landfill sites. Contribution to ozone depletion through the use of CFCs, halons, etc. Indirect pollution arising from increased demand for agricultural or manufactured goods in the area, thus stimulating pesticide and nitrate use or industrial pollutants.

Degradation:

- Of natural resources, heritage sites and cultures caused by influx of a large number of people visiting sensitive areas.
- Through construction of car parks, buildings, landscaping work and visitor facilities in fragile areas, which may lead to a reduction in species diversity and disruption of local ecosystems.
- Reduction in landscape quality as a result of steady urbanization and commercialization in areas otherwise not affected including building and widening of access routes.
- Of local cultures through commercialization and artificial re-enactment of local tradition and rights.

Environmental opportunities for the sector

The major opportunity is to act positively as guardians of a destination's environmental resources in the broadest sense that many attractions reflect and communicate a society's values. In terms of business operations, cost savings are the major impetus behind the development of many voluntary programmes in large-scale commercially operated attractions, but for major environment resources such as Olympia in Greece, the Uffizi museum in Florence, or the Pyramids in Egypt, conservation of the attraction depends heavily upon which visitor revenue generation depends plays a stronger role. (See the Ironbridge Gorge Museum case in Part Four.) Specific opportunities that can be gained from environmental improvement programmes in this sector include:

• *Improvements in product quality.* This is the primary opportunity for all resource-based attractions. For some sites, such as the Horniman Museum in London, environmental interpretation and technology programmes have offered an opportunity to diversify the 'visitor product' elements, for others they have offered an opportunity to improve the quality of service in a similar way to that identified for the accommodation sector.

• *Increased staff motivation and loyalty.* Evidence from resorts such as Disneyland indicate that significant improvements in staff morale can be gained from environmental programmes in this sector as will as the accommodation sector.

• *Cost savings.* Programmes to reduce consumption of energy and water and reduce waste production will cut the utilities bill significantly, especially for attractions which include leisure rides, *Improvements in community relations.* For g some companies, such as the visitor centre established at the Sellafield Nuclear Plant in Cumbria, tackling environmental issues head-on has offered an excellent opportunity to improve customer communications, for others it has opened routes to undertake presentations in local schools or involve local people in recycling or landscape improvement programmes. The majority of visitor attractions run special programmes designed to draw in as many schools as possible as part of an outreach and educational programme.

• *Improvement in relations with local authorities,* although most attractions are much better placed to be proactive and some are owned or part-funded by local authorities.

• *Increased attraction to customers.* The increase in interest in environmental and cultural issues has presented visitor attractions with a considerable marketing opportunity. From the proposed Earth Dome in Leicestershire (UK) and the Sea World attraction in Florda, the environment in all its forms pro vides a powerful motivation for visitors and seems certain to continue to do so.

• *Long-term destination development.* Most visitor attractions rely on leisure tourism for a major percentage of their revenue generation and have an even larger vested interest than accommodation businesses in partnership activities to ensure that their area remains environmentally attractive into the future.

Regulatory background

Environmental regulations have not been adopted specifically for visitor attractions. As for accommodation, the activities of this sector are subject to the wide range of more general environmental and environmental health and safety regulations to that exist. For attractions aiming display and use traditional machinery and processes, modern legislation can create significant obstacles, however, and normal disability access requirements may not be feasible in heritage structures. The regulations which impact on the attractions sector are 'essentially the same as those affecting accommodation. They include:

- Planning and building regulations.
- Environmental health and safety regulations.
- Regulations governing the use and disposal of potentially hazardous materials.
- Regulations governing the responsible dis posal of wastes.

Self-regulation in the sector

As noted above, the characteristics of the sector mean that coordinated self-regulatory initiatives for environmental purposes have been slow to emerge in the visitor attraction sector, and those which have emerged have been pioneered by individual companies, rather than through trade associations and their equivalents. On the other hand, in most developed countries, there are long established national and regional statutory bodies and/or membership associations for specific groups within the sector, such as national parks, museums and galleries, and historic houses. Most visitor attractions are also members of destination and area marketing consortia, including those established by local or area tourist boards. In other words, the principles of collaboration and the exchange of information and communication of good practice for sector purposes are well established. The future lies in developing the existing links more proactively for environmental purposes. Specific self-regulation procedures include:

- Developing, monitoring, and communicating examples of good environmental practice for the benefit of all attractions.
- Developing codes of environmental conduct equivalent to those already produced for the accommodation sector.
- Purchasing policies, especially as regards favouring locally produced products for sale in retail and catering outlets, selecting nonchemical cleaners wherever possible, and the use of organically grown agricultural produce.
- Advice on the use and disposal of potentially hazardous materials, such as chlorine bleaches, PCBs and CFCs involved in operating visitor facilities.
- Development of alternative transport modes, park and ride, etc. to reduce the impact and pollution of car traffic.
- Integration of the community into the attraction's environmental programme, through local educational initiatives, organization of volunteers and friends, donations to local charities, or initiatives to clean up local landscape areas.

- Collaboration with other partners to promote environmental interpretation both on and off-site.
- Cost saving areas of energy, waste, and water management.

Only a small number of guidelines and manuals have so far been specifically developed for visitor attractions, largely under the aegis of broader environmental initiatives such as WTTC's Green Globe programme, which applies the principles developed elsewhere for visitor business operations more generally.

Summarizing the environmental issues for visitor attractions—the way ahead

It is no accident that most of the managed visitor attractions developed internationally in the last decade are based on environmental or cultural

Resources. It is no accident either that the attractions identified are increasing rapidly in most countries. It demonstrates the real strength of the motivating power of the natural and cultural environment for visitors, and their interest and healthy curiosity in knowing more about it. The construction of new attractions specifically designed to communicate environmental themes, and the adaptation of many existing attractions to incorporate such themes, is one of the most interesting developments in this field. In the UK it has been greatly stimulated in the last five years by the availability of national lottery and Millenium Commission funding intended to facilitate environmental awareness generally.

Within this buoyant demand context, the main issue for the environment reflects the fact that managed attractions have a most important role to play in interpreting, explaining, enthusing and interesting visitors so that they better understand what and why the environment at particular destinations is important and how best to appreciate and enjoy it without causing damage.

From a tourism perspective, resource attractions have the greatest vested interest in the long-run health and quality of the environment at a destination. They are, in effect, standard bearers or leading organizations for sustainable goals, which most of them typically express in their mission statements and objectives. They are in the vanguard of shifting visitor attitudes and behaviour in sustainable ways.

Four specific environmental roles are identified :

- To develop and channel their special knowledge as inputs to destination partnerships reflecting their responsibilities as guardians of local heritage resources. For example, taking initiatives with accommodation businesses reflecting their joint commitment to a destination. There is much more that managed attractions could do to develop their main messages which could be communicated initially to visitors by partners in transport and accommodation businesses and by tour operators. Resource-based attractions have the most to lose if the partner organizations, which they cannot control, do not deliver their own sustainable strategies for a destination.

- To extend their knowledge of visitors and marketing processes in order to improve their level of influence and control over the selection and management of targeted visitor segments. Typically, most resource-based attractions have not yet developed their marketing skills because they feel their first commitment is not to a market but to the resource. The growing nature of competition in tourism suggests that marketing skills provide the best available set of tools for achieving their resource objectives.

- To participate with other local resource-based attractions to achieve mutually sustainable objectives for a destination, cooperate in marketing, and to influence and support the management skills of smaller attractions.

- To maximize and use the revenue that is gained from receiving and communicating ; with visitors to underpin the long-run sustainability of the resources they manage (preserving the intrinsic values).

Sustainability - the marketing perspective

It summarizes in note form the extensive role and power of marketing available to managed visitor attractions to support their sustainable objectives. Larger attractions with more than, say, 150 000 visits a year are generally capable of developing and using all the marketing tools directly. Most smaller attractions will only be able to draw on professional marketing skills when networked with larger attractions and local tourist board, but all need to collaborate as they all have a common interest in sustainability of resources at the destination.

By the nature of their operations resource-based visitor attractions are key players in sustainable development from a marketing perspective. Their marketing decisions strongly influenced and in some cases directly control:

- The specific customers targeted for promotion and distribution (from among those staying at a destination and others within, easy day-travelling distance).
- Overall design and quality of the experience which the attraction provides.
- The most direct 'hands on' experience of environmental resources accessible to most visitors.
- Communication of information explaining and interpreting the nature of the attraction/resource and its significance.
- The specific presentation of objects, stories and themes, and all the forms of display provided for visitor .
- Opportunites for visitors and residents to meet on equal terms; qualified local guides and interpreters can perform a key role in this process.

- Prices at which visitors are admitted including any promotional and discounted offers.
- Product offers put together with other destination partners such as accommodation and local public transport operators.
- Evaluation of customer profiles and satisfaction through customer research.
- Customer profiles held on databases for analysis and future marketing.
- Marketing objectives, visitor volume targets, budgets and programmes.

This combination of influences, all of them part of the moderm process of marketing for visitor attractions, is especially important where the attraction being managed is a core part of the environmental quality and appeal of a destination, for example a castle, a cathedra a museum or a national park. Non-commercial attractions such as museums have a special role to play because of the authority and extra credibility often attached to their communications.

13

The Culture Agents

Chester Seveck was a man of the past, born in 1890 along the coast north of Kotzebue. His father was an umelik (captain of a whaling boat), and famous for having landed 22 bowhead, one 40 feet long. From him, Chester learned the traditional life skills. By age 18 he was already an experienced doghandler and that winter he sledged alone the 190 miles south to the gold fields at Nome to take frozen fish to hungry miners. He hoped to be an umelik like his father but times were changing. . . .

At 17 Chester became a lay reader at the Episcopal Mission in Point Hope, and remained a staunch church member all his life but he also learned some shamanistic lore of Inuit angakoks. In later years, his peers considered him "different" because of his travels; some believed only a "powerful" angakok could have done so much in his life. There was jealousy and older Inuit were a little afraid of him.

Chester was the kind of young man you knew you could depend upon. In 1908 when the Federal government introduced reindeer into Alaska, Chester was invited to become a herder. This was his introduction to "White man's world" of paychecks and bureaucrats. He herded for 46 years and retired in 1954 with a government pension. Then he took up his new career as culture agant and tour guide.

Chester visited the Smithsonian Museum in Washington DC soon after the 1969 lunar landing, and saw the rocks Armstrong and Aldrin had brought back. He loved to tell tourists about his trip to the moon and the rocks he saw, because they were identical to the ones the astronauts had obtained. Inuit shamans sometimes did visit the spirit world for power to cure illness and group dissension. Inuit family sitting in a darkened igloo could hear them fly out through the smoke hole, and feel the whirlwind of their exit and re-entry. [Western skeptics might argue such extra-earth experiences were sleight-of-hand but traditional Inuit cosmology held the belief that shamans had such power. . . . see Weyer, 1969, p. 460]

The tourists who visited Kotzebue between 1954 and 1980 found in Chester a charismatic living symbol of the Eskimo stories they had read as school children. Thousands, perhaps millions, saw him (and Helen) on TV and in public appearances in Europe and Latin America and were inspired to visit Alaska, and Kotzebue, because of that marketing exposure. Chester was never a charlatan. He was a culture broker who independently decided the aspects of Inuit life he would share. He never spoke to tourists about "wife swapping"(sexual hospitality), incest, or homosexuality, as these topics were not openly discussed then in the guest's culture, either. He shared his knowledge of Inutt culture as he had lived it, as a "marginal man.'Tbe visitor-guests were richer for the cross-cultural understanding they gained of human adaptation to the Arctic while be guided them around Kotzebue.

Marginal Men and Women

Marginal men and women are cross-cultural mediators between Western and indigenous societies. Usually bilingual, some special circumstance (or interest) has afforded these individuals the opportunity to know, to move and to live in and between two cultures, as Chester did. A few other North Alaskan Inuit of his generation were also "marginal men" and understood western ways.They became the 1960's political leaders who pioneered the Native Alaskan Lands Claims Settlement Act.

Outside metropolitan Kotzebue there are numerousArctic locations where non-Inuit have chosen to live in the North as an alternative to urbanism. Some have investment capital to start up charter air services, or to construct lodges and promote hunting, fishing, and the wilderness experience. With long-term occupancy and close affiliation with Inuit staff, these settlers are other genera of "marginal men"and women affiliated with ecotourism.A somewhat parallel example includes Africa's "White hunters" who work closely with their native staff and interpret indigenous culture to their clients. Others may derive from an ethnic minority, as some Chinese have became the "marginal men" (or women) guides in Dyak villages of Borneo.These "go-betweens" are found in many locales and serve important functions of cultural interpretation, often with a level of detachment that is sometimes difficult for members of the indigenous cultures to attain.These bicultural informants fit the traditional interpretation of guides as pathfinders, mediators, and animators (E. Cohen, 1985).

The Culture Agents

The term culture broker increasingly appears in the tourism literature but there has been little analysis of its significance. The discussion here identifies the responsibility of the culture broker as the mediator between hosts and guests, responsible for ethnic imaging and cultural trait selection. At the local level, guides are culture brokers, but as tourism has grown from a business to an industry, others including travel agents, government at all levels, and international agencies have assumed the leadership.

Webster's New World Dictionary of the English Language (1988) defines a broker as an "intermediary, or an interpreter, who negotiates between or brings together buyer and seller."A culture broker is the mediator between the demand and the supply sides of tourism (Figure 13.1).The culture brokers are primary decision-makers, selectively identifying segments of the culture content to be shared with outsiders, and many also serve as guides. Chester Seveck filled both roles. First, as culture broker he chose from the entirety of Inuit culture those traits that he felt would most interest the tourist, given his contact time with them was only an hour or two. With a degree of ethnocentrism, his projected images should also reflect well on Inuit society. Second, as guide he described the hunting skills, stewardship of the animals, and family values. He demonstrated male dancing, as a hunter in pursuit of game. Helen showed the social dances of women, and demonstrated her skin sewing skills in the manufacture of Inuit fur boots *(mukluks)*. This local-level culture brokering is still operative in many areas of the world. The quality of the experience relies heavily upon the integrity and knowledge of the local guides. Chester benefited from his "marginal man" status, and the airlines were able to offer the traveling public an unusual and quality experience.

On a regional scale, and dating to a century ago with Thomas Cook and his peers, early travel agencies scouted for new destinations to extend their activities. When they discovered something "new," as culture brokers they chose from a range of visible culture traits one or two distinguishing characteristics to "define" this society and used them in their advertising. When tour operators "discovered' Tana Toraja in Sulawesi in the late 1960s (Crystal, 1977), three elements of this culture were striking: the "thatched boat-like houses," the "princely heritage" of the people, and their emphasis on elaborate rituals. "Princely heritage" was difficult to symbolize, and throughout Indonesia there are many dramatic house styles. Therefore, the tour operators cum culture brokers established "hanging graves" filled with mortuary statues as the definitive trait for Torajan culture. Kathleen Adams (1984, p. 472), in her fieldwork in Sulawesi, recognized this arbitrary selection process, and labeled the travel agents "brokers in ethnicity." As a consequence of the advertised emphasis on the death effigies, many tourists now ask Torajans about their graves but almost none inquire about the houses or the significance of their "princely" heritage. The emphasis on the "hanging graves" also had an unintended effect on the world art market, for each wooden icon stolen from the graves is now valued at US$30,000 or more as a collector's

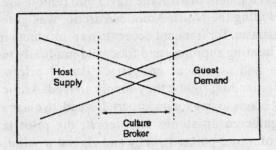

Culture brokers as mediators.

item.Torajan youth with little conscience or interest in heritage are known to have removed the crudely carved statues and sold them for small sums of money to buy their "aspirational wants" of T-shirts and Walkmans.

In yet another example, after NANA purchased the Kotzebue tour operation, the elected corporate leaders became the Inuit culture brokers in support of their own tourism enterprise. In deciding upon the type of exhibits for their Museum of the North, they chose to identify their Inuit ethnicity with the theme of animal and human migration from Asia into the New World. Alternately, they might have used their giant spirit, "Maniilaq," or they could have designed museum exhibits to illustrare'their role as hosts of important Bering Sea trading rendezvous. Culture brokering on this level involves the conceptualization of culture norms, and a process of cultural selection and presentation.

Before Mass Tourism

Mass tourism began in the early 1970s. Prior to that time tourism was a relatively small-scale business. Individual travel agencies formed networks through international associations; hotels were primarily family owned and family operated. The essentials of tourism were independently handled with little supervision from governmental institutions.

The development of airplane travel into remote areas of the world, including the North American arctic, was greeted with great enthusiasm, for it meant access to new products including medicine, hunting supplies, and food, and gradually motorized generators and electrical gadgetry. "Bush" pilots did not negotiate for landing rights; they simply arrived. Arctic villages didn't float bonds to pay for an airport. Instead, to clear a runway, villagers gathered up stones and debris; the pilot laid out a perimeter of white-painted rocks and rigged a windsock. The usual terminal was a three-walled shack to provide weather protection. When Wien airline initiated tourism to Kotzebue in the late 1940s they bought an old warehouse from the local trading post, converted it to a dormitory, and the white station agent lived there and served as guide. In that era, when industrial nations listed their export earnings, they measured their worth in the heavy industries of iron and steel, mining and petrochemicals, followed by agriculture and manufacturing. Tourism was too insignificant to count.

Indicative of tourism in this era, in Hawaii in 1959 (the year of Hawaiian statehood, and the first jet flight to Europe but not to Hawaii) the Matson Steam Navigation Company, which operated the passenger liners and cargo ships between the US mainland and Hawaii, owned the four leading hotels on Waikiki Beach. They included the famed Royal Hawaiian, Surfrider, Moana, and Princess Ka'iulani, and none were over four stories in height. The 1959 visitor count to Hawaii was 250,000. The company was so discouraged by poor occupancy rates and the limited prospects for expanded tourism, even with advent of the airplane, they sold all four properties for US$ 17.65 million (Hibbard & Franzen, 1986). The number of visitors doubled within the next 5 years.

The institutionalization of tourism began in this era, and with it culture brokering was nationalized. Investment loans from the World Bank and International Monetary Fund to newly independent nations were granted on the premise that tourism was a potential source of employment and foreign exchange. The new postwar air carriers and their affiliate hotels now dealt with *governments* for traffic rights, construction of airports, and land for new hotels and other facilities. Governments became the cultural mediators—Do we want tourism? Will it benefit our country? Most nations took advantage of the loans and exercised their legal right to offer attractive inducements, including tax credits, and free or greatly reduced prices for land to attract airlines and hotel chains to serve their country.

Excitement and discussion on the future of tourism began to resonate and ripple. The American Anthropological Association symposium on tourism, which became the genesis for the first edition of *Hosts and Guests: The Anthropology of Tourism* (Smith, 1977), was held in 1974. That same year, the East-West Center in Honolulu sponsored a workshop to assess the impact of this (then) new business. The opening sentence to the resulting publication (Finney & Watson, 1975) asks, "Why do so many Pacific Island *governments* [emphasis ours] choose tourism as a major industry for economic development of their countries? (p. 1). Kloke (1975) opens his essay with "A number of South Pacific island *countries and territories* [emphasis ours] have made substantial commitments to the development of a new industry: international tourism" (p. 3). Robineau (1975) details the development of tourism to Tahiti by explaining that "until 1959, Tahiti could not be reached by plane except from Fiji over the 'coral route' ... by seaplane via Apia in Western Samoa and Aitutaki in the Cook islands.""Since 1961, the opening of the Tahiti-Faaa international airport has made it possible for the big air lines to serve the territory," followed by the construction of the Club Méditerranée, and major hotels. He continues, "it was around 1965 that, in order to coordirate the Territory's tourist policy, a *Tourist Trade Development Office* [original emphasis] was erected. From that time on, a tourist policy was progressively elaborated and tourism was promoted to the rank of great pillars on which the Territory's economy was to repose"(pp. 61-75). The same era and publication carries the now-classic essay by-Fijian John Samy (1975), "Crumbs from the Table? The Workers' Share in Tourism, in which he alleges that the development of "luxurious, multi-million dollar resort hotels creates not only resentment but also confirms prejudices" (pp. 111-124). Hiller (1975, pp. 238-246) pointed out that by 1972 the Caribbean was already the foremost region of the world depending for its development on the benefits of tourism. To illustrate his point, and the not-so-benign influence of government, he cites from a 1972 issue of *Travel Trade* (a North American travel industry journal) that the success of their industry depends on how the Caribbean Hotel Association "can persuade government it is in the overall interests of the islands' economy to grant exemptions and other assistance to the economy."

Government everywhere silently and effectively assumed control of tourism and became the national culture brokers, deciding when, how, and with whom they would interact in its development. Governments can do so, because only they have the legal right to control entry through their borders, to admit some individuals by grant of a visa and restrict others. Strongly Islamic nations still prohibit admittance to anyone whose passport contains an Israeli visa, irrespective of the traveler's religious affiliation. Saudi Arabia prohibited all tourists until 1998, and both China and Russia denied visitor visas to Westerners for decades after World War II.

Through their hirelings who generated policies and programmes, governments initiated selective choices concerning the nature of their tourism in relation to their resources. As an example, the Seychelles islands are noted for their beautiful beaches and warm seas. In the late 1970s a German tour operator talked convincingly to government officials of the desirability of charter tourism—one plane a week would fill the hotel, ideal for noise abatement and limiting bus travel over their narrow roads. Several years later the government realized the extent of the financial leakage, as airline and hotel operations benefited the same company with virtually all the revenue. Guests were on full pension, just laid on the beach in the sun, and spent very little money in the community. The government subsequently cancelled the charter agreement, and the hotel was sold to a local company. The Tourist Board changed their promotion to upscale tourism using expensive small boutique "guest houses" and gourmet restaurants. The result was fewer visitors, but more revenue was more equitably distributed through the island (personal communication, Seychelles Tourist Board).

With control of tourism vested in government, including the mediating role of culture broker, reverberations began to echo. Kent (1975), discussing tourism in Hawaii as a "new kind of sugar" (a parody on their premier agricultural export) reports from the *Honolulu Advertiser,"* One morning recently, one Hawaiian resident remarked to another that the one-millionth tourist of the year would arrive in Honolulu by air that afternoon.'Let's go out to the airport with a shotgun'was the response"(p. 169).Another comment from the same source describes a 1970 flyer distributed at the Honolulu airport, to discourage tourists, "Please, don't visit Hawaii until we can save what's left." But the official (government) 1974 Hawaii Visitor Bureau slogan read, "We've come a long way and it's important to keep the momentum goingg."

After Mass Tourism

The success of mass tourism, registered in arrivals and receipts, is illustrated best in the 1998 emergence of tourism as the leading source of foreign exports (Figure 13.2). The international emphasis of long-haul air carriers and multinational hotels chains further extended government authority at all levels. Competing airlines bid for traffic rights. Hotels sought land for convention centers, and subsequently cruise lines needed dock space, and bargained for cruise terminals that would increase local handicraft sales. Governments in turn allocated funds to NGOs to develop national images that would distinguish their culture and scenery. Culture brokering moved beyond mediating the hospitality needs of hosts and guests to selectively creating cultural icons (stereotypes) of national (or regional) destinations that would attract visitors.

The dynamics of this tourism growth eventually backfired, first in environmental degradation, either actual or potential, and second, as individuals and culture groups realized their voice of self-determination was fading, if not already lost. Numerous conferences revealed a heightened awareness of the necessity of landscape preservation. In addition, the Brundtland Report echoed across the world, mandating local input and advocating bottom-up administration. These were powerful wake-up calls, to break a spiral of unabated and undirected growth. From these movements a new international culture broker emerged, in the World Tourism Organization (WTO) and its affiliates: World Travel and Tourism Council (WTTC), Earth Council (EC), Green Globe, and LA21. Each entity has a mission statement, but in broad perspective WTO works toward mediating the sometimes flagrant competitiveness filled with disregard for everything except revenue. WTO addresses the needs of all member

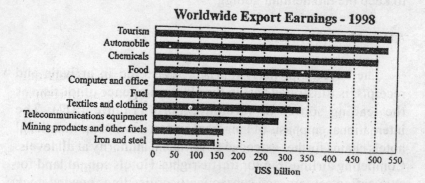

Figure   Worldwide export earnings: 1998. (Source: Tourism Highlights, 2000. WTO, reprinted with permission.)

countries to participate in tourism. Their brokering for the supply side is to raise the standards of service through tourism training and education (their Themis programme). They have also mediated cultural themes suitable for regional development, including Mundo Maya, the Silk Road, and the Slave Route. The centrality of these historic populations and their movements opens a vast range of individual ethnic symbols that can be effectively used for promotion. These new destinations will sustain increased employment in global areas where comparatively few tourists have traveled to date. As culture broker, WTO is broadening the geographic and cultural base of the supply side of tourism. Further, by training marginal workers for more skilled employment as hosts in tourism, those individuals are expected to ultimately enjoy a greater measure of discretionary income and leisure time. These employees, in turn, will become guests themselves, either at home or abroad, and support increased demand.

On the demand side, WTO is facilitating free movement for tourists (without visas), seeking to minimize terrorism and crime, and supporting expanded tourism among specific groups including the aged, handicapped, and youths.

Museums

Museums are increasing in importance as globalization appears to induce cultural homogenization. These heritage storehouses offer unique educational opportunities to the public, to school children, and especially to foreign tourists, all of whom are often drawn to them for visual validation of natural history and ethnography. The curators are culture brokers with multiple obligations: to provide historic time lines, to develop sequent occupancy, and to display natural resources as information for residents and tourists. In addition, to keep the museum active and encourage repeat visitations, curators are expected to mount special exhibits of narrower perspective but of timely importance.

Richard Kurin, Director of the Smithsonian (US National Museum) Center for Folklife Studies and Cultural Studies in *Reflections of a Culture Broker* (1997) introduces a theme of supply-side provider or "host culture" and demand-side guests, in relation to museum operations. Many museums are dependent on state-supported funding and must rely on attendance (in essence, popularity) as part of their evaluation, to secure the budget needs for the following year. Kurin (1997) observes that

> culture brokers study, understand and represent someone's culture (even sometimes their own) to non-specialized others through various means and media. 'Brokering' also captures the ideas that these representations are to some degree negotiated, dialogical, and driven by a variety of interests on behalf of the involved parties, (p. 19)

As Kurin documents, the development of displays can have controversial undercurrents. To prepare a Christmas exhibit in Jerusalem must involve representative input from Palestinians, Israelis, differing faiths, and also atheists. In the face of these contrasting philosophies curators as culture brokers must select from their collections the items to be shown and decide how they shall be displayed. The accompanying text and possible catalogs may provide an arena in which some of differing points of view can be detailed, further illustrating the mediation role of brokering. Special exhibits can be oriented toward age, gender, special interests, and timely topics such as wars and ethnic cleansing. The Anne Frank House in Amsterdam has evolved over a 50-year period with differing emphases and interpretations. As Graburn and Mathers (2000, p. 691) affirm,"cultural interpretation *does* require expert mediation" [emphasis theirs], and "brokerage underscores the customer/ client relationship."

Conclusion

Culture brokering is historically known as early as the 4th century AD, when local guides helped pilgrims find holy sites in Jerusalem (Sumption, 1975). The subsequent expansion of their activity as decision-makers is closely correlated with the growth of tourism and its increased politicalization. Now most culture brokers learn their craft in university courses. Many work in diverse offices, devising plans to heighten the visitor experience in ways that are environmentally sensitive. Others are professionally involved in tourism and guides are now professionally trained and licensed by virtually every host government. The emergent role of the WTO as global culture broker has set a new and higher performance standard for quality instead of kitsch, with emphasis on education at all levels. WTO programmes, which are still new and formative, bod well for the future.

14

Philippine Tourism Development

The commitment to develop tourism is a policy decision fraught with politics but almost always couched in economic and social rhetoric. So it was in 1972, when President Ferdinand Marcos declared martial law in the Philippines and almost simultaneously declared that he was making tourism development a priority sector.

What followed was a transformation of Manila's skyline and the harnessing of this new policy sector to the President's political agenda. Perhaps no nation better exemplifies the use and abuse of tourism for political advantage than the Philippines. Prior to 1972, tourism had been a low-key interest, enjoying slow growth and modest expectations. All that changed after the onset of martial law.

Martial law was ostensibly declared to deal with Communist and Muslim insurgencies and labour and student unrest. The President also saw it as an opportunity to forge what he called a "New Society" of constitutional authoritarianism in which technocrats backed by Marcos would make the hard management and social decisions that the increasingly nationalist Congress was unwilling to pursue. Some critics ungenerously saw in the President's action a desire to postpone his tenure beyond his two-term limit, which would have expired in 1973. Press control, roundup of political opponents, and the dissolution of the Congress assured such criticisms had little exposure.

The President had a delicate problem. The situation had to be serious or else martial law would look like overkill, but the political environment also had to become generally stable quickly or foreign investment might dry up and foreign opposition to the "shattering of democracy" might emerge (Day, 1974). Tourism proved a useful response. It might seem counterintuitive to launch a tourism blitz upon declaring martial law, but President Marcos did just that. The government tourism slogan made martial law seem especially benign: "Where Asia Wears a Smile."

A Cabinet-level department was created to implement the new policy effort. In the next 8 years tourism arrivals quadrupled. No effort was spared to create a veneer of stability and attractiveness that might reflect positively on the Marcos Presidency and the martial law era. With the hindsight of more than 25 years, it is clear that the policy proved ruinous and that succeeding administrations found in the politics of tourism their own opportunities and problems.

This chapter examines the Philippines primarily since 1972 as a case study in tourism development from which one can extrapolate some hard-won lessons that may prove helpful to other leaders and nations engaged in tourism development. Scores of nations are increasingly "banking-on tourism for economic and political gains. It can be a chastening experience unless authorities recognize that this new policy sector is no panacea, is volatile, and is extremely vulnerable to bad news from any quarter.

The Philippines paid dearly for the tourism development President Marcos launched, but it may still reap future benefits. Moreover, the lessons one can learn from the Philippines are not that tourism is bad, unworkable, or a mistaken strategy, but rather that tourism can unravel as fast as it develops and there are ways to assure that "Where Asia Wears a Smile" is more than a bittersweet slogan.

In the first section, six political "lessons" of Philippine tourism are laid out. These are derived from the Marcos era. They do not exhaust the insights one can take away from this period, but they highlight major points relevant to scores of other nations. the second section the Aquino and Ramos tourism policies are examined. The conclusion identifies continuing problems and opportunities for the Philippines in utilizing tourism for national development.

President Corazon Aquino, wife of Marcos' political rival
who was assassinated in 1983, came to power in early 1986
following a discredited election, defections in the Philippine
military, a popular uprising in Manila, and the forced exile of
President Marcos. She governed during a time of great
expectations, democratic resurgence, and political threats from
both the left and the right.

In 1992, former General Fidel Ramos, who had served
President Marcos until his 1986 defection and served Aquino as
Secretary of Defense throughout her Presidency, became the
first President elected under the new Constitution. He won a
just-completed 6-year term with a very slim 24% plurality in a
seven-way contest (Richter, 1993). The very different political
environments of Aquino and Ramos allow one to assess the
usefulness of the "lessons" of the Marcos period and to identify
additional factors and constraints.

The Lessons of the Marcos Era: 1965-1986
Lesson One. Tourism Can Be a Versatile Tool of Political Leaders

President Marcos was not the first autocrat to see the tourist
as a useful visitor. Franco of Spain in the 1930s also used tourism
to soften the nation's fascist image (Pi-Sunyer, 1979). Most
tourists stay in relatively few tourist areas and therefore what
they see and do is controllable. Cleanliness, beautification, and
security, a good exchange rate—these can be assured within
tourist zones. Particularly under martial law, special courts
assured tourists increased protection and criminals more severe
sentences for crimes against visitors. Efforts to keep areas
pristine were rewarded by favorable travellers' reactions that
could be quoted at length in the locally controlled papers. Tourism
could thus generate publicity for domestic consumption as well
as the country's external reputation (Richter, 1980).

Tourists do not seek out political controversy but rather use the media for information about weather, the country's attractions, or news from home. They are typically unaware of what is being censored, what the real social and political conditions are, and the fate of dissident groups (Richter, 1980,1982a).

Despite the fact that tourists generally avoid unpleasant topics, visitors still harbour the illusion that they've seen a destination.This is true even when they have moved in the narrowest of circles, Thus.the happy tourist is quite useful for his or her remarks about a trip because these impressions can generally be manipulated to reflect well on even the worst government.

Tourism proved politically useful in other ways as well. The typical development effort requires—as it did in the Philippines— the creation of a new infrastructure.The government can use the granting of loans and licenses as a marvelous opportunity for patronage. Under Marcos, government plans for phased development of tourism were shelved in favour of crash development that built in anticipation of influential mega-conventions. More than 12 five-star hotels were constructed in Manila in 1974-1976, though planners confidentially acknowledged it would be more than a decade before such capacity was needed.

The Philippines was not the first nation nor the last to use a prospective conference, fair, or mega-event as an excuse to bypass regulations and favour supporters, but the Philippines today stands as perhaps the saddest cautionary tale because of the lengths to which government institutions were raided to reward the President and his allies (Richter, 1989).

The facade of modernity did attract foreign aid and investment despite the fact that government insurance money was being used to build more luxury hotel rooms than public housing. While planners were horrified at the distortion of scarce resources,from the standpoint of the political elite, the crash development showcased the leadership and the ability of the government to transform the appearance of the key cities in ways readily apparent to outside investors, lending institutions, and loyal regime supporters.

Tourism also was a way to control real or imaginary opponents. A selective use of privatization policies by the President was justified in economic terms but primarily served the political advantage of the President. The crash hotel building and the changing fortunes of Philippine Airlines are just two examples of how the President proceeded (Richter, 1982a).

Lesson Two. Rhetoric Aside, Regime Politics Dominate Economic Policy

The Marcos government's primary objective was to turn around and stimulate Philippine tourism so that it would help legitimize the administration at home and abroad. Several key decisions illustrated the domination of political over economic considerations. First, the government launched the Balikbayan and the Reunion for Peace Programmes. Both provided subsidized travel and preferential tourism benefits to Philippine visitors.

The Balikbayan Programme was designed for those of Filipino ancestry and their relatives. The idea was to bring back those who had left the Philippines for a fresh look at the country under martial law. What was lost in money—most returning Filipinos stayed with relatives and did little touring—was more than made up in the use of statistics showing Filipinos flocking to the homeland. The Secretary of Tourism actually went so far as to declare martial law a tourist attraction (Richter, 1982b).

The Reunion for Peace programme adopted a concept used by another formerly authoritarian government, the Republic of Korea. It subsidized the travel of former service personnel who had fought in the Philippines during World War II. Both groups could be assured to find the Philippines looking much better than they had remembered. Both groups had credibility in commenting upon the Philippine scene. Though most tourism based on nostalgia has "to sell the past to the future" (Dann, 1994, p. 65), in this case the sales job was to sell the present to representatives of the past.

Other decisions shaped the character of Philippine tourism in less benign ways. To boost tourist arrivals quickly, the Philippines unleashed a media blitz that promised "a tanned peach on every beach," that used suggestive advertising and the waiving of the curfew to facilitate a proliferation of sex tours to the islands, and that resulted in the development of pedophilia tours from several Western countries.The latter also stimulated the growth in child pornography videos.

To boost tourist investment from within the nation, the administration gave supporters up to 100% loans for hotel investment. When the banks balked at such loans, the government agreed to guarantee them. To garner foreign investments the government made still more enormous economic concessions.

This is a temptation most governments face in a competitive environment like tourism development; but insecure governments and poor nations are notoriously poor bargainers. The Philippines under President Marcos was both. To attract outside capital, investors were given great latitude, small equity requirements, tax holidays,guarantees of labour peace, waived or lax import restrictions.The political needs of the regime led to lopsided negotiations that brought few economic rewards.

Still, tourist arrivals soared. Measured only in arrivals, bed nights, and gross rather than net foreign exchange, tourism was a high-profile success—albeit not enough to fill up the new hotels. A succession of mega-events beginning with the 1976 IMF-World Bank meeting lured convention delegates with superb convention facilities and rock bottom rates (Richter, 1980).

Lesson Three. Luxury Tourism Often "Costs" Too Much

Under President and Imelda Marcos tourism marketing was targeted primarily for the "beautiful people," the sexually promiscuous male business traveller, and the politically useful.

But there are problems with such a narrow focus. Lavish facilities for such clientele are costly to build, disproportionately need scarce foreign exchange for development and ongoing operations, exacerbate the "demonstration effect" on the population, lose value more quickly than modest facilities, and tend to use more capital than labour-intensive counterparts. As such they are a particular drag on developing nations.

The more affluent the tourism target, the more foreign exchange is lost in leakage for imports for the industry. Local products are seldom emphasized. Rather, the emphasis is on food, transport, entertainment, and facilities familiar to the guests. Once the regulations are waived for tourism imports there are no incentives for not importing items. For many Marcos cronies imports were lucrative not only for their tourism establishments but also as a way to obtain and then resell unneeded imports. Because there was no problem but rather an opportunity for the Marcos family and allies, the financial costs to the public were ignored.

The more affluent, "jet set" tourists the Marcos regime favoured also reinforced the "demonstration effect"—the economic and social gap between hosts and guests. All this was happening in the context of worsening poverty for the average Filipino.Tourism was beginning to be controversial.

The more luxurious the tourism development, typically the less labour intensive it becomes, the shorter the time frame for maximizing high revenue returns, and the less flexibility tourism infrastructure has for alternative uses. It may seem strange that luxury tourism—particularly the large-scale five-star liotel—actually employs fewer people per guest than smaller establishments, but most studies bear this out. From self-service elevators to automated cleaning, food processing, and recreational services, luxury facilities need fewer personnel. Such establishments may also seek nonindigenous management in the entertainment and transportation sectors, with local people serving in menial jobs.

Luxury tourism, especially resort tourism, tends to follow a cycle of discovery, seasonal occupancy, and decline as newer resorts and destinations appear. Middle-class and less affluent charter tourism then comes in and gradually numbers are sustained only by massive cost-cutting. The very ostentatiousness, remoteness, and imports to sustain such establishments make it very difficult to switch to nontourism uses.

Lesson Four. Dependence on International Tourists is Risky

Reliance on a few fickle international markets is dangerous. A nation's tourism industry needs a domestic market as well. The Philippines, in part because of the political interests of the Marcos regime, built its tourism during those years around the United States and Japan, the major aid-giving and corporate investors. The Philippine government was quite outspoken in stating it wanted influential visitors, not students, campers, or budget travellers. US tourists consisted overwhelmingly of Balikbayans now residing in the US and of US service personnel from the major bases then at Clark and Subic Bay.

Eighty-five percent of Japanese tourists were male and became associated with the public with the infamous sex tours. The Japanese were not necessarily more involved than other tourists in prostitution, but the language barrier and a propensity for organizing collective outings made their activities more obvious to the public, many of whom still remembered a brutal Japanese occupation during World War II (Benigno, 1993; Richter, 1994).

The Japanese government is unusually vigilant about the welfare of its citizens abroad and Japanese travellers are equally attentive to their government. In any event, Japanese tourism can turn on or turn off with alarming speed. A cholera scare or security issues can empty tourist establishments.

When international tourists for one reason or another did not come, there was no domestic tourism base to take up the slack. Precisely because the administration had made luxury tourism such a high-profile industry and had invested so much in it, the decline in tourists caused not only economic but political problems for the regime.

The government's reactions made matters worse. In desperation, the government became indiscriminate about the type of tourism that came. Certain towns became infamous for permitting child pornography and sex with international travellers. Then the government sought to keep Filipinos in the Philippines by levying heavy departure taxes. These met stiff resistance, in part because they were selectively applied. Both the public and the outbound tourist industry were furious.

Outbound Filipinos could not save the Philippine hotel industry even if they had been so inclined. The problem was overcapacity even if the international market had stabilized and grown slightly. The hotels were always on the verge of bankruptcy unless the government snagged a major convention. Because there were so many in financial danger, it was rather like the savings and loan scandal in the US in the mid-1980s. The hotels couldn't go under without dragging the economy down with it. As in the US scandal, the government took over much of the property and bailed out the rest. The political elite were not hurt. The Philippine economy and the government pension system were.

There were only feeble attempts to organize and promote domestic and student tourism and these were done largely for their public relations value. Even efforts such as Nayong Filipino, a cultural theme park, that highlights the religious and ethnic diversity of the Philippines was built next to the Manila international airport, making it clear just whom it was built to entertain and educate.

In fairness to the government, promoting domestic tourism is not easy in a developing nation short of forbidding nationals to travel abroad or strictly limiting such trips, as Korea and

Taiwan did for years. Complicating domestic tourism in the Philippines are the logistics of traveling in a nation that is an archipelago frequently necessitating boat or air travel. Also, there is no tradition of religious pilgrimage except among the Muslim minority and that is directed toward taking the *Haj* to Mecca!

The importance of domestic tourism in underdeveloped countries has been the subject of some debate. No one questions its desirability but rather the likelihood of it being successful (Archer, 1978; Wylie, 1993). Unless one is dealing with a nation like the US that has over 95% domestic tourism or a nation like India whose enormous size includes an upper class of over 40 million people and a tradition of religious pilgrimage, the domestic market is not readily substitutable in attractions and accommodations for the international one (Richter, 1989).

This is particularly true in the Philippines, where the problem is exacerbated by the way the industry was organized around affluent travellers, conventions, the military bases, and far-flung resorts. Prior to martial law some modest government-owned hotel and hostels were built in nonurban settings. They were successful with foreign and domestic travellers until political insurgencies since the late 1970s made their operation problematical.

Lesson Five: Tourism "Success" is Not Necessarily Evidence of a Wise Development Strategy

Resources directed to tourism development must always be weighed against alternative uses of those monies, even when tourism itself seems to be profitable. Assessing the opportunity costs associated with one type of developmer   ategy over another was not done in the Philippines. This was not because it couldn't be done. It could. The Philippines has sophisticated planners and economists. It wasn't done because the administration wanted to develop international tourism and it wanted an economic rationale for doing so.

The Philippine tourism industry was never a genuine success story. It was a facade of development; but it fooled many, which was after all the point as far as the government was concerned. The Secretary of Tourism, Jose Aspiras, was selected to head the World Tourism Organization for a time, so impressed was the travel industry with the Philippine "tourism miracle" (Richter, 1989). Even as late as 1993, there were some ready to give Aspiras a "lifetime achievement" award. The howls of protest in the now free press persuaded then-Congressman Aspiras to decline the award ("Aspiras Alibi," 1993; Benigno, 1993, p.9).

Precisely because tourism is so manipulable, it is attractive as a measure of a nation's desirability. What tourism departments calculate—bed nights, length of stay, foreign exchange, convention use—are easily quantifiable and, as noted before, can be inflated with aggressive marketing, questionable promotions, and/or concessionary rates.

However, the industry's "success" also needs to be measured in terms of its impact on AIDs rates, prostitution, unwanted children, truancy, crime, and the exploitation of children for child labour, sex, and pornography. Yet, there is no mechanism or incentive in tourism departments anywhere in the world to monitor such developments. In many countries no government department tracks these issues. It is left to small, impoverished interest groups, churches, and human rights organizations to call attention to such problems (Con'curs, 1983-1995). Frequently, as under martial law in the Philippines, they cannot operate without harassment.

It was only when the negative impacts hurt the tourism industry, as in the case of AIDS or crime, that belated attention was paid. Even when governments have acted, typically their concern has been for the tourists' safety and health rather than the powerless child or the discredited prostitute.

Some will argue that this account is too harsh, that tourism can do much that is positive, by showcasing the arts and beauty of a country, providing a market for the performing arts and crafts, and generally enhancing opportunities for employment and the protection of otherwise economically nonviable places of historic or scenic value (Swain, 1993).This is, of course, true, but the characteristic measures of tourism "health" are too crude to assess this very well.

Still, politically it seems worthwhile that tourism foster such creative and artistic activities even in the absence of clear economic data as to its value. Such performances, crafts, and historical conservation become important if they are a means to sustain ways of life and skills central to the cultural identity of particular groups. This is especially important if, as with most minorities, they lack political influence except in terms of their collective identity and the value put on it by others.

Tourism has given tribal and Muslim groups in the Philippines more visibility than would probably have been possible without the industry. Indonesia is an even better example.An authoritarian Muslim government has been much more willing to exempt the Hindu island of Bali from its Islamization initiatives given its ability to exchange culture for cash through tourism. (It may also help that many Muslim communities have profound misgivings about the cultural impact of tourism!)

There are costs as well as opportunities to such tourism for all the groups involved.The culture and crafts will also be shaped by such exposure.The initrusiveness of strangers, bastardization of rituals, "airport art," and tacky souvenirs are endemic to mass tourism (Greenwood, 1989; Richter, 1989). Still, modernization, even without tourism, has had much the same impact. Further, one can be overly sentimental and romantic about other peoples' traditional lifestyles, while ignoring their desire to raise their standard of living (Harrison, 1993, pp. 19-34).

Lesson Six. Government Effectiveness Determines Tourism Viability

Effectiveness or what Samuel Huntington (1968) calls "political capacity" is not the same as whether government is "good" or "bad," democratic or authoritarian. It has to do with whether the government has the adaptability, resilience, cohesion, and skill to ensure order and guarantee basic services. In most developing nations such power does not penetrate the entire nation and may in some cases scarcely extend beyond the capital.

Stable and safe environments are important in ways the Philippine political elite tried to ignore (Richter, 1982a, 1989, 1993). In the Philippines, as in so many nations, tourism is promoted to provide the political and economic capital the government needs for development. Ironically, the industry requires a political capacity in place for law, security, and public interest legislation that is often sorely lacking. Studies from the Philippines and Thailand illustrate (Richter, 1989; R. Smith, 1992; v.. Smith, 1992a) that too often sound plans are not implemented by government either because the resources or the necessary political will are absent to enforce meaningful regulations and critical standards.

Tourism not only needs political stability, it is more vuilnerable to any form of insecurity than most policy areas. This is because it is built around the premise of pleasure. Even so-called adventure tourism is based on controlled excitement. The fragility of tourism has been demonstrated repeatedly over the last 15 years (Richter 1982a, 1989, 1993, 1997; Richter & Waugh, 1991). Tourism is a discretionary activity that can be pursued in scores of locales. That makes the industry both competitive and vulnerable.

Disaster, natural and man-made, can crush tourism. Disease, earthquakes, and typhoons ideally require competent emergency management skills, enforcement of sound health and safety codes, and a thorough risk assessment prior to tourism development and marketing.

A more common problem, however, relates to government expectations that tourism success will make the political system healthier and more secure. This almost never happens. Tourism, even well-developed tourism, is almost always destabilizing to some degree (Nunez, 1977). Hasty, ill-conceived development that accentuates the lifestyles of the elite and the foreign in contrast to the average people is a recipe for hostility.

Under President Marcos not only was there crash hotel development with few safeguards for the government financing involved, foreign aid also was diverted to build the properties that would be "owned" with little equity by those close to the regime. Few Filipinos could afford the grandiose hotels; those employed by the hotels were at the bottom of the employment ladder in most cases. Other government budgets at both the national and local level were raided to support the tourism effort. Prostitution soared (Richter, 1981).

All this tourism activity was taking place without public debate, in a country under martial law, at a time of enormous human rights abuses.Tourism became the target of the opposition.The "Light a Fire" movement torched several five-star hotels. The American Society of Travel Agents (ASTA) Conference was bombed, making a mockery of the speech President Marcos had just given the delegates on how rumors of unrest were media hyperbole! (Richter, 1989). In the insurgent South, Japanese tourists were kidnapped. And there was no backlash to the violence because few Filipinos had a stake in the industry, certainly none more than Marcos. Further, because most of those affected were primarily foreign, it was impossible to censor and control reports about what had happened.Tourism plummeted.

While attacks on tourists are rare, an industry that has thoughtlessly ignored the political and economic environment can be quickly undone. The Philippines also was an example of a more common political problem: general unrest and sporadic rebellion, even far from the tourist centers, may create an image that repels tourists. After the assassination of Marcos' rival, Benigno Aquino in 1983, capital flight, immigration to the US, and a falling GNP discouraged both business travel and discretionary visits.

Can these problems be avoided? Not entirely. However, tourism's contribution to the overall situation can be minimized.

It is common for tourism planners to do attraction inventories in attempting to determine their tourism plans and priorities.As has been argued elsewhere (Richter, 1994), it is probably more important to do a political risk audit. Such an audit would attempt to assess political factors to be considered that may affect the pace, scale, and type of tourism that is desirable. For example, even quiet recognition of insurgencies could encourage planning and marketing that avoids such areas. In many parts of the Philippines tourism infrastructure is inaccessible because of Muslim separatist violence or other guerrilla activities. (Martin, 1994, pp. 36-37).

Since labour peace is critical to the industry, encouragement of indigenous hires, training, small-scale labour-intensive establishments, and progressive labour-management relations are important for securing popular protourism attitudes. Similarly, a slower pace of development and more modest facilities could have been less disturbing, provided more opportunities for adjustment and corrections, and proved less costly in both economic and psychological terms.

Even with a deteriorating situation, the tourism infrastructure would have been more capable of alternative uses for offices and apartments if it had not been built on such a luxurious scale and often in such remote areas. Ironically, in a country like the Philippines, even under a repressive regime, tourism development could have used resources better, assured more secure short-term success, and avoided tourism becoming the source of controversy it eventually became. Neither Marcos nor the Philippines benefited from the lavish excesses and the country is still coping with the tourism-related problems spawned in the Marcos era (Hall, 1992b; Richter, 1987a, 1987b, 1989,1993).

Learning the Lessons. Picking up the Pieces: Tourism Policy in the Aquino and Ramos Administrations

Tourism was not President Corazon Aquino's only (nor even major) problem when she came to power in February, 1986.

President Marcos had stolen an election so blatantly that neither his own military, the public, nor the international community was willing to look the other way. His ouster was street theater at its finest. When he was finally whisked away to Hawaiian exile by the US military, Aquino took over a government whose very institutions had been disbanded or co-opted. Her political tasks were the restoration of democracy, the development of a new constitution, and the restoration of basic services (Richter, 1987b).

To do that, she had to simultaneously capitalize on any revenue-producing sector that could ease unemployment and garner precious foreign exchange.Tourism was a logical priority. Moreover, the government had become the largest owner of hotels in the country.As the five-star hotels went bankrupt in the 1980s, it was the government that was left holding the properties because the legal owners were the Marcos family or cronies without substantial equity in the properties. The hotels and resorts had to be made profitable either through the restoration of tourism and/or their sale to private bidders confident that the government could rejuvenate tourism.

There is evidence that the Aquino administration learned well the lessons of the Marcos era. But it wasn't easy to undo what should have been prevented in the first place. Three examples clearly demonstrate how difficult it is to correct problems of inept, corrupt, or socially flawed tourism.

First, the Aquino government tried to garner domestic and international confidence by adhering to a rule of law in the disposal of Marcos properties. An Assets Privatization Trust was established in 1986 that, along with other efforts, sought to sell nonperforming assets, which were mostly tourism properties or assets of the former President.Yet clear title to the properties was often difficult to obtain. In the meantime, 17 of the Marcos homes became tourist attractions open to the public. To encourage public trust,Aquino stipulated that funds collected would be used to fund the languishing agrarian reform programme. Opportunities for joint ventures between the government and the private sector also made it less risky for investors to participate (Garcia, 1990, 1991).

Second, the tourism secretary struggled to get control over a bureaucracy bloated by patronage appointments from the Marcos era. In 1987, the number of employees was reduced from over 1300 to 700. Separation pay was generous and all procedures followed. Nonetheless, those fired filed a class action for reinstatement and won. In 1991, they were ordered back on the payroll with back pay! His successor, Secretary of Tourism Nazalina Lim, inherited a department with severe morale as well as financial problems (personal interview with Nazalina Lim, 1992).

Third, the government sought vigorously to reorient the marketing of the Philippines to put the emphasis on culture and scenic attractions rather than sex tours and pornography. Desleazing was not an easy or particularly successful effort, but by 1986 there was an added urgency to the task: the threat of AIDS.

Tourist-generating governments were warned that pedophilia tours sent from their countries were not welcome. Individuals would be prosecuted in Philippine courts. Philippine communities, like Pagsanjan Falls, that had acquiesced to pedophilia activities were removed from government tourism brochures and maps (personal interview with Nazalina lim, 1992). ECPAT, a child advocacy organization, remained critical of the government's approach, ehich they said singled out a few poor people for economic penalties, when it was poverty that had encouraged participation.The real offenders were seldom punished (personal interview with ECPAT, 1992).

Tourist promotions abroad and marketing efforts by the government junked suggestive posters and an emphasis on the beauty of Filipinas for more wholesome advertising. In conjunction with that, the government tried to discourage foreign men from acquiring mail-order brides or visiting the Philippines only to bring home a Filipina (Kruhse-MountBurton, 1990).

The Mayor of Manila was zealous in his crackdown on unsavory tourist belt establishments that encouraged prostitution, but there is evidence that the problem has moved elsewhere in the metropolitan area and is flourishing in Cebu (personal interview with Nazalina Lim and personal observation, 1992). Many upscale hotels continue to charge a "lady guest fee," though blatant advertising of sex tours in Japan and elsewhere has declined.

The Aquino administration applied Lesson One from the start. It demonstrated how tourism can serve to legitimize the new government even as it discredits the old one. Aquino needed tourism for many of the reasons Marcos did: to influence domestic and international political elite.

In her case, the agenda was to highlight the excesses of the Marcos years and contrast them with her own lifestyle and plans for the future. She hoped to project democratic values and economic good sense deserving of investor confidence and increased foreign aid. That was critical, for many influential leaders and investors had been badly burned by the Marcos debacle.

To do that, she took five steps. First, she refused to live in the bulletproof Malacanang Palace, but instead turned it into a museum of the Marcos excesses. There visitors could see Imelda's 1000 pairs of size 9 shoes, the 17 mink coats, the vault filled with empty jewelry boxes, and all the other luxuries somehow accrued on the President's $10,000 salary (personal tour, 1987). For 6 years, the Palace both earned money and demystified the Marcos family while providing a contrast to the more spartan lifestyle of Aquino.

Second, by putting the other 17 Marcos palaces on display she could again accentuate the corruption of her predecessor and earn some money until she could unload them. Third, Aquino and the story of her rise to power became a tourist attraction. The Department of Tourism developed a "Freedom Tour" that included stops at places in the Manila area that figured prominently in the overthrow of Marcos and in Aquino's personal history.

The DOT began a major promotional campaign aimed at criticizing the old regime while highlighting the new one. "Come to the New Philippines" demonstrated Aquino's adeptness in shaping the political uses of tourism to her own agenda, which fortunately for the Philippine people no longer included raids on the treasury or a personal financial link (Richter, 1987a).

Fourth, the government also attempted to diffuse economic opportunities in tourism and to enhance low-cost domestic and international tourism with a Home-Stay programme. Unfortunately, the government could not provide enough training to help the fledgling entrepreneurs so the program remained small (personal interview with Nazalina Lim interview, 1987). Efforts were focused on social tourism and historical preservation, particularly at Corregidor and within the walls of Old Manila (Garrucho, 1989, p. 194).

The government was generally successful in assuring that tourism revenues subsidized other efforts like agrarian reform rather than negotiating bad deals for the sake of prestigious foreign investment. Import restrictions were tightened somewhat and duty-free stores were expanded to encourage more purchases within the country.

At first these initiatives seemed to work. Tourism improved after years of stagnation as the political system stabilized and the economy grew. Unfortunately, tourism in democratic regimes proved no more immune than in authoritarian ones to political unrest. Seven coup attempts during her 6-year term crippled Aquino's ability to do much more than hang on (Richter, 1990, p. 534; Richter, 1997).

While Aquino's government could not fully undo the errors of the Marcos period, it made an important start in insisting tourism pay its own way, that economic gains not be sacrificed to political expediency, and that national identity be tied to the culture not the exploitation of its women and children. She also made certain that tourism serve to legitimate her power and the extraconstitutional way it was acquired.

Ramos had just the opposite problem from Aquino. She took power in a euphoric environment with the press treating her almost as a saint. She could never fulfill the hopes of her followers and she soon would become a target for would-be usurpers. The Ramos administration ironically benefited from the low expectations held for it. Ramos was an earnest and colorless leader, elected in a seven-way presidential contest. He was not a "new" face, but rather was associated with both the Marcos and Aquino governments. Nevertheless, he presided over some major economic and political progress.

Ramos built on the tourism foundation laid by Aquino. He continued a Tourism Master Plan developed in 1991, which was designed to be a blueprint for tourism until 2010. (Chon & Oppermann, 1996, p. 35). He continued and expanded privatization efforts, sought to link tourism development with support for rural areas, and linked tourism to his ambitious "Philippine 2000" programme.

The latter was designed to make the Philippines a Newly Industrialized Country (NIC) by the millennium. Within the programme 19 key areas were identified as priorities because of the positive spillover effect they would have on the entire economy. Tourism was one of those so identified. Several of the infrastructure and transportation components benefited tourism, but more importantly they were integrated into the overall development of the nation.

There was also an attempt made to diffuse tourism development throughout the islands by promoting clusters of attractions in several areas. That had been done and undone during the Marcos years, but this time it was coupled with efforts to develop Cebu's international airport and other regional airports as a means of bypassing the polluted and crowded capital. So far, it has not worked. Over 92% of all international tourists continue to visit Manila, though arrivals to Cebu are encouraging (Gaborni, 1997a).

The President was also not able to diminish the problems associated with sex tourism. The sex industry once erroneously linked primarily to the US bases was always more closely tied to tourism. Currently, the upsurge in tourism has been matched with a dramatic rise in prostitution. In fact, as AIDS spread into Asia, the problem of child prostitution became much more serious. Increasingly younger and younger prostitutes are sought so that tourists feel less vulnerable to AIDS. In reality, it does not protect them and it certainly does not protect the children (Hall, 1992b;"Metro Manila Declared Hot Spot for HIV" 1994). By 1995, the United Nations Children's Fund estimated that there were over 100,000 child prostitutes in the Philippines, or 10% of the world total.

The Philippine government has encouraged tourist-generating nations to crack down on child abusers and has sent one high-profile sex tour boss to jail (Boseley, 1996, p. 7).The Internet and other global communications have facilitated the sex tour industry and the exploitation of children, making international efforts imperative. ECPAT and other international groups have kept up the pressure and publicity on the Philippine problem, but much more needs to be done.

What President Ramos did succeed in doing was to provide the political stability that allows tourism as well as other sectors to flourish. That is perhaps the most important lesson to be learned from his predecessors and surely the most difficult to assure. Under his tenure, international tourism arrivals reached 2.2 million (Gaborni, 1997a;WTO, 1997a).

Conclusion

Philippine tourism continues to struggle with the legacy of the Marcos era, but two successor governments have made clear to the public the high price of those policies. Lessons drawn from these policies h.'.ve been important for shaping subsequent plans. Aquino particularly recognized the political usefulness of tourism (Lesson One) to legitimize her administration and discredit Marcos.

Both Aquino and Ramos, while supporting tourism rhetorically and financially, have sought to guarantee that tourism programmes subsidize general development rather than vice versa (LessonTwo).They did this by decreasing government ownership of Philippine Airlines and hotel properties through privatization where possible. Ramos has also been adamant that tourism be strategically integrated into other public investments in infrastructure that benefit citizens as well as tourists.

Both leaders have deemphasized luxury tourism in favour of tourism programmes targeted at a broader clientele. However, unloading the luxury hotels of the Marcos era continues to be a slow, costly process. Similarly, though Aquino recognized the desirability of a domestic tourism market and the fickleness of international tourism, she inherited an infrastructure geared to foreign markets. She tried to control sex tourism, but undoing a thriving industry proved impossible. She was also dependent on the US and Japan, both countries central to tourism generally and prostitution specifically, for aid and assistance in controlling rebel factions.

Ramos, on the other hand, took office as the US bases were being dismantled. In the process, the radical left was losing a powerful symbol for organizing opposition to the government. He has not led on the sex tourism issue, but he has been a tireless advocate for new markets, including those for tourism. Currently, Japan and the US each generate less than 20% of the tourist arrivals—a much healthier balance than before (Kobayashi, 1997).

With less dependence on any one market, it should be possible to control sex tourism without crippling the tourist economy. However, Ramos'tenure (1992-1998) coincided with the enormous growth of the Internet, which has created an advertising outlet for sex tourism that has been increasingly difficult to control (ECPAT, 1997).

Finally, Aquino's policies demonstrated that the reverse of Lesson Five is also true: erratic tourism arrivals are not necessarily evidence of a poor development policy. She took

many positive steps to foster tourism's role in Philippine development, but she did so at a time of great political unrest. Every
coup attempt derailed tourism initiatives for months. She knew
that overall government effectiveness determines tourism's
viability more than mere attractions, but her administration was
trying to restore the economy, rehabilitate a political system,
and garner international credibility even as two guerrilla
movements and numerous military factions challenged her rule.

Ramos had fewer internal challenges and by the end of his
tenure in 1998 his relentless protrade approach was paying
political and economic dividends. However, the sudden financial
crisis in East and Southeast Asia, which began in 1997, threatens
the Philippine goal of Newly Industrialized Country status by
the year 2000. Despite an erosion in the nation's economic
prospects, the Philippines has not fallen as far or as fast as
other nations in the region where speculative investments had
been more prominent. Moreover, tourism to the Philippines
continues despite a decline in intraregional arrivals.

The 1990s represented a new era for the Philippines in that
the US no longer had bases in the Philippines. For the first time
in over 350 years, no foreign troops were on Philippine soil.
Conversion of the bases to nonmilitary use has accelerated. As
the Philippines becomes more attractive for investment, it is
hoped that the efforts of the Aquino and Ramos administrations
to assure that tourism supports the growth of nontourist jobs
will continue. Planned diversification is critical (Mak, 1993).

A new variable in Philippine tourism development is Joseph
Estrada, the newly elected President of the Philippines. He was
Vice-President under President Ramos, but he is from a different
political party and his political moorings and background
are far different from those of recent presidents. For example,
he lacks a college education and is best known as a movie actor.
Business elite are dismayed at his populist rhetoric while the
powerful Catholic Church is horrified by his macho, womanizing
image.

So far, Estrada has offered no clues as to the course he will pursue vis-a-vis tourism policy. His crackdown on crime while Vice-President was popular but not terribly successful. Based on his rhetoric, he is likely to be more sympathetic to tourist industry labour groups and to have around him confidantes less enamoured with external investment and more protective of indigenous businesses.

Finally, the Philippines is very much a part of the global effort to "reinvent government "through increased privatization and a major restructuring of the public sector to decentralize power. Both experiments are from outside modern Philippine culture and history, which has emphasized government involvement in the economy and until recently a highly centralized state (P. Kelly, 1997; Kobayashi, 1997). If the nation can develop wise tourism policies at all levels that integrate the industry into the broader needs of the population then the Philippines will provide still more lessons—this time in sustainable development—from which we can learn.

15

Tourism at Lake Balaton, Hungary

Recently, when an image seemed to be present in the glass windows of a new, Clearwater, FL, office building, someone interpreted the image to be an image of Mary, the mother of Christ. Soon thousands of people, often from far away, flocked daily to the location to marvel at what many perceived as a miracle.The visitors had defined the cultural significance of this site. Whether this site continues to develop as a tourist attraction depends on the guesists continuing to value a certain interpretation of the site. Access and growth of thfie site will also depend on the commitment of the hosts to sustain the tourism at the site.

Sustainable tourism depends as much on hosts' and guests'cultural definition of a tourist destination as it does on the desire to protectet the environment. The negotiation over the definition of a tourist destination has an impact on the environment and on the host culture and society.The removal of local people from a newly established "national park" directly affects the environment because park-development may have more impact on the environment than previous human activities. Can tourism be sustainable, that is, can tourism be developed while minimizing changes to both the environment and the local culture and society? The degree to which sustainable development thorough tourism is possible depends on the negotiation among hosts and guests as to which interpretation of the touristic value and meaning of the destination predominates.

Defining Tourist Destinations: Guests Versus Hosts

Sometimes the guests have more control over the up cultural destination of a site. When I travelled in 1995 with some

Hungarian friends to Transylvania in Romania, I found another interesting destination that had been culturally constructed by tourists: Dracula's Castle (Bram Stoker's 1897 fictional mixing of Hungarian folk thems with a 13th century historical figure, Vlad Dracula, a Walachian Prince who had constructed an eerie castle on a desolate mountain in Transylvania, then part of Hungary). Before setting out from Hungary by car I had read a guidebook entry about Vlad's castle. Raised on a steady diet of Bela Lugosi and Boris Karlof horror movies, I insisted we see it during our excursion of this famous region.

Although the castle of Stoker's fictional Dracula was located near the Ukrainian border, it is the restored castle ruins of the historical Vlad in the village of Aref, central Romania, that has become the tourist attraction. As we got closer to Aref, my Hungarian friends kept asking Romanian ethnic Hungarians along the way to find the castle. Apparently, much was lost in the translation of "Dracula" to these local citizens, because they only scratched their heads in befuddlement at the question. Only with repeated reformulations of the question did people finally understand where we wanted to go. We knew we had finally arrived at the place when we saw the castle rising above a small village that was crowded with cars with foreign license plates and rife with handcraft booths. Official Romania is not happy with Vlad's association with Stoker's Dracula and so the interpretation signs in the castle only made favourable references to the historical Vlad, but the local tourist art entrepreneurs had no reservations. It was only here that the Stoker Dracula connection was made. I had finally found satisfaction after the long trip to Aref, because I wanted to believe that I had found and seen "Dracula's castle!" I had contributed to the construction of a tourist site with special meaning for the fictional Count Dracula's fans.

Another instructive case is the *Alarde* ritual of the Spanish town of Fuenterrabia described in a case study of Davyyd Greenwood (1989).The *Alarde* is an ancient, commemorative ritual re-creating the town's victory over besieging French forces in 1638. The color and pageantry of the ritual attracted lots of tourists, so many that in 1969 the municipal government decided that the ritual should be performed twice in the same day to give all the onlookers a chance to see it. This public recognition of the economic importance of the event to the town severely stunned many of the participants. Two years later, Greenwood reports, the *Alarde* ritual was on its last legs, abandoned by the dozens of volunteers who had supported the ritual every year.

By ordaining the *Alarde* a public event to attract outsiders into the town to spend money, the municipal government made it one more of Fuenterrabia's assets in the competitive tourism market. But this decision directly violated the *meaning* of the ritual, definitively destroying its authenticity and power for the people (Greenwood, 1989,p.-179). In this case the hosts who performed the ritual refused to renegotiate with the guests a culturally significant event that had become a tourist attraction. They preferred to abandon it rather than to change its meaning for the benefit of tourism.

Negotiating a Definition of a Tourist Destination

There are some cases where neither the hosts nor the guests have full control over the site's cultural definition. The interaction between hosts and guests is really the process of negotiation. It is in this context of constructing a cultural definition of a tourist destination that I would like to discuss the case of the Lake Balaton resort region in western Hungary. A review of this case shows that host communities who are heavily dependent on the economic component of the definition allow the guests to define the site. The hosts may accept or reject the guests' definition as long as they accept the consequences—that the tourists might not come back. Communities that have a diversified economy will be better able to control the cultural definition of their tourism destination. The host community may have initially defined their locality in specific ways, but once tourists have gained control over the definition of the site, changes to the site are dependent on the guests' reaction—in effect, a negotiation process. If protecting and sustaining the environment becomes a part of the negotiation, the level and mechanisms of environmental protection will be those that maintain or enhance numbers and/ or spending levels of tourists.

Sustaining tourism does not mean protecting the natural environment, because decisions about environmental protection are made in political and economic contexts. As political and economic contexts change, and as the tourists change, what gets sustained may change, too.Sustainable tourism must include three basic elements: first, the cultural and economic significance of the site to the hosts; second, the value of the site to the guests; and third, the level of commitment and cooperation needed to maintain the site at a physical and cultural level acceptable to both hosts and guest. In the end, sustainable tourism depends on what is important to both the hosts and the guests. In the rest of this chapter, I will explain how Lake Balaton provides a clear example of how the cultural constructions and

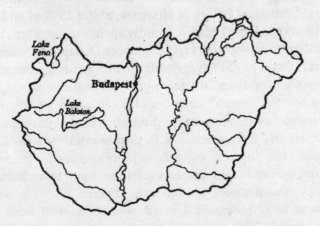

Figure   Map of modern Hungary with Lake Balaton. (Source: Martha Lampland, *The Object of Labor: Commodification in Socialist Hungary*. Chicago: University of Chicago Press, 1995)

negotiations among hosts and guests over time affect the development of a nature-based, recreational tourism destination.The analysis presented here is based on three summers of ethnographic research largely between 1993 and 1995 at Lake Balaton and the surrounding region (Figure 15.1).

Lake Balaton: The Hungarian Sea

Hungary is about the size of the state of Indiana and has a population of 10.2 million.There were at least two tourists for every Hungarian, since over 20.6 million international tourists visited Hungary in 1996, making it the fifth most popular tourist destination in Europe, and eighth in the world (Figure 15.2).

Earnings from tourism account for approximately 25% of total exports. Between 250,000 and 300,000 people are directly employed in tourisn, and another 200,000-300,000 jobs in other sectors are indirectly connected to tourism (Eullul, 1994, p. 55).

Lake Balaton is Central and Western Europe's largest freshwater lake. It is located about 100 kilometers from Budapest and is reached by road and rail along both the hilly northern and flatter lower lying southern shores.After Budapest, it is Hungary's most visited tourist destination. According to the Central Statistical Office of Hungary, about 25% of all foreign tourists stay at Lake Balaton, usually spending more hotel nights there than tourists who visit Budapest (Kozponti Statisztikai Hivata, 1994a, p. 151). Nearly all the tourism is concentrated in a 6-week period from July to August. Its shallow depth, lack of waves, many "beach" areas, and wide array of diversions, restaurants, rooms, houses, and apartments to rent around the lake currently have made it a desirable attraction for Central European families seeking safe swimming sites for their young children during their summer vacations. Each town builds and controls its own *strand,* a small strip of green, grassy area giving access to an abbreviated 2-meter sandy shore in front of the lake's waters. During the high season the *strands* are very crowded with children running around the shore area, roasted

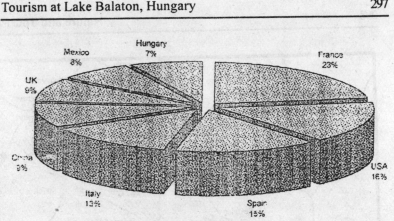

Figure   Top country destinations for international arrivals: 1996. (Source: WTO Tourism Highlights, 1997.)

bodies sizzling in the sun and dozens of snack shops with long lines of men in Speedo bathing suits stretching out in front of them. The principal attractions of the Balaton today are family-oriented, recreational activities connected with water: swimming, sunbathing, sailing, and relaxation.

Most of the guests in the high season are international, usually German speaking, who stay in private homes and apartments. Local officials estimate that only about 20% of all tourists stay in hotels. This makes it difficult to determine the exact number of tourists visiting Balaton, because most private citizens do not report income from their tourism lodging activities. It is estimated by local government biologists that about a million tourists a day visit Lake Balaton during the high season.

Geographically the lake is uniquely shaped. Its 598 square kilometers of surface space is elongate somewhat like a long zucchini cut in half. Except for Tihany (Figure 15.3), a small peninsula jutting into the water on the northeast shore (Figure 15.5), its width varies between 10 and 14 kilometers, while its length is 77 kilometers. The lake is very shallow throughout—averaging about 3 meters—except at Tihany where it is deepest at about 12 meters. The shallowness has distinct advantages and

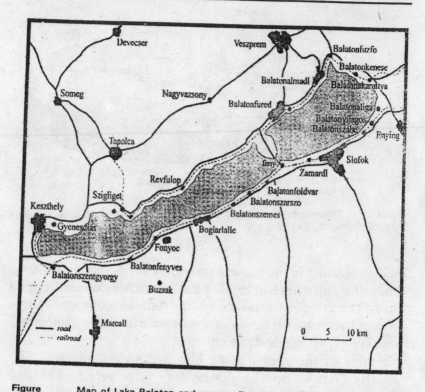

Figure   Map of Lake Balaton and surrounding towns. (Source: T. Sebestyon.
Balaton. Budapest: Corvina,

disadvantages. It warms quickly, from at least 16°C by mid-
May through early October and as high as 25-27°C in mid
summer.There are no waves and the depth changes very
gradually, so parents generally need not worry much here about
the safety of their children when they enter the water. The
disadvantages also stem from its shallow depth. If the water
gets too warm and stagnant, oxygen levels can get so low that
massive fish kills occur. Tourists don't like to see dead fish
floating by when they are swimming. The lake bottom sediment
is so close to the surface that the swimming churns up the muddy
bottom, making the water cloudy. Many tourists think muddy
water is bad for them, but local people regard the lake's mud as
mildly curative.The water warms the low mountains on the north

shore and gives the region a near Mediterranean climate during the summer, making it ideal for vineyards.

Early History

Historically, the hilly northern shore has been noted for its vineyard., wines and fishing, while the flatter, marshier, boggier southern region was known for its grain and stud farms. The Romans introduced vineyards. Roman ships plied Lake Balaton— Lacus Pelso, as it was called on ancient Roman maps. Later, Slavs settled in the area and gave it its modern names.

The invading Magyars, not related to the Huns, arrived from Central Asia around 896 AD, eventually settling the old Slavic village sites or building new ones and constructing churches and monasteries. Alliance with the Austrians brought a baroque renaissance to the region, still reflected in many church buildings and in the religious art that adorns them (Keresztury, 1989, p. 1). One of the best examples of baroque architecture in the area is Festetics Castle, the palatial estate of the Festetics family from the 1700s through the end of World War I (Figure 15.4). They supplied the best racing and stud horses to the nobility of Europe. One of the oldest structures in the country still standing is the Abbey at Tihany (Figure 15.5), where the first document with writing in Hungarian was penned. There are many other important historical sites throughout the region.

The Beginning of Balaton Tourism

The history of the Balaton tourism begins on the north shore in Balatonfured in the late 18th century when the villagers had their lakeside thermal spring waters tested and certified that they were medicinal and hired a spa doctor. The golden age of the town, built around the spa treatment centers, began shortly thereafter as the prominent cultural and political figures of the era began to spend more time here. At the eastern end, the first Balaton steamer was put in operation out of the Balatonfured

port in 1846, connecting with Szantod, a few kilometers from
the modern city of Siofok. Later a ferry connected the northern
and southern shores at the western end from Fonyod to Revfulop.
Eventually another, separate rail line reached the towns on
northern shore in 1909.

Keszthely (Figure 23.6), located at the western end of the lake,
is considered by most Hungarians to be the cultural center and
unofficial capital of the Balaton due to its size with 22,000 population;
the large number of resident artists and academics; its 200-year-
old agricultural university (PannonAgartudomanyi Egyetem); its
Catholic Church's 13th century frescoes and the palatial mansion
of the influential Festitics family (now a national museum)..

Festetics family palace near Keszthely. (Photo by Tim Wallace)

From the Adriatic Sea to the Hungarian Sea

For much of the early modern period (18th and 19th centuries), the real Hungarian sea was the Adriatic Sea, as Hungarians controlled what is today Croatia within the Austro-Hungarian Empire. The wealthy of the era built their vacation homes there and spent summers enjoying the Adriatic sun and sea. During this time, the Balaton region was primarily agricultural. There were almost no bathing areas and what few tourists cime were usually more interested in visiting and relaxing in the spas, tasting the local wines, and fishing the dense reeds that surrounded the lake. This was to change dramatically, however, after World War I.

As punishment for their role in World War I, the Allies removed two thirds of the Hungarian territory and awarded it to

The Abbey at Tihany overlooking Lake Balaton. (Photo by Tim Wallace)

Hungary's neighbours. Hungary was singled out for greater punishment than any of the other Axis allies. At one swoop of the pen, in a document called the Treaty of Trianon, Hungary's economy and national pride took a severe hit. Many historians say this lopsided concession was a major factor in Hungary's decision to participate in World War II as a German ally. With the creation of Slovenia and Croatia, an additional consequence of the Treaty was the removal of the Adriatic Sea coast as an internal tourist destination for Hungarians. The nobles and other wealthy Hungarians began to build more of their summer homes, cottages, and wine cellars around Lake Balaton, as the region started its growth as an important site for domestic tourism.

After the installation of the Communist governments in the postwar period, the fine estates, summer villas, large cottages, private resorts, and tracts of land were expropriated, nationalized, and redistributed to party officials and workers'

Keszthely, cultural center of Lake Balaton. (Photo by Tim Wallace)

unions. Up to this point, Balaton tourism had primarily been for the upper and emerging middle classes.After 1945, the government encouraged the construction of public resorts and holiday homes for the working classes.These actions changed the nature of the tourism around the lake and increased the density of both built structures and tourists within a short time. Reed and marsh strands were cut, beaches were built, and the rocky bottoms converted to sand. Homes, hotels, and restaurants were built very close to the water line as Lake Balaton began to attract larger numbers of tourists from East European countries. Hungary was attractive to citizens from these countries because, arguably, it was the most prosperous and least restrictive country in the Warsaw Pact countries. Adding to the attractiveness of the sand, sea, and sun was the fact that goods often available only in the West could be purchased here. On the other hand, tourists from Western European countries found Hungary an inexpensive bargain, albeit one with a lower standard of tourism infrastructure. After the 1960s the Janos Kadar regime gradually relaxed travel restrictions on incoming tourists from both the East and the West (Borocz, 1996, p. 143). Western tourists made expenditures that satisfied a need for hard currencies, while the Warsaw Pact tourists brought a lower paying, higher volume of tourism .The potential disruptiveness of the Western tourist presence was gradually accepted as a consequence of economic realities.

Balaton From the 1980s

Lake Balaton's reputation as an inexpensive, mass tourist resort destination to swim, sunbathe, eat, drink, and relax was fixed by the 1980s. In 1980 Hungary recorded 10:45 million tourists. By 1990 that figure had doubled to 20.5 million (Hungarian Central Statistical Office, 1992, p. 164). Less restrictive tourism policies allowed travellers from Western countries to become much more numerous than before.

Lake Balaton also became an important meeting point for tourists from West and East Germany. It was easy for them to meet here and nearly impossible to do so in Germany. German tourists soon became the most important and highly visible tourists at Balaton, and Hungarian hosts adjusted their tourism programmes accordingly, offering information in German, having German-speaking staff available, and improving the standard of services. Hungarians especially enjoyed the West Germans, whom they perceived as cultured and wealthy (and likely to spend a lot of money and be less demanding than the "less cultured" East Germans).

In the majority of commercial establishments tourist amenities were basic and far below international standards. Service was slow, uniform, and unresponsive. The few, major hotels in the region, often tied in with the spa resorts, were slightly better appointed with a more experienced staff only because their clientele were primarily from Western Europe. The vast majority of guests (ca. 80%) stayed in private homes and apartments (Borocz, 1996, p. 157).

The Hungarian political system after the 1956 revolution came to be known as "goulash communism," referring to an odd mixing of a state-dominated, socialist agricultural and industrial sector existing alongside a lively individual, informal, capitalist sector. Income from home activities was not regulated by the state. Individuals were able to acquire enough money to buy cars and small vacation homes, but were not allowed to invest in land. However, Balaton homeowners were able to rent their rooms, apartments, and vacation homes to tourists, keeping the cash from lodging transactions unrecorded. With 80% of all foreign tourists staying in noncommercial establishments, the income derived from lodging guests in the informal sector generated a growth and dependency on tourism among the working classes that had never been experienced before at Balaton.

The end of Soviet hegemony after 1989 also spelled another change for Balaton tourism. In the term of guests, fewer tourists from Warsaw Pact countries could afford to visit Hungary; West

Germans suddenly did not need to visit their East German cousins, their cousins came to them. All travel restrictions were removed and Hungarians were easily able to go to Western European destinations for their holidays. The hosts now found themselves with a changing cliente.e and most of the paying tourists increasingly were East Germans. The length of the tourism season began to contract, decreasing from 2.5 months (mid-June to August) to about 5 weeks July to mid-August).

Shortly after 1989, the economy changed, too, with Hungarians experiencing for the first time in decades high unemployment and inflation rates. The government could no longer afford the economic safety net they had provided everyone during the communist era (free education, health, generous retirement plans, employment for everyone, time off for informal sector activities, and so on), forcing - Hungarians who previously had used their free market activities as an income supplement to rely on them as primary economic resources. The euphoria at the end of communism combined with the realization that the economy was changing led many of the people who owned property in Balaton to spruce up their homes and flats, construct new ones with renting in mind, open up new restaurants, and offer new services. Unfortunately, tourist arrivals in Hungary seemed to have peaked around 1993-1994 and have begun to level off and even show a small decline, especially at Lake Balaton. Recent investments are in jeopardy, even as people continue to clear scenic vistas to construct more on rental houses. With the decrease of agricultural and manufacturing output and jobs, the privatization of the economy and the drastic cutback in government subsidies to individuals, tourism has become the backbone of the local economy. Dependency has replaced economic diversity.

The rapidity of tourism growth at Lake Balaton between 1960 and 1990 produced some very big environmental problems, especially in terms of the lake's water quality. The fact is there are too many tourists using Lake Balaton in the summer. The carrying capacity of Lake Balaton is about 600,000 tourists per day. In the summer, there are often over a million people using it. The problem cannot be corrected cheaply or easily. Even if it is fixed eventually, tourism receipts may have declined by that time anyway. Any decrease in tourism receipts would probably produce an economic crisis for thousands of Balaton residents.

The next section explains in some detail the environmental problems that may be leading to a crisis. I will try to outline the key factors contributing to it. In the process we will see how in the short run sustaining tourism is not necessarily compatible with sustaining development. Environmental planning for tourism growth should have occurred sooner than 1980. Even today, government officials in Hungary are doing little to repair the damages and not enough to prevent a worsening of the environmental problems.

The Ebb and Flow of Water Quality Issues in Balaton Tourism

Lake Balaton presents very complex issues in sustainable tourism when it comes to the physical environment. Sustaining the environmental component of tourism in the Lake Balaton case refers primarily to protecting water quality, the local fauna and flora, and the traditional landscape along the shore. All of the water quality problems are ultimately traced back to damaging human activities begun in the last century. At the outset of this discussion, it is important to keep in mind that until recently Lake Balaton was just another rural area in a country dominated by agriculture and animal husbandry. Balaton was not considered a mass tourism destination until the mid-20th century.

Lake Balaton is about 20,000 years old. The depth and size of the lake have changed significantly over the centuries. For example, the Medieval period was much wetter than today and Lake Balaton was much wider. As the rainfall declined, the formerly flooded areas became wetlands, important not only for bird and other mammal habitats but also the lake itself. The largest source of the lake's water, about 40-45%, is delivered via the Zala River from western Hungary snaking its way past large agricultural fields, water-hungry manufacturing plants, oilfields, and refineries. The rest of the water comes from rain running off the increasingly reed-bare campgrounds and resort-cluttered surrounding countryside. Hungarian limnologists (lake system biologists) observed the first serious signs of an impending water quality crisis around 1960. Excessive algae were seen at the western end, near Keszthely, where the Zala empties into the lake. The Kis-Balaton wetlands near Keszthely provided a natural filtration system for lake waters, removing pollutants and excessive nutrients from agricultural and livestock waste up river. In addition, the river water stayed long enough in the wetlands for it to separate its solid material and settle there. The heavy reed growth absorbed excess nutrients from its major water cleansing and sediment removal apparatus, a mechanism that' limnologists (freshwater biologists) later decided was indispensable for the health of Lake Balaton. In effect, between 1860 and 1960 a hundred years of additional sediments and excess nutrients had been dumped into the Keszthely end of the lake as a result. This caused a toxic algae problem to arise. The algae also depleted the shallow lake of its normal oxygen levels-, seriously affecting other marine life and causing massive fish kills (especially carp and eels) in later years.

The western end of the lake is currently the most polluted area. If this part of the lake is unhealthy, the whole lake will suffer eventually. Prior to 1800, the water around Keszthely was as clear as drinking water according to old documents. Deliberate draining to increase agricultural lands took place in the early 1920s, so that nearly all of what was once wetlands disappeared .This is an indication of the little importance most of the region had placed on tourism relative to agriculture and animal husbandry. As late as 1960, landowners and even the state tried to drain additional wetland areas. However, the marshy area closest to the lake mouth was never adequately suited to agriculture and was eventually abandoned. Unfortunately, the removal of wetlands had a disastrous effect on Lake Balaton.

A second environmental problem for the lake arose after the construction of the southern rail line in 1861. The tracks were built close to the lake—some places within about 50 meters of the shoreline. After the first flood, rail owners complained to the government The response was the construction of a channel and dyke at Siofok to control the water's depth. Government engineers set the high level at 104.5 meters above sea level. Buildings and cottages were constructed nearby along the rail line. Now the lake level cannot be raised without flooding homes and businesses. Barring an unforeseen rainfall or drought of catastrophic proportions, the lake level will always be within a few centimeters of the high mark level. The shallowness of the lake reinforces the problems created by the destruction of the wetlands: lower oxygen levels and increased muddiness. Unfortunately, the worst effects of these two problems (lowered oxygen levels and muddiness) are more likely to occur at the height of the tourist season. The hotter it is, the less oxygen there is for the lake's aquatic creatures, sometimes provoking a massive fish kill as there was in 1994 when thousands of fish died during a July heat wave. The hot days also bring out more bathers, who are not happy seeing dead fish floating by as they wade in the very warm water with their children. In addition, the greater the number of bathers, the more the muddy sediment on the lake bottom is churned up, making the water cloudier and less appealing to tourists.

The third major environmental problem for the lake has been the disastrous leveling of the reed stands that existed for eons around the lake. Reeds soak up the excess nutrients flowing into the lake from fertilizers and other sources of nitrogen, slow the entrance of polluted runoff into the lake, protect delicate flora, serve as nests for birds and other animals, and in general contribute greatly to the overall biotic structure of the lake's complex ecosystem. The reeds were traditionally used as thatching for cottage roofs, a practice today mostly abandoned in favour of ceramic or asbestos tiling, although a few, newly restored homes are reusing them as an attraction for tourists looking for lodging in a more "authentic" Hungarian cottage.

Following the expropriation of the redistribution of properties around the shoreline, home and resort builders cut down reeds, which they saw as a nuisance, and planted trees. Dirt from the construction site often was just dumped into the lake. This sometimes added a few more meters to the shoreline property. Tree planting only worsened the problem, because their shade inhibited reed growth and allowed runoff to head into the lake unfiltered by denser plant life.

These three problems have together contributed to a significant decline in water quality. Although a major effort has been undertaken to solve some of these stubborn problems, my field school students in 1994 and 1995 could only find harsh adjectives for the lake's water. For example, one of them wrote in 1995, "The environmental problems of the lake become apparent when one looks at the nice, murky, brown color of the lake. This could be a devastating blow if the lake becomes so polluted that nobody wants to swim in it anymore" Jaeger, 1995, p. 34). Another student wrote, "The water quality is poor and on any given day one may find dead fish floating or grounded on the beach" (Broomfield, 1995, p. 53). Although they generally did not mind sitting at the "beach" areas, most of them were reluctant to enter the water due to the dead fish, the cloudiness, and the water's stillness. They concluded they might contract some kind of a disease if they swam in it.

Germans, also, are uncomfortable with the same things and German newspapers monitor Balaton water quality to their readers. In 1994 and 1995 several German newspapers reported the Lake Balaton fish kills and cloudy water problems shortly before the German school holiday period. Both years Balaton business owners and residents reported noticeable declines in German tourist arrivals and length of stay. By their shorter visits or even their decision not to visit, German tourists were signaling their demand to Balaton hosts that maintenance of water quality was so important to them that they might not come back. In 1995 the Keszthely Bay was dredged to remove sediment. For the 1996 summer season, the Hungarian Water Authority tried to keep water levels as high as physically possible to lessen the possibility of fish kills and improve the colour of the water. Recently, many towns are expanding the amount of *strand* area to give more space to sunbathers and children. Thus, it is clear that Hungarians took notice and are concerned about the situation.

The large scientific and water engineering communities have been doing research on Lake Balaton and monitoring its water quality for decades. But the combination of destruction of wetlands, fixing the water level, cutting the reeds, and building more small resorts, homes, and cottages up to the shoreline could produce an environmental crisis for the lake. Today, the infrastructure is so dense around the lake and in the Kis-Balaton it would be impossible to restore the lake to its pre-1800 environment. Nevertheless, the government has undertaken some projects to ameliorate the consequences of these human social, economic, and political decisions of the last 200 years. These include the reconstruction of the Kis-Balaton wetlands, the continued dredging of the Kis-Balaton Bay, and declaring much of the shoreline and Xetlands as protected nature areas.

Germans and Austrians are far more interested in the recreational elements of the lake than are tourists from greater distances. Lake Balaton is relatively close to Germany, and Austria is a border state. German tourists want comfortable accommodations where they can relax and play, swim, sunbathe, eat, and drink, not unlike most American tourists visiting the beach towns of the US Atlantic, Pacific, and Gulf coastlines. They are not greatly interested in ethnic or cultural tourism. It is the very rare German tourist that can speak any Hungarian and few even attempt it. Balaton hosts and guests communicate in tourist German. The number of German-speaking tourists has become so great that most of the signage and restaurant menus are bilingual, and signs and menus in other languages are hard to find, much to the frustration of other foreign tourists.

Americans and British, in contrast, are much more interested in ethnic, cultural, and historical tourism. Eight times as many British tourists stay overnight in Keszthely as in Siofok, probably because Keszthely is noted in the guidebooks as the Balaton city with the most cultural attractions and programmes. I once spoke with a Keszthely resident who taught English at the local university and moonlighted as a tour guide. She found British and American tourists to be remarkably different from Germans and Austrians in their touring preferences. On a weekend tour the latter wanted to taste the wine from north shore wine cellars, take a horse-drawn wagon ride through a picturesque village, visit the beach, and eat and drink throughout the afternoon and evening. The English speakers, in contrast, insisted on visiting as many churches, famous buildings, museums, and castle ruins as possible within a weekend. She said she far preferred guiding Germans because the "Brits and the Americans always leave me exhausted."

But there are many workaholic Germans that are so taken by the slower pace of life that they now seek to invest in a piece of it. They are changing the terms of negotiation over the definition of the site. The foreign purchase of the country vacation homes has become very common throughout Balaton communities, even in more distant areas such as the Kis-Balaton. Each summer seems to find more real estate for sale to foreigners and fewer native farmers staying behind. This is also having an interesting consequence for the physical environment. A colleague at the university in Keszthely found that his research is showing greater concentrations of native flora reappearing in fields around the Balaton. He attributed this occurrence to the large number of abandoned agricultural fields. He noted that in his recent travels in the area he found dozens of communities with abundant restored homes, newly painted with well-kept gardens. "Unfortunately, no one lived in them," he said. "They are like ghost towns" because the homes are owned by-foreign guests who appear infrequently for a short vacation (Figure 15.7).

Tourism in the Kis-Balaton

About 20 years ago, prior to the wetlands reconstruction project in the Kis-Balaton, the national petroleum company, MOL, was digging for oil in Zalakaros, a small community near the Kis-Balaton. They found an underground hot spring instead. Hungarians love thermal baths, and soon construction was under way to convert this small farming community into a spa center. The Kis-Balaton reconstruction project, the beginning of tourism in this area, started in the 1980s. Several farm communities sacrificed their land to this project, for which they

Figure   Balaton farmhouse with thatched (reed) roof restored by German vacationers. (Photo by Tim Wallace)

received some financial compensation.Today, the wetlands project looks like a small lake in a very rural setting. Many species of birds have returned, white storks from Africa regularly return to summer over here, and various kinds of fish flourish in the waters.The peaceful, bucolic setting amidst old farming communities has attracted Austrian and German tourists seeking quite month-long vacations in a "natural" environment.At first, these tourists lodged with local families in their farmhouses. Recently, it has become very common for the tourists to buy a farmhouse, restore it, and use it as a vacation home. German families first find out about Hungarian village homes through advertisements in their newspapers. German and Hungarian real estate agents operate in the area to show them available homes for purchase.

More Cracks in the Negotiation

Balaton residents are not riveted by the prospect of forever serving German tourists. East -Germans are especially resented, because they are seen as *declasse* proletarians and peasants without social graces. But the dislike of Germans is generally well cloaked, except among local youths in the 15-25 age range. We determined this by pairing field course participants with Hungarian students and asking them to interview together both hosts and guests during their 5-week programme of study. On one occasion some Hungarian and American students were at a beach at Gyenesdias, a town near Keszthely.They wanted to interview Hungarian vacationers, but when they walked across the hot,crowded strand along the water's edge they were unable to find a single one. One of the Hungarian students remarked in a very serious tone to one of the Americans that the absence of Hungarians "makes the vacation town undesirable to him." He felt like a stranger in his own country (Massa, 1994, p. 119). Over and over again, the Americans reported a brooding sense of alienation among the young Hungarians with whom they were working.

It was clear from our research that local Balaton Hungarians responded more positively to tourists who took the time to learn some Hungarian words, wanted to visit cultural sites, and wished to participate in local customs. Hungarians were uncomfortable with the vertical, asymmetrical relationship characteristic of tourists who visit less developed countries. They preferred guests who were flexible in their expectations as to time, accommodations, and food and who were willing to treat Hungarian service personnel as guides to interpreting Hungarian culture, rather than as servants.

Conclusion: Processing and Sustaining Tourism

Tourism development is an ongoing process of negotiation, so it is inevitable that a tourist destination changes to fit the needs of both hosts and guests. Sometimes, the hosts are in control and sometimes the guests are in control. Sustainable tourism is a misnomer, as it assumes there is a single, original state at a particular moment in time when the destination was in its ideal environment, and social and cultural condition. Tourism is in the eye of the beholder—that is, the tourist, the hotel owner, the waiter, the real estate agent, the travel agent, the politician, the citizen, and so on.

One of the great fears of the Balaton residents dependent on tourism is that there will be massive fish kills in late June, just before the Germans arrive. A fish kill means a poor tourist season. Several tourist seasons in a row will hurt not only the hotel owners but the thousands of average residents who depend on the rental of the apartments and houses in order to survive inflation and difficult economic conditions. Residents want to know the secret for getting the "perfect" tourist—the one who is going to have the least impact and leave the most money. The negotiation between hosts and guests continues at Balaton. The post-1989 decline in agriculture and manufacturing in the region has made local residents overly dependent on tourism, so the hosts hold the upper hand for the moment in the definition of Balaton tourism. The national government is not committed to major changes in funding formulas to help Balaton. The problems afflicting Balaton are minor compared with the economic problems facing all Hungary. People living in other parts of the country where there are few tourists hope that some of the tourists visiting Balaton will come their way instead. The irony is that, or balance, fewer tourists at Balaton will probably have a positive effect on water quality and crowding, which may make the guests happy, but not the hosts who depend on tourism for income.

As the economy and the tourists change, so also will the cultural definition of Lake Balaton as a tourist destination change. If there are no tourists, then there is no tourist destination. However, when tourists arrive and interact with local residents, the process begins and starts to affect the social, cultural, and physical environment. Balaton is being tremendously affected by mass tourism. Few tourists stay in hotels. Most live in Hungarian homes and apartments and deal face to face with the hosts. These interactions saturate the day-to-day lives of the hosts throughout the summer, affecting the local culture to varying degrees. I was told by many of my Hungarian friends and acquaintances how nervously they awaited the arrival of the tourist season and how relieved they were when it was over.

Tourism in the 1980s and early 1990s had been confined primarily to the shores of the Balaton and only for a short 6-8-week season. Today, the purchase of vacation homes in areas distant from the Balaton shore is going to create perhaps more profound changes. As Butler (1990) points out, the true local environment can still be found in areas into which tourists do not penetrate,

> To disperse tourists in space and time, i.e., to extend the season to peaking, could and in some cases has, resulted in far more profound and permanent changes over a wider area, than when tourists are confined to small areas in huge numbers for clearly defined seasons. (Butler, 1992, p. 45)

Now, communities are even selling their vacant farmlands to foreigners seeking to build new houses. The Kis-Balaton will eventually become linked not only by the wetlands and the Zala River but also by the creeping development of these new residences to mass tourism at Lake Balaton. As one of my students recently asked rhetorically,"Will the Hungarian Sea become the Austro-German Hungarian Sea?"Just as English-speaking tourists are affecting the little Romanian village of Aref to find their fictional Dracula and tourists are seeing the Virgin Mary in an office building window in Clearwater, FL, so also the process of transformation of the Balaton continues as it has been doing for centuries since the time of the Romans. Sustainable tourism probably should not mean sustaining tourists, but rather assuring that the process of it be orderly, with minimal culture shock for the hosts. Hungarians must ask themselves how will they respond to these changes. "How should we sustain our Balaton? How do we retain our cultural heritage at Lake Balaton?" But if they change too much they also have to wonder "Will tourists come back again?"The cultural definition of a tourist destination is the result of a long process of negotiation among hosts and guests. Sometimes the former hold the upper hand and sometimes the latter do. There are multiple factors that determine whose definition takes priority, not the least of which are economic ones. As Hungary moves beyond the difficulties of the transition period of socialism to a new system, economic diversification may make it possible for Hungarians at Balaton to welcome tourists more on their own terms, or perhaps welcome a different kind of tourist. Even then, they will have to renegotiate the cultural definition of the Balaton.

16

Tourism Development in Nottingham, England

Myths and legends often form the basis of cultural tourism as in Nottingham (UK), whose tourism industry earns in excess of *f*256 million per year and employs 15,000 people, largely dependent upon themes based around the medieval story of Robin Hood. Despite doubts about the historical validity of the character, the legends and associated locations have been successfully packaged to attract a wide range of visitors. Visitors to Nottingham have an image of place derived largely from Robin Hood feature films, which have always been shot elsewhere. This, combined with the doubtful historical basis of the legend, may be thought to detract from the visitor experience at the destination, but in practice the reverse seems to be true. Visitors to Nottingham apparently either do not care whether the legend was authentic or expect Robin Hood to be a myth and are agreeably surprised to find some historical foundation. Nottingham's tourism received a measurable boost from the 1991 release of two Robin Hood films, but recent promotion has tried to diversify the cultural tourism product.

The Legend of Robin Hood

Nottinghamshire and Sherwood Forest are synonymous with the legendary medieval hero, Robin Hood, an outlaw dressed in Lincoln Green who supposedly robbed the rich to give to the poor. The accoutrements of the myth, characters such as Little John, Friar Tuck, Will Scarlett, and other Merry Men are familiar to all, and Robin is frequently depicted as an heroic figure standing up for oppressed peasantry. Despite skeptical claims that Robin Hood was actually the invention of sensation-seeking

medieval minstrels (S. Davis, 1991) who tapped popular resentment, the character has remained universally popular for
centuries, regardless of its historical validity. Today, thanks to
extensive film versions of the Robin Hood legend, the hero is
both instantly recognizable and firmly stereotyped. It is, unfortunately, very difficult to identify the "real" Robin Hood who
forms the background for the stories.Wandering outlaws of
similar predilections certainly existed (J. Holt, 1982), but many
authorities claim that Robin Hood merely represents an amalgam
of different mytns. In medieval times major stones of the day
were told by traveling minstrels and the earliest written mention
of Robin Hood occurs in a poem called. "The Vision of William
Concerning Piers Plowman" by William Lagland, considered to
have been written around 1377. Several original ballads suggest
that a Robin Hood character was active in the 13th century or
even later (Dobson & Taylor, 1989), although a 16th century
historian (coincidentally called John Major) wrote in 1521 that
Robin Hood was active in the early 1190s during the reign of
Richard I (the Lionheart).This 12th century identification has
remained the most popular in cinematic representations.
However, there is much contradictory evidence.

Nottinghamshire tradition says that Robin was a native of
the village of Loxley in the 12th century, but this probably
represents an amalgamation of two characters. Indeed, although
Nottingham is the major area connected with the modern legend,
in early ballads (Dobson & Taylor, 1989) much of the outlaw's
life is set around the area of Barnesdale in Yorkshire. Other
sites connecting Robin to York-shire include Kirklees Priory
where he is supposed to have died and been buried. Nor are all
the elements of the Robin Hood story contemporary. Maid
Marion and FriarTuck were later additions to the tale, the latter
not appearing until the 1500s, probably as part of May Day
plays.This has to cast some doubt on the validity of the claim
that Robin Hood and Maid Marion were married in Edwinstowe
Church, Nottingham, some 300 years earlier. However,
Edwinstowe is still a major tourist attraction.The legend strongly

identifies Robin with Sherwood Forest, fragments of which still exist today. In the 14th century primitive forests covered more than 30% of England with some, such as Sherwood, being owned by the King and guarded by royal rangers. Forestry laws were harsh and cruel, and the Robin Hood of legend defends oppressed local peasants both from rangers and from royal officials such as the Sheriff of Nottingham (Figure 16.1).

Robin Hood is one of the most popular film heroes of all time. Between 1908 and 1922 more than 26 major films have been made around the Robin Hood theme, starting with silent pictures, in addition to innumerable television series, commercials, cartoons, etc. (Turner, 1989).These have served to establish a picture both of the man and his contemporary environment in many people's minds, the exact image being related to the age of the consumer and thus to the film version with which they are most familiar.The most famous early portrayal is certainly the 1922 film *Robin Hood* starring Douglas Fairbanks, Jr. In 1938, Warner Brothers made Adventures *of Robin Hood* with Errol Flynn, widely regarded as the definitive Robin Hood movie. Most of the film was shot in Chico, CA, some 500 miles north of Hollywood. Ironically, part of the shooting did indeed take place in Sherwood Forest, although this was not the Nottinghamshire original but a Californian forest near Los Angeles that had been renamed at the time the 1922 film was being shot there.

Other significant Robin Hood films include *Robin and Marion* (1976, starring Sean Connery) and the 1973 Animated Disney cartoon In the UK the television *"Adventures of Robin Hood* ran for I 13 episodes between 1956 and 1960. By this time there can hardly have been anyone in the Western world who did not know what Robin Hood looked like or that he lived in Sherwood Forest, near Nottingham, and in recent years this association has formed the basis for most of Nottingham's tourism industry.This was greatly helped by the release (in 1991) of two films: *Robin Hood* (starring Patrick Bergin) and *Robin Hood Prince of Thieves* (with Kevin Costner).The latter was

Statue of Robin Hood outside Nottingham Castle

the more successful and was utilized as the basis for a massive
Robin Hood promotion in Nottinghamshire despite the fact that
none of it was shot in the county. Some of the landscape shots
actually featured Hadrian's Wall and the Scottish lowlands.

Myths and Heritage Tourism

Myths and legends are frequently used as the basis for a heritage tourism product (Prentice, 1993). The visitor may be unaware that the character or story is invented British examples include Scottish Highland tartans (a Victorian elaboration) and the creation of Sherlock Holmes (a fictional character). Perhaps the best parallel for Robin Hood comes with the legends of King Arthur and Camelot, equally historically doubtful but still the basis for much of Cornwall's cultural tourism product. Because contemporary images of a mythical or pseudohistorica! character are generally derived from film or television portrayals, the potential tourist has a definite destination image that might differ markedly from the image he would have created in his own mind from reading a book. Many non-UK residents unfamiliar with such stories are unable to distinguish fact from fiction, hence the numbers of disappointed visitors each year trying to find the mythical 22I b Baker Street, London residence of Sherlock Holmes.

In the case of Robin Hood, continuous media exposure has resulted in a firm image of both the character (complete with longbow, peaked hat with a feather, and green tunic) and his environment (the oakwoods of Sherwood Forest). Such pictures of the Greenwood, the battlements of Nottingham castle, and rural villages of medieval England create expectations in the minds of visitors that cannot possibly be realized, although they attract large numbers of visitors to Nottingham (Figure 16.2).As we know, destination images influence tourist behaviour (Echtner & Ritchie, 1991) and strong positive images are preferred in the travel decision-making process (Woodside & Lysonski, 1989). Myths and legends are often used as the basis for a heritage tourism product and can create powerful and romantic subliminal images. When reinforced by heritage themes these are widely used to create images in advertising and may be combined into powerful marketing devices for tourism. Once at the destination, visitor satisfaction depends on a comparison between image and reality, which, in the case of Nottingham, might be thought to be disappointing (Chon, 1990). Myths are cultural products and as such may themselves become commoditized. It is often assumed that tourists desire culturally authentic, rather than potentially mythical, experiences, yet authenticity is a socially constructed concept.The tourist may be unable to recognize authenticity, making himself "damned to inauthemicity" in MacCannell's famous phrase (MacCannell, 1973). One could argue that the portrayal of mythical heritage is no less authentic than the staged authenticity of many tourist settings.

D. Pearce (1988) sees the term "image" as describing an overall mental picture or destination stereotype. Each individual will have a unique mental picture of the destination, although certain images will be held in common. In the case of Nottingham these shared images generally involve forests, castles with battlements and drawbridges, and medieval villages.The landscapes of today's Nottinghamshire are dominated by deserted coal tips and pitheads rather than castles, with the heritage of the city center heavily influenced by the Industrial Revolution.This is not to say that nothing medieval survives but rather that it may take a determined visitor to find it.

The formation of this destination image begins with the development of a mental construct based upon a few impressions chosen from a flood of information. The potential visitor to Nottingham can thus make his own selection from a wide variety of potential images. In the early stages of image formation (Gunn, 1988). the image is generally formed from nontouristic information including general media, films, and books.Tourist information such as brochure literature forms a second stage. The destination image of Nottingham is particularly strong as a re-suit of the Robin Hood films, although these are totally misleading because none were actually made in the county. However, few tourists seem to be aware of this fact and are attracted to the area because of its associations with the legend rather than any landscape qualities.The association of Robin Hood with Nottingham is generally accepted quite uncritically.

Poster of Robin Hood. (Photo by Myra Shackley)

Research suggests that the final phase of image formation is acquired after a visit has modified the image (Phelps, 1986). One might therefore expect that because the reality of Nottingham and Sherwood Forest falls so far short of expectations that it would affect the quality of the visitor experience. This, however, does not appear to be the case.

Nottingham and Robin Hood

Nottinghamshire has based a very successful tourism
industry on Robin Hood and is now trying to use the positive
image of place it has acquired from this process in the
development of new products. At present, estimated tourism
spending in the county exceeds £256 million per year (East
Midlands Tourist Board fEMTB], 1993), attracting domestic
visitors predominantly from London, the southeast and east
Midlands. Overseas visitors are predominately German (18%),
French (14.6%), or American (13.3%). Not surprisingly,
attractions based around the theme of Robin Hood dominate
Nottinghamshire's tourism product. Today's visitor is met by
"Welcome to Nottinghamshire" "Robin Hood County" signs at
the boundary and invited to visit nearly 50 sites that claim some
association with the mythical outlaw. These include Nottingham
Castle, which is marketed on its Robin Hood connotations
although the medieval original was totally destroyed during the
English Civil War and replaced by a Ducal mansion in 1679. It
is now a museum and art gallery, which attracted 741,891 visitors
in 1992 (EMTB, 1993). Another popular destination is the
Sherwood Forest Visitor Centre, a favorite spot for walking in
one of the few surviving remnants of the once extensive
Sherwood Forest.This received major refurbishment in 1993 with
the inevitable Robin Hood theme.The Major Oak, legendary
haunt of Robin Hood's Merry Men, can still be seen, although
foresters consider the tree to be no more than 300 years old
and thus it postdates Robin Hood by anything up to 500 years.
Visitors may also glimpse the current Sheriff of Nottingham
(holder of a political office) or go to the Tales of Robin Hood, a
purpose-built themed medieval adventure (appropriately located
on Maid Marian Way in Nottingham) that opened in 1989 and
attempts to recreate the atmosphere of 13th century Nottingham.
Here a cable car ride takes visitors through forest settings in
search of Robin Hood followed by extensive exhibits related to
daily life in medieval times, plus a critical appraisal of the

legend. There are also a number of related festivals and events, including the Robin Hood Festival (held in Sherwood Forest)), the Robin Hood Pageant (Nottingham Castle complete with jousting), and a new attraction, The World of Robin Hood, which opened in 1991 utilizing the scenery from the Kevin Costner film plus supplementary material from a failed heritage center called the Crusades Experience. Those still not satiated with the world's most famous outlaw can search for the church where he was supposedly married (at Edwinstowe) or Friar Tuck's Hut (at Rainworth).

The release of two major Robin Hood films in 1991 provided an opportunity to measure t˙ effect of this boost to the destination image. Nottingham gained very considerable benefits from the Costner film and associated promotions despite having failed in a bid to attract the actor himself to Nottingham for the premier of the film. Sherwood Forest Visitor Centre received a 47% increase in inquiries directly after the film was released, and visitors to the Robin Hood Festival and Robin Hood Pageant increased by 20% and 27%, respectively. Inquiries and souvenir sales at Nottingham Tourist Information Centre increased by 45% between July and September (Nodding, Berresford, & Alexander, 1993). A special Robin Hood rate accommodation promotion generated £34,000 in bed nights plus additional spending, and an additional investment of £8,000 by the County Council on a promotional video generated free TV commercials worth £120,000 and greatly increased awareness of Nottinghamshire tourism.

In many ways, although Robin Hood has undeniably been a most successful ambassador for Nottinghamshire, the overemphasis on Greenwood products has made it difficult for marketeers to diversify. Nottingham has a lot else going for it, including major visitor attractions associated with Lord Byron and D. H. Lawrence, and an interesting industrial heritage based around lace making. The overpromotion of Robin Hood illustrates how heritage themes may swamp a region, becoming overworked and difficult to escape from. This theming reduces the complexity of urban history to a few instantly recognizable simple marketable devices. However, boredom thresholds differ between hosts and guests. Nottingham locals are tired of Robin Hood while visitors remain interested in seeing places associated with the legend.

Because of the failure of many Robin Hood sites to live up to their image, great attempts have been made to compensate. In the case of Nottingham Castle, for example, visitors often record disappointment and the management is trying to forestall this by providing extra information on the significance of the site in the English Civil War (Liepens, personal communication) and by opening new attractions such as the network of underground tunnels. The city won the UK award for Holiday Destination of the Year in 1993, partly for its Robin Hood promotions but also for events marking the 350th commemoration of the English Civil War and for the development of new attractions associated with Byron, Lawrence, and lace making. The Robin Hood theme is more extensively used in overseas marketing. Rod Nipper, Nottinghamshire's Principal Tourism Officer, said in 1994 in the course of a promotional visit to Arizona that "We found that Robin Hood was a particular attraction to Americans, but they had little idea of the geography of Britain." Despite the success of Robin Hood promotions, the limits of innovation have almost been reached. Today's promotions are increasingly trying to diversify and link Robin Hood with other local characters (including Byron and Lawrence) fighting against authority or institutions. But in the mind of the average visitor, particularly visitors from overseas who have no alternative images, Nottingham remains firmly associated with Robin Hood.

Does Authenticity Matter?

Within the UK Nottingham scores highly in most "quality of life" tests. It is famous as an urban shopping center, center of sporting excellence, and for having excellent pubs and nightclubs that cater to the huge student population (20% of citizens, during term). Recent unpublished surveys commissioned by Nottinghamshire councils suggest that visitors to Nottingham are generally motivated by an interest in history (particularly if they come from overseas).They are highly aware of the Robin Hood legends but not of the individual visitor attractions. They generally have an image of place that is generation dependent and usually formed by the Costner film, or by the earlier Errol Flynn film, depending on their age. In the case of children, popular breakfast-cereal commercials with a Robin Hood theme are also significant in developing a mental picture. Visitors report high levels of satisfaction with all Robin Hood visitor attractions, except Nottingham Castle, which few realized had been destroyed. The most surprising result in recent surveys was that before their visit tourists had thought that Robin Hood was a mythological character (but didn't care). This conditioned their expectations of Nottinghamshire tourism and when they found that there was a reasonable historical basis for the Robin Hood legend they were pleasantly surprised. The net result was that expectations were exceeded and the visit rated as highly satisfactory.The inauthenticity of Robin Hood sites or the doubtful basis of the myth itself does not, apparently, matter to the heritage tourist. The crucial factor would appear to be the quality of the visitor experience, it would be possible to argue that the overpromotion of this mythical theme has led to commoditization of local culture (Greenwood, 1977), replacing authentic cultural products with staged authenticity (MacCannell, 1973). E. Cohen (1968) noted that not all tourists are seeking authenticity in the ethnographic sense and that recreational tourists are generally less concerned with authenticity and may be prepared to accept as authentic a cultural product or attraction that concerned cultural tourists (applying stricter criteria) may deem unauthentic.This is certainly true in Nottingham, where some tourists will see adequate evidence to support the myth but the majority will remain unconcerned. The staged product can be acceptable to some if it contains some resemblance to the real thing. The visitor may be aware that an attraction is not real but be able to achieve a high quality of experience by compliance with the fantasy. This, after all, is the reason for the success of historical recreations such as Colonial Williamsburg. What matters to Nottinghamshire visitors is not whether Robin Hood was a real character but whether they can have a good time trying to find out. And they can.

17

European Union Cross-Border Cooperation: A New Tourism Dimension

The Austrian-Italian-Slovenian Three Borders Area is a perfect example of an area partitioned after World War I that is now attempting a common future under the new unified Europe. The European Union offers superb opportunities to develop multicultural tourism in peripheral areas such as Three Borders Area, where three major European ethnic groups (German, Italian, and Slavic), cultures, and languages meet. The unsuccessful bid for the Winter Olympics in 2006 (after a first try for 2002) united these disparate entities for the first time in history towards a common goal. Their coalition for a cause demonstrates the latent power of multinational cooperation for this unique location with its slogan *"Senza Confini"* ("Without Borders"). The creation of a transnational cross-border tourism region, rich in historical and cultural tradition and set amidst spectacular natural beauty, is a new research concept that holds promise for other European areas and elsewhere, such as idyllic but troubled Kashmir.

In contrast to its positive aspects of diverse cultures and natural beauty, the border area still retains strong national perspectives. However, the emerging economy of the European Union (ETU) follows its own rules of internationalization despite public opinion. European history and tradition have created a variety or cultural identities. What will happen to the many cultures of Europe?

European Culture is marked by its diversity: diversity of climate, countryside, architecture, language, beliefs, taste and artistic style. Such diversity must be protected, not diluted. It represents one of the chief sources of the wealth of our continent. But underlying this variety, there is an affinity, a family likeness, and a common European identity. Down through the ages the tension between the continent's cultural diversity and unity has helped to fuse ancient and modern, traditional and progressive. it [the culture] is undoubtedly a source of the greatness of the elements of our civilization. (European Community, 1983)

The Three Borders Area lias been a region of long-standing tension and conflicts: the World War I battles at the Isonzo River, the fights over borders, the division into three nation states followed by forced nationalization and ethnic cleansing The creation of a unified tourism region that will introduce theme oriented tourist attractions into a peripheral area, and improve a stagnant economy, is a challenging research project.

The Research Team

The research to date has centered on a pilot area consisting of 12 communities along the European Union's internal borders between Austria and Italy and the external borders between Slovenia and Austria/Italy (Figure 17.1)

The research design is interdisciplinary, involving cooperation between two leading research institutions: the University of Graz Department of Human Geography and Regional Studies, and the University of Klagenfurt Department of Southeastern European History.Additional contributions have been made by the Geography Departments in Ljubljana (Slovenia) and Trieste (Italy), and tourism experts, decision-makers, and local opinion leaders added practical experience.

European Union Regional Policy and Tourism Development

Two important EU policies are very supportive and decisive for tourism development in the pilot region. First, the "European

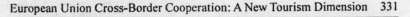

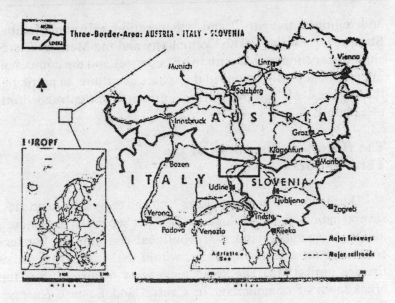

Location map of the Three Border Area

Union Regional Policies" initiated under the European Community (EC) Treaty (Rome, 1957) stated in part three, Title XIV, Article 130a:

> In order to promote its overall harmonious development, the Community shall develop and pursue its actions leading to the strengthening of its economic and social cohesion. In particular, the Community shall aim at reducing disparities between the levels of development of the various regions and the backwardness of the least favoured regions, rural areas, (see also http:// www.inforegio.org/wbpro/agenda2000/compare/04_en.htm)

Second, the EU is producing a new European culture, a "unity in diversity "Article 128 of the Treaty of Maastricht provided a framework that encourages the "flowering of the cultures of the Member States, while respecting their national and regional diversity," and "cooperation between Member States. . . ." Further, "The Community and the Member States shall foster cooperation with third countries and the competent international organizations in the sphere of culture, in particular the Council of Europe" (http://europa.eu.int/en/record/mt/title2.html).

The Historical Dimension of the Three Borders Area

During the national era of the 19th and early 20th centuries, several nation states developed in Europe. Separatist tendencies, national hegemony, and sharp political and cultural barriers continued for a long time (e.g., within the Austro-Hungarian Empire until 1918).The same tendencies occurred after the breakdown of communism in Central and Eastern Europe. Border regions became peripheral and economically marginal. In the course of European integration, these areas will find new challenges and new opportunities as border functions disappear.

The location of the Three Borders Area in a European context is characterized by centrality. Major traffic routes, freeways, and railroads meet here, connecting Northwestern Europe with the Balkans and Northeastern Europe with Italy and the Iberian Peninsula. The location is a crossroad of two major European trade routes and a living textbook of European history. Romans settled here, followed by Celtic-Roman tribes, the Slavs in the 6th and 7th centuries, Germanic settlers, and wars against the Turks in the 15th and 16th centuries.The French wars at the turn of the 18th and 19th centuries left major impacts in this area. World War I was : disastrous. Between May 1915 and November 1917 the 12 "Isonzo battles" were fought and more than half a million soldiers—members of various European nations—were killed in this mountainous terrain.There are many remnants like museums, cemeteries, and literature commemorating these days .

Until World War I, this region was still a culturally diverse area of many languages. Nationalism, nationalization, and ethnic cleansing began after the peace treaty of St. Germain 1918-1919. This process was supported by Mussolini and Hitler and by the Yugoslav authorities after World War II. Contrasting political systems of Yugosiavia (Communist),Austria (neutral in 1955),and Italy (NATO and EC member) have caused political, cultural,and economic tensions. However, evidence of cross-border cooperation began with the opening of Yugoslavia's borders (mid-1960s), the independence of Slovenia in 1991, and the recent membership of Austria in the Eu (1995).The meeting point of three European cultures, languages, and ethnic groups, shaped by centuries of European history,can be offered as the main tourism attraction for guests in the Three Borders Area.

Tourism Attractions Focusing on Culture and History

Trends in international tourism disfavor peripheral areas.The process of globalization in tourism has increased markedly since the late 1980s. Globally advertised bargains from airlines, hotel chains, and tour operators tend to benefit tourist sectors that can accommodate mass tourism, such as winter travel to Spain or the Canary Islands. While large corporations cooperate with each other to their economic advantage, border regions have been disadvantaged. Smal-and medium-scale enterprises are unable to compete on the international stage. Tourist motivations and destination preferences change; independent young singles and active senior citizens expect excitement, adventure, and entertainment; the price advantages of charter discounts (mass tourism) contrast with the relatively high prices of individual trips; the constant pressure for high quality, comfort, and innovation and the increasing importance of environmental issues add to the list. These industry trends create a need for action with new development strategies.

The Tourism Dimensions of the Three Borders Area Tourism Supply

Tourism development in a peripheral area should introduce the concept of *complementary supply.*Three Borders Area has great potential for winter sports activities such as alpine skiing, snowboarding, and cross-country skiing, especially in an area that is less crowded than the major winter sports regions farther west (Figure 17.2).Additionally, ice-skating,sleigh-riding, indoor pools, and a casino can be offered.The facilities justify international winter sports events including world-cup ski-jumping, downhill racing, and a major cross-country skiing event across borders. The summer season offers national parks and other protected areas for hiking, mountain climbing, water-sports activities (rafting, kayaking, canoeing) cycling, mountain biking, golf, tennis, horseback riding, and parachuting.

The *accommodation sector* offers about 4000 rooms with regional differentiation. The Austrian section, located at the edge of the Corinthian Lake region, is based on small family-owned hotels and bed-and-breakfast establishments of average quality. The Slovenian part was developed under the Yugoslav government and is a planned tourism development area. Kranjska Gora especially could attain international status as a tourism destination.The war of independence in 1991, the conflicts in Bosnia and Herzegovina, as well as the recent conflict in Kosovo have had a tremendous impact on tourism in Slovenia. Not only was the number of tourists cut in half during the last couple of years, but also the privatization of formerly state-owned hotels led to a complete restructuring process in the region. Thus, large hotels have come under private company ownership and a huge number of small family-owned restaurants, hotels, and bed-and-breakfast enterprises have appeared. The Italian part of the region is characterized by a very limited number of accommodations. However, the Italian region is well known as a second-home area for people living in southern Italy. Strategies for future cooperation among suppliers to provide services for various demand sectors are needed.

Tourism Demand

Parallel to the diversity of area attractions, tourism demand is also very diverse. The Austrian region annually hosts about 200,000 overnight stays: one third Austrian, one third German,

Figure   Skiing in the Three Borders Area. (Photo provided by Friedrich Zimmermann)

and one third other foreigners. Activity in the Slovenian region peaked in 1990, when more than 700,000 overnight stays were registered but declined due to regional hostilities to fewer than 400,000 overnight stays in 1993.The guest count rebounded and by 1998 overnight stays reached 500,000 (50% of whom were domestic, 15% Italians, 10% Germans, 2%. Austrians).The Italian region is dominantly short-term tourism, about 250,000 annual overnight stays, and day visits. Visitation to the Italian region tends towards stagnation, with a 40% domestic demand, followed by Slovenians and Austrians (about 10% each).

Strengths and Weaknesses

Natural beauty is one of the main components of the area within the Alpe-Adria Region. There are many natural areas, especially the Triglav National Park, nature parks, and protected areas. Limestone mountains wilh a very sensitive karst system also occur.

The Three Borders Area, located at a main transportation crossroads, has a very good *infrastructure*. International freeways make the region accessible for 20 million visitors within a radius of about 100 miles. The internal traffic system is well equipped, and there are attractive mountain roads with many panoramic views Ski lifts for summer viewing and hiking are also available in all three parts of the region.

To date, *cultural attractions* have been marginal for tourism in the Three Borders Area. There is no one major site of international interest. However, various cultural attractions could be combined as regional day trip tours including the culture and history of the three major ethnic groups. This concept is inherent in the EU philosophy of national diversity in regional unity, and future cultural tourism will be dominated by a multicultural European approach in this region.

Organization and cooperation in the supraregional sense is not yet well developed. However, the bid for the 2006 Olympic Winter Games clearly demonstrates the vitality and validity of the cross-border projects that combine the Olympic concept with the present idea of a culturally and historically important Three Borders Area. At present, there are no cross-border *tourism* organizations, but the model for cooperation exists and needs to be reinforced.

Cross-Border Tourism as an Innovative European Concept

Holism and sustainability offer many new opportunities for small-scale tourism. In the past, tourism developed differently because it was heavily influenced by a national orientation with political/economic frameworks and varied recreation mentalities. Now the EU influence supports international competition, regional development strategies, and transnational cooperation. The former differences are of less importance. Postindustrial society favours a uniformity of tourism demand and supply. The application of tourism sustainability of small-scale tourism is especially suitable for peripheral areas as a special response to competition with transnational corporations that use aggressive tourism promotions.

Sustainable tourism needs multiple alliances and approaches. First, there should be a partnership between economy, society, and the environment. Decision-making must foster a democratic approach that includes the local population. The interests of both present *and* future generations should be considered with equal importance.

The peripheral location of the Three Borders Area offers a number of cooperative ideas and development options. Even though tourism to date is small scale, the area has great potential in terms of its untouched natural setting, the persistence of traditional lifestyles, and its historical uniqueness. The EU regional policy recognizes the need to provide external support for peripheral areas, and private investment is available from individual nations, states, and the EU for pilot projects. In the Three Borders Area, development must include the creation of cross-border nature protection areas, including expansion of Triglav National Park and comparable areas elsewhere in Italy and Austria. The existence of a unified administrative unit would increase the tourism exposure and marketability of the area as a summer tourist destination.

Cooperative marketing could offer various tourism packages with minimal new infrastructure. This integrated partnership might establish a type of holistic "Tourism Lifestyle" combining nature, history, culture, life, and economy that could bring new vitality to the region. Success for a sustainable tourism project

will depend on strong political support. The 2006 Olympic Winter
Games bid demonstrated that such support is attainable, and
can overcome cross-border financial, legal, organizational, and
social problems.

The Tourism Keystones

The tourism keystones, or unifying marketing themes, are
designed to create a feeling of history, exemplified by the
contemporary unification of a formerly divided region. Slogans
such as"Europeus Sine Finibus," A Region at the Crossroads of
European History," or "Divided Past—Common Future"
emphasize the cross-border tourism image favoured by European
Community Regional Policies. They can be marketed as
historical tours and adventure trips by car or bus as well as
adventure trips by bike.

Thematic biking tours express different lifestyles during
the experience of crossing borders. Hiking can offer recreation
in a natural and/or cultural landscape for which slogans could
be: "Unlimited Hiking Tours." "A Way for Everybody," "Hike
Europe," or "All Ways Lead to Europe." Hiking paths "could
be designed according to thematic to thematic approaches:"A
Bee's Hike, "Aipine Living and Lifestyles," or "A Day in the
Life of a Soldier of the First World War," "A Day in the Life of
a Miner," "A Day in the Life of a Hunter," or "A Day in the
Life of a Smuggler."

The *winter sports* keystone follows the Olympic Games
concept—the cross-border use of jointly regulated and promoted
available resources. The Winter Olympics slogan *"Senza
Confini"* (Without Borders") confirms the desire and need to
grow toge er within the region. The cooperative strategy could
market a " kiing Experience Without Borders."

Summer sport activities could also promote thematic
regional images such as rafting golf, horseback riding, hiking
and mountaineering, and regional spas and health centers.
Advertising could feature "The Blue-White Waters of the Three

Borders Area," The Enjoyment of "Adrenaline" (or may be "TheAdrenaline Experience"), "Mountaineering Without Borders," "Triathlon in the Three Borders Area," and "Sports and Peace."

Multicultural food events should feature local, regional, and national food specialties, presented as "A Food Experience of Multiculturality." With an organized network of local restaurants offering specialties of Slovenia, Friuli, and Carinthia, the partnership could establish quality control and cooperate with local agriculture. Coordinated marketing could strengthen gourmet tourism.

Marketing Issues

As an international development project, marketing would include two target groups: residents of the outlying region and those close by. The wider target region would include the Adriatic region, the Carinthian Lake region, and the winter sports areas in Southern and Western Austria and Northern Italy. Short-term tourism and day trips would be appropriate for Italians living in Trieste, udinc, or Venice, Slovenians and Croatians living in Ljubljana. Maribor, Zagreb, and as far as Rijcka and Split,and Austrians living in Carinthia and Styria. Special packages could be marketed within a "radius of 100 miles.

The stunning natural beauty and contrasts of the Three Borders Area holds appeal for long-distance visitors including Eastern Europeans (Hungarians, Czechs, Slovaks.'Poles, and Russians), Scandinavians, Britons, or inhabitants of the BENELUX countries. Special discounts for studentgroups and the local population could lead to insights relating to market elasticity.To initiate marketing, representatives from the Three Borders Area communities must form a tourism promotion organization, develop detailed marketing plans, guarantee cooperation of the partner countries, and procure start-up funds. From this base, promotion will stimulate greater international awareness of thc Three Borders Area.

Conclusion

Many border areas in Europe suffer economically as a result of being peripheral to the important economic centers. The Regional Policy of the EU recognizes these problems and supports structural changes that can benefit peripheral areas, and especially those that border Central and Eastern European countries. The Austrian-Italian-Slovenian border area is particularly well suited for development as a tourist region because of its uniqueness. Here, cultural and ethnic highlights, natural beauty, and an incredible history of war and conflict can be fused into a new type of sustainable tourism that will bring disparate European parts together in peace. The holistic approach that unites different societies and economies in partnership serves both today's needs and the interests of future generations. Tourism development features product clusters including those dealing with (1) historical tours, (2) mountain climbing and hiking, (3) winter sports, (4) adventurous summer activities, and (5) multicultural food events. The goal for Three Borders tourism is to overcome divisiveness by strengthening cultural pluralism or "Unity Through Multicultural Diversity."

18

Tourism Problems of the 21st Century

At the Elder's Workshop (Inupiat Paitot) in 1976, three Inuit men, all in their 80's who had known or known of each other since childhood, sat with coffee cups in hand, remembering. . . . Chester Seveck, the tareurmiut (salt water man) from the coast;Joe Sun, a nunamiut (inland man) from the Kobuk River near tree-line where Indians once lived; and Puto Vestal who had worked in gold mining camps near Nome all his life quietly listened to these "men of the land." joe Sun recalled,

Wood was always one of our most precious possessions. If we couldn't find enough driftwood along the river (and Chester added, "or the beach"), someone must trade with the Indians who controlled access to the forests. We didn't trust the Indians. They called us "Eskimo"or "eaters of raw meat," so we named them "Irkillirk." or "eaters of body lice." My grandfather told stories about the old times [of his great-grandfather?] before. White men came, when Inuit and Indians had many wars. Indians waited untill our men Went hunting, then they sneaked in at night and threw torches into our igloos to set them afire. When the women and children ran out, Indians shot them with arrows, or took them prisoner. Then our men sneaked to their camp to set their tepees afire, killed the Indians, and rescued our women. It went on like that, back and forth, for a long time. Inuit wore "armor" or chest plates of caribou ribs to stop arrows. Later, Inuit men figured out a trap (like "land mines"). They buried tiny pieces of very sharp sticks in the ground before it froze; after snowfall you couldn't see them. When an Indian stepped on one, the point cut his moccasin and his foot. He went away howling. Of course we knew where to avoid the points, in a circle beyond the igloos. Later, I think it was before that Russian came [see Zagoskin, 1967], we knew we were killing each other off and soon there would be no one left, so some Inuit and Indian men met, and decided no more wass. Now, one Kotzebue man [Elwood Hunnicutt] is married to an Indian lady, and they have sixteen kids.

Puto, had been turning pages in a little diary, then looked up, saying "life is like a book; many chapters, yon close one. . . ." He turned open a blank page, "I wonder what that page will write for my grandchildren?" (Inupiat Paitot field notes, January 1976).

Tourism as a global industry faces new challenges at the millennium, the most important of which is the need to look carefully at the limit's symbolic blank page, and plan for more expanded tourism. This chapter initially examines the three critical factors that will influence the future of tourism—namely (1) the economic and demographic factors that favour increased tourism and its global distribution; (2) the limited resources—namely energy and water—to sustain profected growth; and (3) the stewardship of fragile environments.

In addition to these fundamentals, globalization is creating new styles of tourism involving ethnicity in urban areas, a new exclusivity in wilderness regions, and expanded virtual tourism. Concerns for personal safety due to intensified terrorism and the global spread of disease are of increasing importance. The fact that tourism is now considered a human right calls attention to the widening disparity in access to tourism between rich and poor, and the need to provide tourism opportunities for the indigent.

Every nation needs to assess its own population growth in relation to resources, identify its capacity to provide quality vacation experiences for domestic as well as international visitors, and effectively plan its own commitment to tourism.

2000: A Psychological Time Marker

The year 2000 was a mental milestone or a bridge in time from which to assess the past and to speculate the future. In retrospect, the advent of modem mass tourism created an unprecedented awareness of travel impacts, and the subsequent research has provided a better foundation for tourism management than was true in 1970. The international bonding of government and industry through the World) Tourism Organization, the World Travel and Tourism Council, the United Nations, and respective governments and their NGOs has provided an institutional framework. As a consequence, tourism has gained stature as an industry but also has become increasingly politicized as governments assume directional roles as culture agents and use tourism as a tool to manage their economy (see Balance of Payments, below). Many countries, especially in the South Pacific, are now proactive in tourism planning, and recognize the need to support sustainable tourism development. They fund conservation and heritage projects, and support university and research institutes. There are more than 415 universities in 58 countries with tourism departments that provide tourism training, and 1213 researchers in 71 countries now ensure a cadre of potential teachers and qualified employees (Baretje, 2000, personal communication).

The ongoing "scientification" of tourism is well demonstrated by publication of the *Encyclopedia of Tourism* (Jafari, 2000) and the article "Annals and Tourism Evolving: indexing 25 Years of Publication" (Swain, Brent, & Long, 1998). The latter examines Index headwords. Even the index of this volume identifies the breadth of studies in tourism. The most valuable single bibliographic source is the Centre International de Recherches et d'EtudesTouristiques, 6 avenue du Grassi, 13100 Aix-en-Provence, France (available http://www.ciret-tourism.com).

Three recent milestones favouring further expansion of tourism have quietly been approved. The comprehensive Tourism

Code of Ethics, which sets performance standards and provides mechanisms for redress, was approved by the WTO at their Santiago meeting in November 1999 Article 7 of this document describes tourism as a *human right* and is an important validation of leisure travel. The Tourism Satellite Accounts were approved at the March 2000 United Nations Statistical Commission, giving tourism the distinction of the first industry to have UN-endorsed international standards for measuring its true economic impact. An important foundation has been structured, but the need now is constructive action at multiple levels of participation, using the strategy "Think Global, Act Local."

2000: A Technological Threshold

Technology at the millennium is transitioning from the Industrial Age of coal and petroleum to the Electronic-Cyberspace Age. This future, to be powered by innovative renewable fuels, is leading the world into the conquest of cosmic space and multiple other frontiers of technological change including wireless Internet, unprecedented use of DNA code, cloning, robotics, and artificial intelligence. The new technologies are already affecting our *worldview:* where we live and work, our concpts of governance, and our attitudes toward travel and recreation. Travel to the Moon and Mars will probably be realized within this century; travel to Deep Space (beyond our solar system) within this millennium. Technology can recreate any environment as virtual reality. The present time is exciting because we understand the processes involved in watching distances shrink as communication and transportation time bring destinations closer.

The Critical Issues
Demographics

World population has more than doubled since the postwar 1950 baseline data of 2.5 million to reach 6.1 billion in 2000, and upward projections estimate 7.7 billion by 2020 and 9.4 billion by 2050. *Vision 2020* (WTO, 1998a) predicts international tourist arrivals in 2020 will increase by 240% to 1.6 billion arrivals, or nearly 21% of the entire world population will be traveling away from home each year. *Vision 2020* further suggests that this volume of international tourism is not evenly distributed, and that many individuals in the MDCs may make more than one (and possibly as many as four) international trip(s) per year. Thirty-two percent of travel will be long haul, transporting tourists to distant, even remote,destinations,and increasing their impact in the air and on the ground. Many air traffic corridors are already overcrowded, causing flight delays. To service these new tourists, European and American aircraft manufacturers have drawing board models for 650- and 800-passenger jumbo jets. With a domino effect, these giant craft will require longer runways, larger terminals, and more ground transport. In many instances, airport relocation to sites farther from urban centers is mandatory. The cumulative effect of larger populations that travel more and farther intensifies the pressures at destinations for recreational space and vacation activities.That pressure will be most heightened in the fragile environments of nature tourism.

In addition to this demographic increase, the future will be also influenced by three further factors:

1. virtually all industrial nations including China (as of May 1999) have now adopted a maximum 40-hour work week, ensuring more leisure time;
2. the new electronic technology that created jobs and prosperity in Asia, the US, and Europe also provides more discretionary income; and
3. the recognition of travel as a human right confirms positive social sanctions for travel.

Thus, the original definition of tourism as leisure time + discretionary income + positive sanctions is further validated for the future.

In the past 30 years, outbound tourism from the industrial West dominated and established then-new popular styles of tourism including mass tourism on motorcoach tours, the north-south flow to the sunbelts, the sun-sea-sand-sex beach and island resorts, adventure tourism,and cruising. Looking ahead, the emerging economies of Asia and their demographics suggest that, in the next decade or two, the Asian population will dominate tourism and the tourism styles will change in response to their cultural preferences.The psychographs of Asian travellers are different, and their importance is still little understood in the West. In part, Boracay is an evolutionary microcosm of Asian tourism that began with local householders hosting families of Western visitors for a beach vacation, and subsequently expanded to mass tourism involving Asians living in foreign-owned hotels on short, cheap air tours with emphasis on shopping. Alternately, the new emerging Asian cruise industry (Singh. 2000) follows the "fantasyland" theme using Carnival Cruises format of mega-ships, but is adapted to Asian cultural preferences. Short 3-, 4-, and 5-day cruises from Asian hubs emphasize shopping more than beaches or sightseeing, and the ships have larger casinos (and more electronic security) as well as private rooms for karaoke (http://www.starcruises.com).

Essentially half the present world population lives in Asia, in the area bounded by the five Asian mega-cities, and many more cities with large populations lie within this perimeter. The addition by 2020 of another 1.6 billion people, of whom almost half will be urban Asian, points vividly to new centers of mass tourism for which planning must begin now.

Population shifts illustrate that among the leading industrial nations (MDCs), only the US and the UK will have population increases in the next 50 years all others decline. Among the LDCs, the greatest *percentages of growth* by 2050 are African (Ethiopia, Congo, Tanzania, and Nigeria), but the *greatest increases in numbers* of residents are Asian, led by India, China, and Pakistan. Rank as the "top 40" is a WTO ranking of nations in terms of popularity as a destination (number of international arrivals) and as an earner and spender of foreign exchange. Comparing the two sides of Table 18.2 illustrates demographic growth in relation to tourism.

The US between 1990 and 1998 heed No. 1 rank as an earner and spender nation but slipped in destination popularity from second to third place. The US also shows the greatest percentage of population growth and presumably will retain a leadership rank because of the popularity of its destination attractions. Increased domestic tourism plus increased international arrivals point to the need in America for serious recreation resource planning. Vehicular traffic to national parks such as Grand Canyon, Yellowstone, and Yosemite already exceeds comfortable carrying capacity.

In that same 8-year time span, China moved up from 12 to 6 in rank as a destination, from 25 to 7 in earnings, and from 40 to 10 as a tourism spending nation. WTO forecasts that by 2020 China will rank first as a destination, with 137 million international arrivals per year, and will rank fourth as a generating area. These projections become important as our data identify China's limited critical resources as well as the nation's new protourism policy.

No other country has shown comparable shifts, although Brazil is gaining in popularity as a destination and also as a

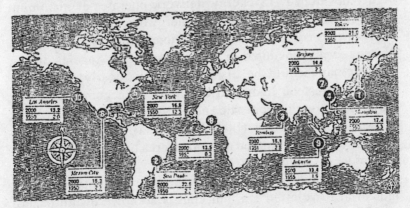

Figure   Mega-cities around the globe. (Source: United Nations, Elizabeth Traynor. Reprinted with permission of Dow Jones from *The Wall Street Journal*, December 11, 1997, p. A20)

spending nation. Some countries are listed because of their high percentages of population growth (Tanzania, Iran, and Congo) but have never appeared in the tourism "top 40" because political instability deters tourism.

Critical Resources

Gunn (1994), a widely recognized tourism planner, views tourism as a system or a series of integrated elements Population dynamics is important but tourism growth that must be matched with the critical physical resources—energy and water—to sustain both a larger host population and increased numbers of visitors. A tourist destination requires a higher per capita share of both energy and water in comparison to the normal use. The after-dark entertainment industries with lighted signage and illumination are heavy power consumers.Tourist water consumption increases for laundry, swimming pools, and the decorative use of water in architectural and interior design.

Energy

Electric energy is vital to modern life and industry. Even the highly developed US energy network operates at maximum electrical output on days of high-energy demand for either heat (on unusually cold days) or air conditioning (during a heat wave). A mega-event scheduled in New York or Los Angeles during peak demand could be disastrous. New, costly, long-term facilities must be budgeted and built to accommodate the projected increasing domestic and tourist population. Elsewhere, especially in the LDCs (Including China), rolling brownouts (limited electricity rotated around an area on a timed schedule) disrupt local services.

Coal was the primary energy source throughout most of the Industrial Revolution era, but coal is a known health hazard causing respiratory ailments and widespread air pollution. At least 800 million rural Chinese still use coal for cooking and the nation still generates 75% of its electricity from this source. Dunn (1999) reports that coal combustion is "the single largest source of CO emissions . . . and greenhouse gases released by coal combustion play a significant role in destabilizing climate . . . extensive ecosystem damage, loss of species and other serious disruptions". The high incidence of air pollution from Asia (which crosses the North Pacific and reaches the West Coast of the US) is convincing the Chinese to shift to natural gas even at the considerable cost for new equipment.

Petroleum was second to coal as an Industrial Revolution energy fuel.The oil crises of 2000 with petroleum priced at US$35 per barrel or more is but a ripple preceding a tidal wave of disruptions, considering that oil production is near total global capacity. Geologists Campbell and Leberrere (1998) report that half the world petroleum supply was exhausted in the 20th century, and future production is expected to peak at 2010 and decline rather steeply thereafter. Because so many nations now depend on tourism as their primary income and employment source, the search for replacement energy is intense and diverse. New sources must be expandable to accommodate the ever-increasing demand

Access to new fuels is an important reason for industrial development in space. The tourism space travel case emphasizes the development of passenger travel. However, the new "race for space" is primarily rooted in potential industrial resources and land for colonization. Noteworthy among energy sources, Schmitt (2000) estimates that a single Atlantis shuttle load of helium-3 brought to earth from the moon could power all the energy needs of the US for a year.

Water

The role of water as a tourist resource dates to prehistory. Aboriginal peoples gathered at mineral springs to enjoy therapeutic baths as did the ancient Greeks and Romans, and travel agents continue to promote spa vacations. "It is for its great value to tourism that water quality and its protection must be seen by all sectors as absolutely essential to tourism's success—economically as well as socially and environmentally" (Gunn, 1994, p . 45).

Although critical shortages are not immediate, water is clearly an important 21st century issue India, China, and the US are numerically ranked as the nations with the greatest potential water deficits (Postal, 1999), despite the fact that all have major watersheds and enormous river basins. With full realization that by 2050 her population may exceed 1.5 billion, China openly acknowledges the problem. China's present total water reserve is the sixth highest in the world but the per capita supply ranks 121st in the world, an amount equal to only one fourth of the world's per capita average (Xia, 2000, p. 6). If population pressure requires that water be allocated to cities rather than to irrigated farming, crop production and its high market value will suffer.The US once joked, some 40 years ago, about a futuristic plan to reroute the Yukon River from Alaska to southern California. Now that then-sleepy Los Angeles has grown into one of the world's mega-cities (Figure 18.1), this idea may reappear as a serious proposal. A similar and controversial project under consideration in China would divert part of the Yangtze River north to the now nearly dry Hai River basin, to sustain its agriculture. To find water on the moon and transport it to earth as ballast in returning space shuttles may not prove to be as ridiculous as it now sounds.

Environmental Stewardship

In 1900 only 10% of the world's population were city dwellers, but by 2000 that figure had increased to nearly 50% . The presence of cities changes the landscape and reduces the amount of open land available for agriculture and for recreation. Each of the five mega-cities of Asia (Figure 18.1) currently exceed 10 million residents, but dozens of other cities in excess of 1 million are scattered through Asia from India to Korea.

Further, the most rapidly urbanizing area of the world is sub-Saharan Africa (O'Meara, 1999, pp. 16-17). From these crowded urban cores, an eager humanity is waiting to pour out into international vacationlands, to enjoy the lifestyle of the Western tourists whose images they have seen on TV Urban crowding is an incentive to spend discretionary funds on tourism, and has been encouraged by Japan and China to equalize balance of payments (see below).

The Japanese have traveled widely for several decades, and other Asians began their overseas travels dominanty in the 1990s.The Taiwanese are believed to have first ventured into the High Arctic on a Russian icebreaker in 1995.Taiwànese and Hong Kong Chinese began to arrive in Kotzebue in 1997 in such numbers that NANA felt obliged to hire a Chinese interpreter to serve them. Asian demand for beach resorts led to overdevelopment of Boracay, and many more Asian beaches in Vietnam, Malaysia,Thailand, Sabah, and Indonesia will certainly undergo similar expansion. African tourism will probably develop in another generation.

Balance of Payments

Asian cultures have traditionally fostered the philosophy of saving, not spending, their surplus income. However, in the new global economy in which national and international culture broksrs increasingly politicize tourism, the economic value of tourism becomes a factor in international trade. In the 1980s, as overseas sales of Japanese products progressively increased that nation's favourable balance of payments, the Japanese government advocated more overseas tourism to partially equalize their income/debt ratios. The Chinese also recently adopted this policy, using overseas payments by Chinese tourists to help offset their mounting export income. The list of countries in which their workers may vacation first included contiguous Thailand and Malaysia, then Australia, and most recently the

US. Chinese travel expenditures in these countries infuse money into the local, economy and, with its multiplier effect, stimulates further purchase of Chinese manufactured goods Tourism has become an export-import commodity, not just a host-guest exchange. As a product, tourism is subject to the criteria by which foreign manufactures such as automobiles or computers might be judged: quality, reliability, style, manufacturer guarantees, support services (here, NGOs, tourist boards, and consulates), and consumer satisfaction.

For the year 2000, China announced creation of three week-long holidays per year, the first in early May. In large numbers, urban Chinese enjoyed holidays by train to historic cities, gardens, and famous shrines, infusing urban wealth into rural poverty. During this week Chinese spent an estimated PMB 18 billion (US$2,068 billion) on travel, mostly for domestic tourism. Zhang (2000) suggests that the government supports this long holiday spending "as a means to stimulate consumption and further accelerate the entire national economic development," expressed in Chinese *as jiart jingji ("holiday* economy").

Cross-Cultural Values

Stewardship is a cultural construct, and conservation of public lands and wildlife is not a traditional global value. The increased industry promotion of ecotourism and adventure tourism for the expanding Asian market holds great appeal but threatens natural preserves. Lew (1998) observed many differences in the Asian-Pacific perception of ecotourism: "Despite the considerable literature defining what ecotourism is or should be, it is the practitioners [tour operators] who make ecotourism a tangible experience for their clients and destinations. In putting ecctourism into practice, they ensure that the often overlooked element of a *bottom line profit margin is calculated into the definition* of ecotourism [italics ours]." irrespective of "the loss of natural environment and traditional cultures that form the basis of many ecotour experiences. This is the price of the modernisation that most countries seek" (p. 93).

Hashimoto (2000) further emphasizes that the Chinese and the Japanese

> love nature and the natural phenomenon only if nature provides benefits for humans and not for nature itself. . . [they] do not understand human-nature relationship as it is understood in the West . . . that humans have to help conserve and renew while utilising the natural environment and resources. Such an anthropocentric view will encourage the exploitation of scenic beauty, and abundant natural biosphere as tourist attractions. Relying too heavily on "natural power" for maintenance and healing of environmental damage, and on technological 'quick fixes' may lead to long-term problems ... it is an essential task for the tourism industry in these countries to understand and disseminate awareness of environmental issues sooner rather than later. . . failure to do so could be placing the environment in severe jeopardy, (p. 143)

The reality of this assessment has already occurred in Thailand where Twentieth Century Fox studio leased Maya Beach on Phi Leli Island (Thailand) to produce a 1999 film, *The Beach*. In violation of their own regulations, Thailand's Royal Forestry Department accepted a use fee of Bhat 4 million (about US$ 108,000), hut did not set effective preservation standards. In preparation for filming, the island— described—as one of the beautiful unspoiled islands in the Pacific—was transformed by bulldozing and the importation of nonnative plants to create a Hollywood version of "paradise "The issue stirred an international controversy from conservationists initiated by a Thai group who photographically documented the desecration (http:///www.uq.edu.au/-ppgredde/index.html).The circumstances illustrate in part the differing cultural concepts of environmental stewardship, and also demonstrate the electronic capability to monitor and mobilize public opinion in defense of sustainable use.

Stewardship by Exclusivity

"Travel has suddenly become such a huge industry that it's threatening to wreck the places we love" according to Tourtellot (2000, p. 110), senior editor of *National Geographic Traveller*. Tourtellot summarizes five options for possible stewardship: Spread Out; Concentrate; Limit Traffic by Quota, by Price, or by Lottery; Ban Access Entirely; and Raise Awareness. However, one of Tourtellot's sources identified the economic reality, "I've never seen a resource manager at the tourism-marketing table" (p. 119).

Tourism planning to protect environmental resources requires the coordination of government, tour operators, and service providers, as shown in efforts to protect the Great Barrier Reef. Two countries, Namibia and the Seychelles, have recently established environmental stewardship priorities, limiting tourists by price. Namibia, formerly Southwest Africa, was renamed for its formidable Namib desert when the country attained independence in 1990. The present government is eager to develop their tourism potential. However, due to water limitation they can serve a *maximum* of 1 million tourist arrivals per year. The Namibian Tourist Board worked with investors and developers to establish a "high-cost, low volume tourist base made up primarily of wealthy Europeans, Australasians and North Americans who have grown weary of the crime and crowded national parks in East Africa" (Swaney, 1999, p. 561). Namibian marketing is directed to these long-haul air travellers, but to avoid a criticism of exclusivity older, lower cost properties remain available for drive-in traffic from South Africa and Angola. This conservation-oriented decision is temporarily costly but long term it should preserve the Namibian desert landscape and its exotic wildlife.

The Seychelles has boldly moved forward to create an autonomous private-public marketing organization to target the upscale market who want and can afford exclusivity. With resort room rates priced at US$1000 per night, the intent is to "place ourselves in a league different from other tropical islands" (Savy, 2000, p. 10). This new conservation strategy to "preserve some of the world's most idyllic islands for the enjoyment of tourists and the prosperity of residents for generations to come"permits only 180,000 annual visitors.The project is managed by Seychelles Tourism Management Authority (STMA), online January 2001.

Globalization

In the 1960s era that was the forerunner of mass tourism, corporations such as Hilton and Intercontinental Hotels, which were in business or had properties in multiple countries but were centered in one home nation, were termed *transnational*. This concept began to change as producer services in finance, consultancy, accounting, and advertising became *multinational* and stimulated broader-based international trade.As capital flowed by means of direct investment into industries, mining, and even agriculture in other countries, business became global. Most automobiles,for example, are no longer manufactured in a single plant but are assembled with component pans imported from specialty factories located in a number of countries.This development of an interactive world economy is now termed *globalization*. It has been accompanied by significant changes in political structure, including deregulation of the airlines and expansion of free trade under multilateral agreements such as the North American Free Trade Agreement (NAFTA), and the European Community (EC).The direct effects of cultural globalization were discussed in Section 1 The specific interest here is the correlation between globalization, urbanization, and tourism

Urbanization

As the Industrial era and colonialism faded, many historic cities lost their **aura** of prosperity and greatness.Their central factories closed and jobs disappeared, leaving empty stores, abandoned churches, and vacant houses. Central business districts "died" as the population moved to the suburbs, started businesses, and patronized new shopping malls with their vast parking areas.

The New Cities

Globalization is widely discussed by social scientists who now see in cities the emergence of new nucleating cores to replace the vanishing nation-state. Globalization entails a shift from two-dimensional Euclidian space with its centers and peripheries and sharp boundaries, to a mufti-dimensional global space with unbounded, often discontinuous and interpenetrating sub-species" (Kearney, 1995, p. 549). World War II cities used to bear a national image in architecture, life style, and place names.The new cities build deterritorialized pinnacles of steel, glass, and mirror, termed "hyperspaces," in locations such as airports, franchised stores, and malls that are so detached from local referents as to have "monotonous universal qualities" (Eco, 1986).

Short and Kim (1999, p.120) describe the new entrepreneurial city as less concerned with former values, such as promotion of local businesses, and more concerned with pro-growth activism, often termed the "growth machine" that believes "bigger is better." In pursuit of this goal, civic leaders may offer free land and tax incentives for new long-term growth enterprises (as national governments did in the 1970s). Cities now advertise for new businesses and new residents in newspapers, including the *Wall Street Journal* and the *Economist,* as well as in magazines as diverse as *forbes, National Geographic Traveller,* and *Historic Preservation.* Cities adopt slogans, such as "Los Angeles: Capital of the Future," which advertises business opportunities, while others advertise quality of life, such as Miami, FL as "perfectly seasoned" (for retirement living) or Atlantic City, NJ, which proclaims itself as "American's favourite playground" (for tourism and gaming).These advertisements also attract new tourism.

Important to the development of the new cities are the information and best practices shared via their networks. In June 1996 representatives from 171 nations and 579 cities met in Istanbul at Habitat II (the second United Nations Conference on Human Settlements). Delegates signed a metropolitan version of Local Agenda 21 "to develop cities that are safer, healthier and more livable, equitable, sustainable and productive "The International Council on Local Environment Initiatives (ICLEI) serves as the clearinghouse, and in 1999 reported more than 2000 cities were engaged in Local Agenda 21, with more than 600 success stories, or "best practices" available for study.

Urban Tourism

As new global cities forge images as centers of political leadership, they attract several streams or categories of residents, four of which are particularly important to tourism: penturbia, internationalists, ethnic refugees, and urban poor.

Penturbia

Penturbia is the fifth urban movement in the US since 1735 AD (Lessinger, 1986). The first was migration within the original 13 colonies, followed by their grandchildren who spread into the Mississippi and Ohio valleys after 1790.After 1845, the third wave built industrial cities, and their grandchildren after 1900 fled to suburbia.Two generations later, after 1960, the Penturbians, wearied of commuting, began renovating abandoned warehouses in the urban cores as upscale townhouses and boutiques. They may even live "upstairs" in a view apartment where they can "go home to lunch, via elevator." Most like and support the cultural amenities of the city, and are important both to domestic and foreign tourism because they have no house or land to maintain.

The New "Internationalists"

The "new" city attracts top-echelon internationalists from global enterprises in finance, insurance, export-import, electronics, international airlines, and the arts. Often Echo Boomers in age, they are well educated, affluent and avant-garde. Manv are single and may support alternative lifestyles or are married "dinks" (double income, no kids). They shun traditional ethnicity except as a veneer to their modeled culture of sophistication and political correctness. They have been instrumental in the development of new technology but find their professional interests are best served by globalization. Their urban presence is often defined by the boutiques and fine restaurants of renovated historic sites, including San Francisco's Ghiradelli Square (in the old chocolate factory), England's Ironbridge Gorge, Capetown's Victoria and Albert Wharf, and in Australia, Sydney's Harbor and Opera district. They are also the Chinese of Shenzhen and other Economic Zones, and the Indians of the computer complex in Bangalore.

Ethnic Refugees

Late 20th century political turmoil in some developing countries led to liberalization of immigration policies (especially for "guest" workers, willing to accept minimal wages). Political refugees from former colonies flooded the "home" land. Others who were suddenly "stateless," "soilless," or victims of human rights violations sought haven wherever shelter was extended, including border refugee camps. The fortunate ones among them benefited from jet travel that speeded the flow of ethnic migration to cities such as New York and London where they filled the now-vacated rooms and opened businesses (Sassen, 1991). A rich and interesting literature describes the "Caribbeanization of the New York City" (Sutton, 1987), the Senegalese in Italy (Carter, 1995), the Turks in Germany (Mandel, 1991), and West Indians and Sikhs in England (Goulbourne, 1991).

A deterritorialization of culture progressed as these recent migrants formed ethnic enclaves built around the convenience of language, and proximity to ethnic food markets, to churches/synagogues/mosques/temples, and to friends and family. The presence of these often inner city ethnic entities further defines the influence of globalization. San Francisco's Chinatown (and the new Chinese community forming in Vancouver, British Columbia) is the largest Chinese "city" outside Asia; the Hispanic community of mega-city Los Angeles is the largest Latin "city" north of Mexico. Their folk festivals and craft fairs are major tourist attractions, and ultimately these urban newcomers also become important reserve storehouses of heritage that is often disappearing from a war-torn homeland.

Tourism and the Urban Poor

Globalization has not as yet erased the polarities between rich and poor. The wealthy can have tourism options whereas most urban poor do not (Sassen, 1998), and few tourism specialists have expressed concern with the tourism of poverty. Rural populations in Africa, Eastern Europe, and South America are often near, if not at, starvation levels, driven from traditional homes by hunger or by an emotional hungering for a better life in the city. Data from the Asian Development Bank (www.adb.org) suggest that, for China at least, the urban in-migrants benefited from increased life expectancy (+9%), access to culinary water (+50%) and sanitation (+120%), and five times (+500%) greater access to medical care. These ratios are not true, however, of many who live in the shanty towns and squatter's huts that ring the outskirts of Lima, Caracas, Rio, Harare, Dacca, and Djakarta, to name some of the most glaring. Attracted to the city in hope, some find jobs but many do not. For these homeless and hopeless, their avenue to escape is regrettably linked to crime, prostitution, and drugs, and not to pleasurable recreation because there is little or none provided or available to them.

If tourism is a human right, then the failure to provide recreation to everyone is a disgrace to a city and a blight on the industry. The editors of this volume are thoroughly mindful of the overwhelming problems resulting from the trauma of ethnic cleansing, of starvation from weather-induced crop failure, and similar tragedies in which only basic needs can be minimally met. Beyond those tragic circumstances, there are avenues to provide recreation, and many are not costly Communities are beginning to learn that funds invested in recreation are repaid by decreased delinquency, less graffiti, fewer gangs, and more potential employees. The London-based Overseas Development Institute (ODI) initiated a programme: *Putting Poverty at the Heart of the Tourism Agenda* (National Resource Perspective, March, 2000). Through proactive research and activities, they hope to halve the number of people Jiving in extreme poverty by donor-supported tourism master plans. ODI reports challenge the validity of nationally reported tourism growth receipts because they lack economic sector analysis. The poverty-stricken currently benefit very little from national tourism development. Proposals to provide training programs that will reach into slums to teach tourism job skills await implementation by WTO as well as ODI.

Volunteerism

To donate *gratis* one's time and talent to helping unknown people is a cultural concept that is little known in Asia, Africa, and even Europe. Old World societies relied on blood relatives as defined by membership in tribe, lineage, clan, and family members to provide crisis support for illness and misfortune. Families who had lived in the same villages, or on the same lands for generations, even centuries, maintained an important obligation of reciprocity and mutual aid.

In the Americas, the picture was different. Aside from the prehistoric migrations of Native Americans, from the time of Cortes and the Conquest of Mexico (1521 AD), all new settlers irrespective of their origin in Europe, Africa, or Asia were immigrants. Most came to the New World as *individuals,* leaving behind family connections and reciprocity. To meet personal crises, lonely Americans turned to neighbours for needed support, and the concept of community aid grew into the now-international service organizations originally founded in America, including Rotary International, Soroptimist, Kiwanis, Lion's Club, etc. Volunteerism is now an integral part of the lifestyle and behavior of millions of Americans, many of whom are retirees. Unpaid, these volunteers donate hours of time each week to assist in hospitals, teach the illiterate, serve as teacher's aides in schools, feed the homeless, and operate boys' and girls, recreational clubs. The new technology will soon create larger numbers of retired workers in LDCs whose volunteer efforts could similarly alleviate some hopelessness among the impoverished in their cities. Volunteerism is a cultural construct that can be implemented anywhere by individuals who are motivated to reach out to others, as did Mother Teresa in Calcutta to ease the pain of the dying.

Other Global Issues
The New Technologies
The Internet

The Internet is a powerful new factor in tourism that provides almost instantaneous access to current world tourism sources. The growing number of individuals who prefer to make their own travel arrangements via the Web soon discover a need for more knowledge of world geography as well as tourism services.The do-it-yourself search for cheaper airfares or last-minute bookings for unsold space on cruise vessels leads to poring over online advertisements for tours and hotels. However, the search is a rewarding exercise for many travellers who often benefit from the additional knowledge about their destinations. What used to be the excitement of going to the travel agency to obtain information and documents is now concentrated in their sense of self-satisfaction.

The travel industry clearly stands to benefit from increased Internet exposure. At a January 2000 WTO Tourism and Cyberspace symposium, panelists urged small enterprises to develop Web sites, which for modest cost enable them to reach global audiences at an advertising level never before attained. Small-scale entrepreneurs, especially home-stay owners in areas such as Pamukkale or Bali (Dahles & Bras, 1999), could develop and have a marketing organization with more income security." On Internet, content is not just king. Content is God.The more information you can give, the stronger you are" (McGovern, 2000, p. 15).

This new found independence in making travel arrangements is not without risk. The world is a huge complex of places, some of which are not served by frequent transportation. Despite the listings of services (such as buses, dormitories, and cafes) in adventure travel magazines and guidebooks, on arrival travellers have found these facilities no longer exist. The convenience of self-planning face at least two risks: quality control and fiscal responsibility. Unless the guest uses a. reputable reservation service or a multinational hotel chain that requires regular site inspections, there are no guarantees of cleanliness or quality of the facilities. As Dann (1996) has repeatedly stressed, travel brochures are merely pieces of paper on which representations can be very misleading, and the mediated images of the Internet can be even more persuasive. Travel agents are the usual first line of traveller protection, and without that, Internet misrepresentation or fraud to individuals may become a legal issue. International litigation is an expensive and cumbersome process.

The Internet also offers the possibility of creating new centers of employment in rural and remote locations. Language facility and a Web site are the basic requirements to participate in global business and thus extend the economic benefits of tourism to outlying areas, often at less cost. Reservations for car rentals, hotel rooms, tours, and cruises can be handled from any geographic location given training and equipment.

Information Technology

Geographic Information Systems (GIS) are proving to be an invaluable new tool, to gather and map data on almost every aspect of land use important to tourism. When combined with the Global Positioning System (GPS), tourist attractions and services can be quickly and accurately located, and even emergency services can be dispatched to a site identified by a call from a cell phone. The pioneering journal *Information Technology & Tourism,* launched in 1998, is an important addition to the tourism literature and often draws directly from the GIS sources and data. Buhalis and Spada (2000) capture the essence of the information technologies (ITs) that "transform the tourism industry to the digital economy. The emergence of destination management systems (DMSs) as 'info-structures' enables destinations to disseminate comprehensive information about resources and services at destinations and local tourism products as well as to facilitate the planning, management, and marketing of regions as tourism entities or brands" (p. 41).

Virtual Tourism

The Internet has also helped to spawn the *virtual tourist,* or an armchair traveller who use to read travel books but now"surfs"his way to a destination, selecting routes and transportation, studying weather maps, and finally enjoying the coloured (and sometimes animated) photos to dream of his stay— all with essentially no expense, no jetlag, and no threats to his personal security. Bristow (1999) suggests that virtual tourism may eventually become the "ultimate ecotourism," capable of incorporating the full range of human senses. Some museums have already developed this capacity, including the odors of decaying fish in Viking markets (at Maihaugen in Liliehammer, Norway andYork, UK). MacCannell, in the concluding case study, raises the penetrating question: if virtual reality is m̄ˉˀ authentic than reality, why should the tourist leave home?

Tourism students (and their professors) are also virtual tourists, gathering information about destinations to analyze its characteristics for their research and writing projects. Their use of the Internet may further instill an interest for *real* tourism, as did *National Geographic* and the stereopticon in the days of their grandparents.

In addition to theme parks, including Universal Studio where MacCannell has been engaged in research, HYPERPORTS are new commercial buildings.They will feature offices and state-of-the-art interactive platforms to display Business Solutions and Education products. The first HYPERPORT will be linked by footbridge to the Mall of America in Minneapolis, to take advantage of their 42 million annual visitors.The US$800 million building sited on 53 acres of land will be anchored by a 100,000-square-foot Sony display of their latest products. Using the theme of educational enrichment, the structural centerpiece will be Space and Discovery Park with a life-size replica of the International Space Station (ISS). Visitors can experience weightlessness and have virtual views of the Earth (Figure 18.2) Success of this ambitious project is expected to expand local tourism, lure more shoppers to the Mall of America, and stimulate construction of HYPERPORTS in other world locations. Space travel thus becomes a form of virtual tourism "shoppertainment."

Personal Security
Terrorism

Personal security is an **element** of mounting concern that has moved beyond criminal **attacks** and muggings for money and personal effects. The heightened terrorist activity of kidnapping and holding tourists hostage to barter their lives for armaments is a chilling deterrent to tourism in many unstable areas of the world. An individual tourist can observe the usual precautions of avoiding dark streets and high-crime areas of a city, but even tourist groups have little foreknowledge of raids on resorts. Unfortunately, incidents of terrorist attacks on tourists are often deliberately unreported or are downplayed, to protect local images and tourist income.The traveller's world is becoming progressively more dangerous, including "hacker" raids on computer software, that can disrupt air service, close airports, derail trains, and cause accidents.

Disease

The spread of contagious disease is of increasing concern as a consequence of tourism, and the rapid transit of infectious diseases between continents can occur in a matter of hours. "We live in a time where there exists a virtual viral superhighway, bringing people into contact with pathogens that affect our adaptation" (Armelagos, Barnes, & Lin, 1996, p. 7). Returning tourists as well as foreign visitors can introduce a new emerging disease that can affect large segments of the population. Many are mutant diseases that may be antibiotic resistant due to indiscriminate medical practices, including the use of subtherapeutic doses of antibiotics in animal feed. The incidence of HIV and AIDS in Africa, now spreading in part via tourism through shared needles and unprotected sex, becomes a tourist threat if hospitalization and blood transfusions are necessary.

Global warming is also identified as a "hidden Health risk" (Epstein, 2000, pp. 50-67), contributing to the spread of diseases to higher elevations than normal, and under the influence of El Nino to areas that were normally arid. Threats of pulmonary infections such as hantavirus and West Nile virus are tourist deterrents.

The PEST Analysis

To complement our macro-view of tourism in the decades to come. Hall (2000, p. 88) has drafted a microperspective, or PEST (political, economic, social, technology) analysis of future trends in tourism. Short term, it offers substantial guidelines with which to monitor and forecast change, and is a worthy addition to any discussion of the future of tourism.

The Future: War and Peace

More than a century ago, Inuit and Indians engaged in ethnic cleansing and used aboriginal equivalents of land mines to cripple their enemy.They finally agreed to a peace process and ceased fighting. Can the modern world also do so? "Peace is the pivotal issue . . and how we handle this issue may determine whether or not humanity survives into the 21 st century but also the quality of life for future generations and the biosphere, and even the course of human evolution "(Sponsel, 1994, p. 2).

Wars of the 18th and 19th centuries were fought on battlefields between armies composed of men trained and equipped for the purpose, and tourists watched its progress (Seaton, 1999).The 20th century wars progressively carried the conflict deeper into civilian space, damaging cities and destroying heritage sites, and unleashed the powerful potential of nuclear destruction.To these, the 21st century in 1968, "Nationhood [is] little more than a state of mind" (cited in Eller, 2000, p. 346).

Slowly, and worldwide, that state of mind changed, as nations began to recognise in their midst special interest groups or the ethnicities defined as the "subjective symbolic or emblematic use of any aspect of culture (by a group), in order to differentiate themselves from another group". These groups constructed individual and separatist social values, which Stavenhagen (1990) suggests "generally involve a clash of interests or a struggle over rights: rights to land, education, the use of a language, political representation, freedom of religion, the preservation of ethnic identity, and autonomy or self-determination". When such conflicts turn violent, as in ethnic cleansing,most tourists flee and do not return to visit refugee camps, to see the maimed and the orphaned whose conditions burden a society and further reduce the standard of living. Only the "danger tourists" in search of excitement, and the *thanatourists* who "travel to a location wholly, or partially, motivated by the desire for actual or symbolic encounters with death" are attracted to such grisly scenes (Seaton, 1999, p. 131).

By contrast, tourists have enshrined many war-related sites, such as the Anne Frank House where 60 years later tourists continue to visit the site of a book written by a child. MacCannell (1976, pp. 44-46) initially described this as a five-step process of sacralization, which involved:

1. the naming phase, *tot preservation* of the site;
2. the *framing* and elevating of the site, giving it special recognition;
3. *enshrining* the site by some type of distinctive display;
4. *mechanical reproduction*, as scale models, postcards, and photos; and
5. *social reproduction*, or the naming of one's group, city, or region to identify themselves with this famous attraction.

Ethnic symbols are also sacralized and enshrined. Nothing is more French than the Tour Eiffel, mere Indian than the Taj

Mahal, or more American than the Statue of Liberty.

Wars leave as their legacy the largest assemblage of tourism attractions in the world but they are best visited when there is peace.

The International Institute for Peace Through Tourism (http://www.iipt.org) works diligently to promote positive avenues to counter these negative trends.

> The world is becoming a global village in which people from different continents are made to feel like next door neighbours. In facilitating more authentic social relationships between individuals, tourism can help overcome many real prejudices, and foster new bonds of fraternity. In this sense tourism has become a real force for world peace. (Pope John Paul II, "Tourism: A vital force for peace," 1988, p. 13).